Israel/Palestine and the Politics
of a Two-State Solution

Israel/Palestine and the Politics of a Two-State Solution

THOMAS G. MITCHELL

McFarland & Company, Inc., Publishers

Jefferson, North Carolina, and London

LIBRARY OF CONGRESS CATALOGUING-IN-PUBLICATION DATA

Mitchell, Thomas G., 1957–
    Israel/Palestine and the politics of a two-state solution /
Thomas G. Mitchell.
        p.   cm.
    Includes bibliographical references and index.

    ISBN 978-0-7864-7597-1
    softcover : acid free paper

    1. Arab-Israeli conflict —1993– — Peace.   2. Arab-Israeli
conflict.   3. Pacific settlement of international disputes.
I. Title.
DS119.76.M583 2013
956.9405' 4 — dc23   2013014437

BRITISH LIBRARY CATALOGUING DATA ARE AVAILABLE

Front cover images: iStockphoto/Thinkstock

Manufactured in the United States of America

McFarland & Company, Inc., Publishers
    Box 611, Jefferson, North Carolina 28640
    www.mcfarlandpub.com

Table of Contents

Preface

In 2011 Palestinian intellectual Sari Nusseibeh published a book declaring that the two-state solution was dead. Because of his reputation as a liberal defender of that solution, Israeli intellectuals on the Left also took their cue from him. After reading the blog of Carlos Strenger in *Ha'Aretz* I decided to investigate the situation for myself and draw conclusions for policy makers. This book establishes, from an analysis of Israeli elections since the outbreak of the Al-Aksa Intifada in October 2000, that no government is likely to be formed in the medium term without the participation of the Likud. I link this with an analysis of Likud/Revisionist ideology and a study of past withdrawals by Likud governments and by a similar government in South Africa. I then look at the conditions that led the Fianna Fail party in Ireland to renounce its country's constitutional claim to the territory of Northern Ireland as part of the Northern Ireland peace process. In the conclusion I draw together these four cases (Sinai, Gaza, Namibia, and Northern Ireland) to draw policy conclusions about what types of withdrawals Likud governments will be willing to support in the future and about the Palestinian willingness to renounce irredentism. Before the conclusion, however, are two chapters of background on how American politics and Palestinian politics affect the peace process.

The conclusion here is drawn from a separate line of reasoning from Ami Pedahzur's *The Triumph of Israel's Radical Right* (which was published in September 2012), which is based upon an analysis of mainly extra-parliamentary politics. My conclusions are independent, but they reinforce those drawn by him.

I would like to acknowledge the assistance of the interlibrary loan staff of the University of Wisconsin–Madison for promptly procuring so many needed books for me, particularly for the chapters on South Africa and Ireland. I would like to thank Stephen Collins of the *Irish Times* for providing me with bibliographic advice for the chapter on Ireland. I would also like to acknowledge the financial assistance of my parents, James and Rita Mitchell, without which I would have been unable to write this book. My father's wise investing and my mother's household economies over the years made this book and my previous one possible.

Introduction

For some years now Palestinians, in particular, and Arabs, in general, have expressed doubt about the viability of the two-state solution to the Israeli-Palestinian conflict. Many on the Israeli Left and in Jewish peace groups in the United States echo this concern based upon the record since December 1988, when the two-state solution became official Palestinian policy. I write this book in order to realistically analyze the likely prospects for Israeli-Palestinian peace, based on several assumptions.

First, as I argue in the next chapter, there has been a major shift in the strength of the Israeli Right versus the Israeli Left in the former's favor since the start of the Al-Aksa Intifada in October 2000. This was temporarily offset or disguised by the emergence of Kadima as a splinter party from the Likud in November 2005, but Kadima retained its strength in the Knesset largely by cannibalizing other parties of the Center-Left in the 2009 election after many of its 2006 voters had returned to the Right. This is unlikely to change in the near future, so that any future ruling government will include the Likud and likely be led by it. There will be no return, for the next decade, of Labor-led or Kadima-led coalitions, coalitions that produced the Oslo peace process and the 2008 Annapolis-process negotiations — which incidentally we should remember both failed. My analysis of this will be laid out in full in the next chapter.

Second, I assume that Likud territorial plans, and thus ability to make concessions, will not significantly change from past territorial concessions made by the Likud as part of peace processes that it has engaged in. The Likud has withdrawn from two pieces of occupied territory: the Sinai in 1979–82 and Gaza in 2005. Because Likud leader Ariel Sharon was unable to win support for his unilateral disengagement from Gaza from the Likud Central Committee in 2004–5, he split from the party that he had created in 1973 to form Kadima, the third political party he founded in his 32-year political career. Thus, I include in this book case studies of the Egypt-

3

ian-Israeli peace treaty and the Gaza disengagement. But because Sharon's political career is over — his coma and age have seen to that even as his body still functions — and because the withdrawal has been deemed a failure by the Israeli public, and also because the Sinai is so unlike the West Bank, I find it necessary to examine a third case. For this, I take South Africa's 1988 agreement to withdraw from Namibia.

I explicitly note here that I'm not comparing South Africa to Israel or the Israeli occupation of the West Bank on the grounds that the latter constitute examples of apartheid. I think that apartheid as a concept for analysis is not useful outside of Southern Africa (South Africa, Namibia, Rhodesia), and even in that subcontinent there are problems with applying it to the Portuguese settler colonies of Mozambique and Angola.

The argument that the Israeli occupation is a form of apartheid usually rests on three lines of reasoning. First, linguistic — because the official name for its defensive barrier is the Separation Fence (*geder hahafrada* in Hebrew) and *apartheid* is Afrikaans for separateness, this proves a link. This by itself only is convincing to those who are predisposed to believe this in the first place. Second is the argument that the fact that there are separate legal systems and legal statuses for Jews and Arabs on the West Bank is proof of apartheid. While this is at the heart of apartheid, it is a feature common to all military occupations. Even in basing its personnel in other countries, the United States has status of forces agreements (SOFA) that spell out whether American servicemen accused of crimes committed in the country will be tried by local authorities or by American courts. The presence of hundreds of thousands of Israeli settlers on the West Bank in practice renders this more difficult and problematic. The third line is that the Israeli occupation fits the UN definition of apartheid. I think that if the UN were required to define a dog it would define it as a "quadruped predatory mammal" and then go on to selectively argue that certain cats — but not all cats — were dogs because they fit this definition. Anyone who has much acquaintance with both cats and dogs will realize that although both are predators, mammals, and four-legged, they behave quite differently. It is the same with Israel and apartheid South Africa.

But this is not to say that they cannot be usefully compared (and contrasted), as I have done in two books in the past and as a whole school of political scientists have done with these two countries and Northern Ireland since 1989. I compare them on the basis of three things. First, both are countries in hostile environments in which they are the periphery and the core of the region is at war with them. In the Middle East, the inner core consists of Sunni Arab regimes, either military or monarchical. The outer core then consists of non–Sunni Arab regimes such as Christian Lebanon or the present Iraq and Syria and Sunni non–Arab countries like Turkey. The periphery consists of those countries that are neither Arab nor Sunni Muslim, such as Iran and Israel. In sub–Saharan Africa, the inner core consisted of black radical military or civilian regimes, the outer core consisted of more moderate regimes and the periphery consisted of white minority regimes and Malawi, the only country to have had diplomatic relations with Pretoria. Israel's Arab neighbors and the Arab League pursued a policy of liberating Palestine (i.e., destroying Israel). The Organization of African Unity and the Frontline States (FLS) pursued a policy of liberating the Portuguese colonies, Rhodesia and Namibia, and ending apartheid and white rule in South Africa.

Because Pretoria was in a similar situation to Jerusalem, the two countries concluded an informal political and military alliance that lasted from 1974 until the late 1980s, when American pressure forced Jerusalem to end it. During that time close cooperation existed between senior military officers and both parties shared strategies of coping with insurgencies.[1] Israel under David Ben-Gurion pursued a peripheral strategy of aligning itself with regimes in the periphery or outer core and with minorities within the inner core such as the Lebanese Christians, the Kemalist military regime in Turkey, the Pahlavi monarchy in Iran, the Kurds in Iraq, and the Christians in southern Sudan. It also pursued a policy of reprisal raids as its prime counter-insurgency strategy in the 1950s and 1960s. Pretoria, influenced by this and by similar strategies pursued by the Portuguese and Rhodesians, pursued a strategy in the 1980s of regional destabilization based on raids, invasions, and supporting insurgent groups in Angola, Mozambique, Zimbabwe, and Lesotho.[2]

Second, they can be compared because both are forms of ethnic democracies that function as democracies, but only in terms of the ruling ethnic group. Under a simple majoritarian definition of democracy as majority rule, Israel is a democracy and the white regimes in South Africa from 1910 to 1994 were not. But Israeli sociologist Sammy Smooha argues that Israel is an ethnic democracy because Arab parties have been excluded from all ruling coalitions in Israel and because there is discrimination in budgetary allocations between Arabs and Jews when it comes to education, health, and municipal infrastructure spending. Some Israeli critics have argued that Israel is really an "ethnocracy" — a third type of regime between a democracy and an authoritarian government.[3] I reject this because Israeli governments are at least as democratic as regimes in the past that historians have commonly considered democratic, such as antebellum America and nineteenth-century Britain. Political scientists have labeled apartheid South Africa a *herrenvolk democracy* (master race democracy) in which the franchise is limited to the ruling ethnic group and possibly to other ethnic allies. In South Africa from 1948 until the mid–1960s, the cabinets were exclusively Afrikaner and gradually select English-speakers were let into less sensitive positions. In 1984 Indians and coloreds, the latter group having been striped of the franchise by Afrikaner nationalists in the 1950s, were given a limited role in a "sham consociational" government in an attempt to co-opt these groups against the majority African population.[4] Thus, in terms of franchise, apartheid South Africa was a herrenvolk democracy, but in terms of the cabinet, it was an ethnic democracy. But in having to answer to an electorate in free and fair elections, both Israel and South Africa were democracies and democracies under siege, or "siege democracies." And the Nationalist Party government that ruled South Africa is comparable to the Likud as the National Party was a conservative populist ethnic party like the Likud.

The main differences between the two are that, as previously mentioned, South Africa was a minority democracy and Israel is a majority democracy, and also the nature of the party systems. South Africa, as a former British colony, had a first-past-the-post electoral system that produced a two-party or three-party system from 1910 to 1994. This is very different from the multiparty system produced by Israel's proportional representation franchise system.

Third, both Namibia and the various Arab territories that Israel conquered in June 1967 were conquered in what the conquerors considered to be just defensive wars. The Union Defence Force under Prime Minister Louis Botha and Defense Minister Jan Smuts, both Boer generals in the Second Anglo-Boer War (1899–1902), conquered South West Africa as part of the Allied war effort against Germany in the First World War. South Africa was then granted a League of Nations mandate in 1920 to rule Namibia as if it were part of South Africa. Smuts, working as part of

6

the Imperial War Cabinet in London during World War II, was too preoccupied to annex South West Africa after the demise of the League of Nations in 1939. By 1946 it was too late for him, and South Africa engaged in a forty-year dispute with the United Nations over the legal status of the territory and the legality of the South African presence.[5]

Likewise Jerusalem has been shielded from an antagonistic United Nations by Washington, which, as a permanent member of the Security Council, has a veto, despite the fact that in the General Assembly, a majority of countries consider the occupation by Israel of the West Bank, Gaza, and the Golan (and before that of the Sinai) to be illegal. Other than Israel, I can think of no other case than Namibia, in the late twentieth century after Portuguese decolonization, of a Western country withdrawing from occupied territory as part of a peace agreement.

Previously Ian Lustick in his 1994 study *Unsettled States, Divided Lands* compared the British process of decolonization in Ireland and the French process of decolonization in Algeria to Israel and the occupied territories.[6] While the study was very interesting, especially given the parallels in party system between the French Fourth Republic and Israel, there are two major defects in this study. First, the two countries being compared with Israel were global colonial powers — with Britain being the superpower of its day. (Israel is a regional military power, but not a major colonial power with several overseas territories). Moreover, the colonies they were withdrawing from were separated from the metropole's territory, by a sea — the Mediterranean and the Irish — rather than being contiguous with the territory as is the case with the West Bank, Gaza, and the Golan. This makes a big difference in terms of security.

Plus, in the Israeli-Palestinian conflict, as with the conflicts in Northern Ireland and the Indian subcontinent, the irredentism that resulted in partition as a solution by the decolonizing British, and also stemmed from it, exists on both sides. Mainland Britain was not threatened by the Irish Republican Army nor France threatened by the FLN (National Liberation Front) in Algeria once withdrawal from the territory was completed. This was also true of Namibia. So we need another case study to represent the irredentism of the Palestinian side, which has been a major factor in Israeli reluctance to give up the West Bank. For this we need to turn to the other conflict that is often compared to Israel, Northern Ireland. The territorial portion of the Northern Ireland peace process was the Republic of Ireland dropping its constitutional claim to the territory of Northern Ireland embodied in Articles 2 and 3. These were rewritten in December 1999 after a May 1998 referendum in the Republic gave the government authority to do so. The delay was so that the new amendments would go into effect at the same time that power sharing began in Northern Ireland. The heart of the Northern Ireland peace agreement — the Belfast Agreement, or Good Friday Agreement of April 1998 — was the mandatory sharing of power between the nationalist and unionist communities in the Executive in exchange for the disarmament of the IRA and the release of security (terrorist) prisoners and the dropping of the constitutional claims.[7] A joint North-South Council between the Northern Ireland Assembly and the Dail Eireann (Irish House of Commons) served as a concession prize for the failed nationalist dream of a united Ireland.

The Irish party that oversaw the Northern Ireland peace process from 1992 to 1999 and after was the same party that wrote the 1937 constitution that was being amended — Fianna Fail. Fianna Fail was the dominant party in Irish politics from 1932 to 2010 and the most successful party in Western Europe in the twentieth century. Ireland until the early 1990s was a conservative, religious and largely agrarian society. Along with Northern Ireland it was the most traditional country in Western Europe, even surpassing Spain and Portugal. Ireland was the Vatican's favorite Western country because of its high church attendance rates and conservative sexual morality, which was reflected in its laws. Ireland was also a very corrupt society in terms of political corruption by business, and Fianna Fail was the most corrupt of all the Irish parties.

I would argue that Ireland and Fianna Fail are good comparisons with rural, agrarian, traditional Palestine and Fatah. The main difference is that since the end of the Irish civil war in 1923 Ireland has behaved as a genuine democracy, whereas the Palestinian Authority may be democratic by Arab standards but certainly not by Western standards. For its first decade under the leadership of PLO leader Yasir Arafat from 1994 to 2004 the Palestinian Authority was a typical Arab autocracy — more democratic than Iraq, Libya, or Syria but comparable to the Arab monarchies. Since January 2005 under the leadership of Mahmoud Abbas, the PLO has been moving towards democracy, but this has been impaired by continuing corruption and the struggle between Fatah and Hamas for supremacy.

In Chapter One I cover the nature of the Israeli political system and the problems that plague Labor, Meretz, and Kadima. Here is where I make my argument that underlies the case studies. In Chapter Two I briefly relate the history of Revisionist Zionism from the Revisionist Party in 1925 to the Likud today. This will provide the ideological background to the case studies.

In Chapter Three I begin the case studies with a study of the Sinai negotiations from 1977 to 1979. In this chapter I look at the attitude of the Likud toward territorial concessions and the role of Labor figures in nego-tiating and passing the agreement in the Knesset. I also look at the reasons for Sharon's decision in 2004 to withdraw unilaterally from Gaza and why his party rejected this withdrawal. He carried out this withdrawal the fol-lowing year and then split the Likud to form Kadima, part of the subject of Chapter One, before suffering a major stroke that has left him in a coma.

In Chapter Four I discuss the history of South African occupation of Namibia and the internal politics within South Africa that impacted on decision making on the territory. I also discuss the Border War of 1966 to 1988 and analyze how the final phase in 1987–88 affected the negotiations in 1988. I look at the negotiations in 1988 and make my argument for why Pretoria decided to withdraw in 1988. I then look at the Northern Ireland peace process as seen from Dublin in Chapter Five.

In Chapter Six I examine Palestinian politics from the mandate era in the early 1920s to the present to see what themes have remained constant and what has changed. In Chapter Seven I look at relations between Jerusalem and Washington and how American politics have affected these relations. I look at America's role as mediator from Nixon to George W. Bush and at the roles of the American Israel Public Affairs Committee (AIPAC) and J Street in affecting the relationship.

In the final chapter I then analyze the lessons of these various case studies for the Israeli-Palestinian conflict and the future of the two-state solution. I examine how likely a future Likud government will be to withdraw from either the West Bank or the Golan. I also discuss how the differences between Ireland and Palestine will impact on ending Pales-tinian irredentism. I then make a few suggestions for American policy in the Middle East based on these conclusions and offer my conclusions on what conditions are necessary for successful mediation in the Middle East, based on a previous analysis of the Oslo and Northern Ireland peace processes.

CHAPTER ONE

The Demise of
the Israeli Center-Left

For forty years the Labor Party has been America's Israeli peace partner in the Middle East. From the Roger's Plan diplomacy of 1969–70, through Kissinger's shuttle diplomacy of 1973–75, to the Camp David Accords and Egyptian-Israeli peace treaty of 1978–79, to the Oslo process of the 1990s, Labor has played a crucial role. Even when the Likud led the government in 1977–80 it was a former long-term Labor minister, Moshe Dayan, and a future Labor minister, Ezer Weizman, who did most of the negotiating with Egypt. And it was the Labor Party that provided the votes in the Knesset to pass the Camp David accords and peace treaty when many Likud MKs were voting no or abstaining.

But from 1992 to 2012, Labor's size in the Knesset has been cut by eighty percent, from 44 seats to nine, and Meretz has been reduced to a quarter of its 1992 size. Whereas it took Labor 29 years to go from the largest party to the second largest and another 29 years to go to number three, it has taken only three years to go from third to fourth largest. This indicates that both parties are presently in free fall.

When Palestinian intellectual doves first conceived of the two-state solution in the early 1970s as an alternative to the Palestine Liberation Organization's official policy of phases (conquering Israel on the installment plan), it was conceived as an agreement between the Labor Party and Fatah. Only Feisal al-Husayni (or Husseini) thought in terms of an agreement with the Likud, and he died in 2000.[1] Can the two-state solution survive the collapse of Labor and Meretz? Before we can answer that we need to examine the nature of Israel's party system and why the Israeli Left has collapsed.

Israel has a proportional representation franchise system with a very low (two-percent) entry barrier. Under this system the entire country is considered a single electoral district with 120 seats. Theoretically each party should turn in to the elections commission a list with 120 ranked names on it. But in practice each party turns in a list that includes a few more names than what it realistically expects to win. Thus a party expecting to win four seats might turn in a list with ten names and one that expects to win 20 seats would turn in one with 30 names. No party has ever won a parliamentary majority in the Knesset (parliament) by itself, and so every government in Israel's history has been a coalition government. The closest to a single-party government was when the new Alignment won 56 seats in 1969 — five short of a majority.

For Israel's first 29 years (actually from 1935 in the prestate Yishuv), there was a single dominant party: Mapai (Labor). Then from May 1977 (or arguably from the creation of the Likud in September 1973), Israel had a biparty-dominant multiparty system that lasted until 2003.[2] This two-bloc system behaved much like a traditional two-party system in a first-past-the-post voting system. Political scientists in Israel and outside have argued since the early 1980s whether the Israeli party system was going through dealignment or realignment.[3] Under realignment the Likud replaces Labor as the single dominant party, whose policies, symbols, and issues define the era. Under dealignment there is simply no dominant party. I argue that the Israeli system is partly going through both: the Likud has become the dominant party but in a much weaker dominant position than Labor once was, and there are a number of medium-sized parties such as Kadima, Israel Beitenu and Labor.

Traditionally Israeli parties have been divided into four main sectors: Arab parties, Jewish religious parties, Jewish Right and Jewish Left. Within each bloc there can be major changes from election to election but the blocs themselves have remained relatively stable. There have been three main shifts. First, in 1973–1981 there was a major shift of the Israeli secular public to the Right as a result of the Yom Kippur War, the longevity of the Left in power, and a change in mizrakhi (Oriental Jews from Muslim countries) voting patterns. Second, there was a shift by Arabs in the 1980s and 1990s away from lists affiliated with the main Jewish parties toward Arab nationalist parties. And third, since the October 2000 Al-Aksa Intifada there has been a further shift of the Jewish secular public to the Right. Plus, there was a shift to the Right ideologically by all of the Zionist parties after 1967 as the victory in the war went to Israel's collective head.[4]

This situation came about for two reasons. First, in the bibloc system from 1974 to 2003 the Likud was the stronger of the two main parties, with Labor *In the Shadow of the Likud*, as one of the two leading English-language studies of Labor (by Neill Lochery) is entitled. In this situation Labor could come to power only as part of a national unity government or when the Right made a major mistake. The latter occurred in 1992 when several competing lists of settler-oriented parties failed to make the 1.5 percent barrier, thus wasting their votes and giving the Left bloc a narrow margin.[5] In 1999 Israelis blamed Netanyahu and the Right for the problems with the peace process and voted Ehud Barak into power at the head of One Israel, a combined list of Labor, David Levy's Gesher party, and the moderate Meimad religious party.

Second, in 1992 both Yitzhak Rabin and Benjamin Netanyahu supported a reform that gave Israeli voters a separate vote for prime minister and the Knesset. It was an ill-conceived attempt by ambitious politicians to combine the parliamentary and presidential systems. Rabin could count on his popularity as "Mr. Security" and Netanyahu on his expertise with television to prevail in presidential-style elections. What neither considered was that this would change the calculus of Israeli voters. No longer forced to take into account how their party vote would affect who would be prime minister, many voters started voting for their ideological choice, thus strengthening the parties on the Left and Right at the expense of the two main parties in the Center.[6] Realizing what was happening, the two main parties voted to repeal the "reform" and restore the status quo ante after the 2001 election. Only three elections were held under this system: Knesset elections in 1996 and 1999 and a prime ministerial election in 2001. But even after the restoration, voters continued to vote like republicans and give their votes to the smaller parties.

The biparty domination was already starting to break down by 1999. Between 1949 and 1999 the two largest parties combined had between 55 and 95 seats out of 120 total. The highest totals were in 1969 to 1988 when the totals ranged from a low of 79 in 1988 to a high of 95 in 1981.[7] From 1973 to 1996 the "competiveness ratio" (second largest party: largest party) varied from a low of .74 (1977) to a high of .98 (1988).[8] Between December 31, 1973, and 1992, the two main parties each ranged between 32 and 47 seats after each election. In contrast, in 1999 Labor had only 26 seats and the Likud 19, and in 2003 and 2006 Labor dipped to 19 seats, while in

2006 the Likud had only 12 seats, with a "recovery" to 27 in 2009. Kadima had 29 seats in 2006 and 28 in 2009 but may dip to half that in the next election. This demonstrates the lingering effects of the double-vote system.

Labor has been suffering from several problems. First, it has suffered from a shrinking demographic base since 1973, when *mizrakhim* (*Sephardic* Jews) began voting in large numbers for the Likud. Since then the *mizrakhim* (Jews from Muslim countries) have continued to vote for the Likud and Shas and the Likud has also attracted a growing share of the Ashkenazi (European Jews) vote away from Labor.[9] The United Party also suffered from this problem in South Africa, as after 1943 it failed to attract new Afrikaner votes and so had to rely on English-speakers and aging Afrikaners, who were dying out. As the Afrikaners constituted roughly 60 percent of the white electorate compared to 40 percent for English-speakers (English, Scots, Greeks, Portuguese, Jews) this left the United Party with an ever-shrinking share of the pie. The Israeli Left draws mainly from the Ashkenazi population originating in Europe (minus the former Soviet Union) and the Americas.

The mizrakhim have switched their allegiance to the Likud for a number of reasons having to do with their absorption experience within Israeli society from the late 1940s to the mid–1960s. First, most mizrakhim were sent to live in development towns and settlements far from the main urban centers, when most of them had been used to living in large cities in the Arab countries and Iran. Second, most mizrakhim come from traditional homes where Jewish ritual is respected, even if they are not considered religious by ultra–Orthodox standards. Mapai was hostile to Jewish ritual as its adherents had consciously revolted against traditional Jewish life in Eastern Europe. Third, absorption and labor officials had discriminated against many of the mizrakhim because they saw them as inferior. By contrast, Begin as Etzel commander, had valued mizrakhim because of their ability to speak Arabic and disguise themselves as Arabs for underground operations. Herut's Central Committee was as Ashkenazi as was Labor's, but it had a different feel for mizrakhim because Begin knew how to speak to traditional Jews.[10]

Second, Labor relied too much on former generals to provide it with electoral charisma. Since Moshe Dayan, Yigal Allon and Moshe Carmel in the 1950s, the component parties of Labor have depended on former generals to attract new voters. Two of the three former generals (Rabin and Barak) who were prime ministers came from Labor. Only two other Western countries had a similar phenomenon of *military politicians*: the United States in the late eighteenth and nineteenth centuries and South Africa in the late nineteenth and twentieth centuries. France had three generals between 1934 and 1969, but de Gaulle's party — which provided two of them — does not compare well with Labor.[11] Each of these two countries produced a party that, like Labor, was reliant on the charisma of former generals — the Whigs (1836–1852) and the Republicans (1868–1892) in the U.S. and the South Africa Party/United Party in South Africa (1910–48).

Relying on generals to provide it with electoral charisma was bad for Labor for two main reasons. First, it led to a neglect of other issue areas besides foreign affairs and defense such as economic and social issues. This meant that it was putting all of its eggs in one basket. Those eggs got cracked when the Oslo peace process began to fail in the mid–1990s due to terrorism by the Palestinian Islamists of Hamas and Islamic Jihad. Then, when the Al-Aksa Intifada began in October 2000, with the full participation of Yasir Arafat's Fatah party — Israel's ostensible Palestinian partner for peace — the eggs were smashed.

The American Whig Party had three generals in its stable to promote as presidential candidates. When the Whigs first ran for the presidency in 1836, two years after being created from a merger of smaller parties, they lacked a single popular figure to nominate as their candidate, so they nominated three regional candidates for the South, the West, and New England. General William Henry Harrison, a hero of the War of 1812, did the best and so emerged as the party's nominee in 1840 and was elected. He died in office of pneumonia only a month into his first term. He beat out Senator Henry Clay and General Winfield Scott for the nomination that year. In 1844 Clay was nominated and narrowly lost to James K. Polk of Tennessee, a former Andrew Jackson protégé. In 1848 Zachary Taylor emerged as a popular war hero after defeating Mexican president Santa Anna in the Battle of Buena Vista in February 1847. Taylor was easily elected but died in office of an intestinal or stomach ailment in July 1850. Scott, a hero of both the War of 1812 and the Mexican War, was the only remaining Whig general. He defeated President Millard Fillmore for the Whig nomination and then was badly beaten in the general election by Franklin Pierce. Two years later the Whig Party began to collapse over both sectional differences and a nativist reaction against immigrants.[12] The Whigs had allowed military charisma to overshadow their economic issues during the 1840s. Later, after the American Civil War, the Republican Party, a successor to the Northern Whig Party, ran politicians who had served as generals in the Civil War for a quarter century starting in 1868. But they ran the generals as part of an ideology of free labor and capitalism so that they had a complete package.[13]

In the Union of South Africa at independence in 1910 the South Africa Party emerged as the largest party. It was an Afrikaner nationalist party that had half a dozen former Boer generals from the Second Anglo-Boer War (1899–1902) in its ranks. In 1913 James Barry Munnik Hertzog, a former general and the attorney general of the Orange Free State Boer Republic, split from the South Africa Party to form the National Party over issues concerning the relations between the two main white groups in the country. When World War I began the following year a number of these generals joined an abortive Afrikaner rebellion in opposition to South Africa's participation on the side of the Allies against Germany, the Boers' former main foreign ally. This eliminated half of the generals, leaving three former generals to dominate politics for the next three decades: Prime Minister Louis Botha, Defense Minister Jan Smuts, and opposition leader Hertzog.

Botha died of disease in 1919. Smuts then took over as prime minister with the support of both English-speakers and moderate Afrikaners. Hertzog defeated Smuts in 1924 by forming a coalition with the South African Labour Party. Hertzog ruled as prime minister for the next fifteen years. In 1933 he formed a coalition government with Smuts's South African Party and a year later merged their two parties to form the United Party. In September 1939 the United Party broke up over the issue of South Africa's entry into World War II. Hertzog basically retired from politics at this point and within three years was dead. In 1948 the National Party, led by Daniel Malan, who had split from the decision to go into the United Party in 1934, invented the term *apartheid,* meaning "apartness" or "separateness," and won the election. Smuts, who had been a major international figure during World War II in London, retired from politics in 1950. The United Party lacked a real leader to replace Smuts and went into decline. A quarter century later, in 1977, the party emerged as the New Republic Party and was viable only in Natal Province. Natal was the smallest and the most English of South Africa's four provinces. A decade later the party was gone.[14]

While there were many reasons for the demise of both the Whig and United parties, the fact that they were both dominated by generals was a major part of the problem. Both Botha and Smuts were interested in foreign policy and defense and not really interested in economic issues. Hertzog was mainly interested in symbolic nationalist issues.[15] The National Party in 1948 and the 1950s managed to combine bread-and-butter economic issues with ethnic nationalism. The Likud was able to do the same in 1977 and 1981 when running against the Labor establishment.

Second, the reliance on generals encourages the promotion of national unity governments, like those that existed in Israel from 1967 to 1970 and from 1984 to 1990, where they blurred the differences between Labor and the Likud in the minds of voters and over time caused much of the electorate to desert to the Right. The original national unity government put into place in June 1967 to deal with the security crisis that resulted in the Six Day War helped to legitimize Menachem Begin's Herut party in the eyes of voters. This made it easier for them to vote it into office a decade later.

This promotion of national unity governments comes about because former generals who have spent their formative years in the military climbing through the ranks tend to look upon politics as a second career that is like their first, only in civilian clothes and with certain different rules. They see a government ministry such as the transportation ministry or the defense ministry as a new command in which they can prove themselves before taking the next step up the ladder to the prime minister's office. When they are in opposition it is the equivalent for them of being without a command — of being on the waiting list for promotion. Once in a national unity government, generals are reluctant to leave. There are at least three prime examples of this. First, Ezer Weizman was very upset with Begin for withdrawing Gahal from the national unity government of Golda Meir in 1970 over Meir's decision to accept Resolution 242 as being applicable to all of Israel's fronts. Weizman had just "parachuted" directly from the Israel Defense Force in 1969 , where he became Herut's first general, to a place in the cabinet as transportation minister. This led Weizman to mount an unsuccessful challenge to Begin's leadership at the 1972 Herut annual convention.[16] Second, Yitzhak Rabin was furious with Shimon Peres for breaking up the national unity government with the Likud in which Rabin was defense minister in an attempt to establish a Labor-led government in early 1990. Rabin dubbed this the "smelly maneuver," and it further inflamed relations between the two Labor rivals during the early 1990s.[17] Third, Ehud Barak split from the Labor Party with a third of its Knesset members in 2010 after there was talk of pulling out of the national unity government of Benjamin "Bibi" Netanyahu. The leading generals such as Matan Vilnai followed Barak into his new Atzmaut (Independence) party.[18]

Third, Labor suffered from a leadership problem because of losing a whole generation of future leaders during the 1974–94 period due to the monopoly on power by Shimon Peres and Yitzhak Rabin. Rabin is now dead and Peres is now out of electoral politics for good as the Kadima president of Israel. The Whigs suffered a similar problem in 1848–52, when President Zachary Taylor died in office and their top three congressional leaders (John Q. Adams, Henry Clay, and Daniel Webster) died. I believe that one of the problems of the United Party is that it did not produce new popular leaders to augment James B M Hertzog and Jan Smuts. The party was suddenly left leaderless when Smuts retired in 1950.[19]

Peres used his insider control of the Labor Central Committee to repeatedly win nomination as party leader from 1977 to 1992. A group of seven or eight leading Labor figures from the intermediary generation ended up either leaving the party for parties to the left (Ratz, Meretz) or leaving politics altogether out of frustration with the twenty-year rivalry between Peres and Rabin, which was an extension of an earlier rivalry between Moshe Dayan and Yigal Allon that stemmed back to 1938. Most of the exits occurred in the 1990s. The first exit was that of Shulamit Aloni, who ran as the head of the Citizens' Rights Movement (Ratz) in 1973 after Golda Meir had her excluded from a safe seat on Labor's list for the Knesset. The next exit was that of Yossi Sarid in 1984 for Ratz. This occured after the Labor Alignment collapsed when Mapam left after Labor formed a national unity government with the Likud. Uzi Baram managed to introduce primaries into Labor in 1988. This allowed Rabin to prevail over Peres in 1992. Baram retired from politics in 2001. Avrum Burg, son of National Religious Party leader Yosef Burg, left to head the Jewish Agency before retiring from politics in 2004. Gad Ya'acobi retired from politics in 1992 after he failed to win a safe Knesset seat; he then served in a number of administrative posts starting with ambassador to the United States from 1992 to 1996. Ya'acobi had a full political career, but others like Baram and Burg were cut out of the top position because of the long rivalry between Peres and Rabin. Yael Dayan, daughter of Moshe, and Yossi Beilin, architect of the Oslo peace process, left to join Meretz in 2003. Both Sarid and Beilin served as leaders of Meretz.[20]

Fourth, Labor suffers from a lack of new policy ideas. For twenty years its foreign policy consisted of close ties to Washington and the Jordanian Option. The Jordanian Option came in two mutually exclusive variants: territorial compromise, or the Allon Plan, and functional compromise, or the Dayan Plan. The Allon Plan, put forward by Ahdut Ha'Avoda leader Yigal Allon in 1967, was for Israel to annex between a third and forty percent of the West Bank — the unpopulated areas in the Jordanian Valley, around the Dead Sea, and the Etzion Bloc of settlements south of Bethlehem. The rest of the West Bank and Gaza would be returned to Jordan in exchange for a peace treaty. The Dayan Plan called for Israel to assume responsibility for security in the West Bank while the Palestinians would be represented in the Jordanian parliament in Amman. The trouble was that King Hussein would not accept either version, as he felt he could not afford politically to surrender any territory to Israel or to agree to any infringement of Jordanian sovereignty. Despite secret meetings between the king and Israeli leaders from 1968 to 1987, no agreement was ever reached.[21]

The option was taken away in July 1988 when King Hussein publicly renounced any responsibility for the fate of the West Bank in response to the outbreak of the Intifada in December 1987. It was only gradually replaced with an attempt to deal with the Palestine Liberation Organization (PLO). At present the two-state solution with Mahmoud Abbas is as realistic an option as the Allon and Dayan Plans were from 1967 to 1988. The problem is that both Israelis and Palestinians prefer to negotiate among themselves about their respective futures rather than with the other party to the conflict. This way they don't need to make painful compromises and risk being branded traitors, but there is no peace either.

The United Party (UP) also suffered from being a "me too" party offering a "kinder, gentler" form of apartheid rather than an alternative. The UP's shrinkage from 1948 to 1988 parallels that of Labor after 2000, except that Labor has shrunk much more quickly.[22] The Whigs also suffered from a lack of new policies after the old economic disputes of high tariffs versus low tariffs and internal improvements became less relevant during the 1850s.[23]

Fifth, Labor has suffered from backlash from the failure of the Oslo peace process in 1999–2000. Ehud Barak failed to negotiate peace with either Syria or the PLO. Israelis hold Labor responsible for the outbreak of the Al-Aksa Intifada of 2000, which the Likud largely crushed from 2002 to 2005. The Ulster Unionist Party (UUP) suffered a similar backlash from 2002 to present for the initial failure of the Northern Ireland peace process after the Irish Republican Army (IRA) refused to decommission (disarm) its weapons as called for in the Good Friday Agreement. The Democratic Unionists (DUP) were given credit for the IRA's decommissioning in 2005. The DUP then entered into a power-sharing government with Sinn Fein, the political wing of the IRA, in May 2007.[24] The UUP shows no signs of recovering anytime soon. The Whigs also suffered after the Kansas-Nebraska Act was passed in 1854, thereby repealing the Missouri Compromise of 1820. Thus, this was seen by many Northerners as the equivalent of a failed peace settlement with the slave-holding South. The Whigs never recovered, and they collapsed in 1856.[25]

Sixth, Labor suffers from a backlash for its poor management during the Second Lebanon War in 2006. Amir Peretz, the Labor Party's first mizrakhi leader, had no military experience above being a captain in the Israel Defense Forces (IDF) in the Yom Kippur War thirty years before. Rather than bargain for the finance ministry or a leading social ministry, the party accepted the defense ministry from Kadima. Peretz was the first "civilian" defense minister since Begin in 1980–81, following the resignation of Ezer Weizman. Before June 1967 civilian defense ministers were the norm, but since then the norm has been for defense ministers to be either former generals or defense technocrats like Shimon Peres and Moshe Arens.[26] Ehud Olmert also suffered even more from the war. Labor attempted to solve this by changing Barak for Amir Peretz in 2007, thus going back to the earlier problem of overuse of generals. Operation Cast Lead in Gaza in December 2008 and January 2009 only partially reestablished Labor's hawkish credentials, but this was canceled out by Barak's defection a year later.

For those who like mathematic formulas the decline of the Left can be expressed in a formula.

L2 + M2= L1

L1 = number of Labor MKs (Members of the Knesset) before the election

L2 = number of Labor MKs after the election

M2 = number of Meretz MKs after the election[27]

Let's look at the numbers[28]:

	Labor	Meretz	Combined Left
1992	44	12	56
1996	34	9	43
1999	26	10	36
2003	19	6	25
2006	19	5	24
2009	13	3	16

This is because Meretz voters have moved to support Labor as both parties have grown weaker and Labor voters have defected to other parties such as the Likud, the Center Party, Shinui or Kadima. There is a floating vote in the Center composed of voters who are prepared to vote for Center parties either to punish Labor for corruption or other sins (ultra-dovishness) or because they want to protest religious coercion when neither Labor nor Meretz is devoting sufficient attention to this issue. They will also vote for the Likud when they feel their security is threatened as occurred in 2001 and 2003 during the Al-Aksa Intifada.[29]

In 1977 Labor lost power to the Likud because about a third of its voters defected to the Democratic Movement for Change (or Dash) led by former chief of staff and famous archeologist Yigael Yadin. It won fifteen seats, too few to allow it to blackmail the Likud into enacting electoral reform, which was its main issue. Dash collapsed after about two years in power as its two main wings drifted apart.[30] In 1999 a number of prominent defectors from the Likud got together with former chief of staff Amnon Lipkin-Shahak to form the Center Party. They won only seven seats in the election and the party collapsed after three years after its leader, former Defense Minister Yitzhak Mordechai, was indicted for sexual assault.[31]

The most spectacular example of an overnight sensation was Tommy Lapid's Shinui. Shinui started out as a protest movement in the mid–1970s before being one of the two wings of Dash. After Dash broke up it remained a small party until joining together with Ratz and Mapam to form Meretz in 1992. Two of Meretz's nine MKs left when Meretz was formed as a united party in 1996 to form an independent Shinui. Tommy

Lapid, a prominent Israeli journalist and television personality, took over leadership of the party before the 1999 Knesset election. In 1999 the party received six seats and in 2003 fifteen seats. Sharon made it his primary coalition partner in 2003. Internal squabbling occurred in 2004. After the party crossed Prime Minister Ariel Sharon in December 2004 he fired all of its ministers and replaced it with Labor. In 2006 it was wiped out after failing to win a single seat.[32]

Those who are supporters of the two-state solution, both in Israel and abroad, needed a new Israeli partner to replace Labor as it lost support. They decided that Kadima would be that party that would anchor the process. But is Kadima a viable enough party to bear this weight?

Giora Goldberg wrote in 2011 that there have been six ways to analyze Kadima:

- As a classic Center party;
- as a neo-centrist party;
- as a centrist party in the Left bloc;
- as a Likud faction;
- as a middle party between the two blocs but not in the center;
- as sui generis.

He goes on to argue that it is in fact *sui generis*.[33] I would argue that it is similar to Dash, except from the Center-Right rather than from the Center-Left and that it has escaped — so far — the fate of the Center parties whose history I have just reviewed only because due to the lingering effect of Sharon's electoral charisma as Israel's third Mr. Security (after Moshe Dayan in the 1960s and early 1970s and Rabin in the 1980s),[34] it managed to win enough seats first time out to avoid the fate of Dash and the Center Party. Initially it was a virtual rebel Likud faction with enough Labor figures (Shimon Peres, Haim Ramon, et al.) to receive some support from Labor voters as well.

Under the leadership of Olmert it began moving leftwards and its bargaining positions in negotiations with the Palestinians in 2007–2008 were similar to those of Barak in 2000 and 2001.[35] It also suffered from a wave of corruption unprecedented since that which brought down Labor in the 1970s. Olmert was forced to step down as leader and resign as prime minister when he was indicted on political corruption charges. Omri Sharon, Sharon's eldest son and close advisor, went to prison in 2008 for political corruption. Haim Ramon was found guilty of sexual assault (forced kissing) in 2007. And Zachi Hanegbi, the son of Tehiya firebrand Geula Cohen and a former Likud justice minister, was excluded from the 2006 government due to his political corruption.[36] These two factors caused about a third of its voters to return to the Likud in 2009, and these were replaced by both the floating centrist vote from those who in the past voted for Shinui and then the Pensioners' Party and by cannibalizing the Left. In 2009 with Tzipi Livni as its leader it received votes from wealthier Labor voters and from Meretz voters — especially women.[37]

During the campaign the Likud ran a campaign against Livni that was personal, sexist, and patronizing. It was meant to appeal to the traditional view that women are not capable of handling security matters, despite Livni's career background as a Mossad officer, and also similar to the Hillary Clinton campaign against Obama in the 2008 primaries.[38] This ended up winning the sympathy vote of many women Meretz voters who abandoned their party for Livni. This had the effect of leaving Meretz with only three seats — the size of one of its three component factions in the 1980s. Labor was reduced to 13 seats — behind Israel Beitenu. Before the election 72 percent of Israeli Jews had defined themselves in surveys as belonging to the Right. For the first time since the 1920s a socialist Zionist party was not a major player in the politics of the Yishuv in Palestine or in Israel.[39]

Livni, who as foreign minister under Olmert had been on quite friendly terms with Secretary of State Condoleeza Rice, was the darling of the Israeli media. By refusing to bow to Shas's blackmail during coalition negotiations in 2008 she had been responsible for the early election in 2009. She then refused Netanyahu's invitation to join his coalition because he refused to commit himself to working for a two-state solution of the Israeli-Palestinian conflict. He would do this a few months later at a speech at Bar Ilan University in mid–June 2009. By letting Labor enter the coalition instead of Kadima, Livni had made a principled but costly decision. She had defeated former Defense Minister and Chief of Staff Shaul Mofaz in late 2008 by a narrow margin of 43.1 percent to 42 percent — comparable to the margin by which Rabin defeated Peres in 1974 for the Labor leadership — and this decision had the effect of exacerbating the enmity between their two camps. Over the next three years she proved to be rather a failure as a party leader and Mofaz easily defeated her for the party leadership in the primaries in 2012.[40]

At the time of the primary, polls were showing the party as likely to receive about half as many seats as it had in 2009. Elections must be held by November 2013, and have been scheduled for January 22, 2013.[41] Mofaz made a surprise deal with Netanyahu to enter the coalition and thus avoid early elections just as a bill to dissolve the Knesset for elections was about to go through its second of three mandatory readings. Mofaz declared that they had a deal to make a decision on replacing the Tal law that exempted ultra–Orthodox Jews from military conscription and to initiate election reform.[42] The deal bought Netanyahu time to deal with Iran before the next election — hopefully by forcing the West to force Tehran into renouncing a military nuclear potential and Mofaz time to do something before his party faced new elections. On June 14, 2012, Livni told the Israeli media that the party would no longer be around by the time the next election is held. Within weeks Haim Ramon, one of the original architects of the party with his "big bang theory" echoed her prediction. And *Yediot Ahronot* reported that in October Kadima MKs farther down the list were looking to join the Likud, or Labor or simply retire from politics.[43]

It is quite possible that in the next election former Labor and Meretz voters who voted for Kadima in 2009 will vote for Labor, thereby ending the latter's slide into oblivion, where it had bottomed out in 2010 after Barak's defection with only nine seats — the same size as Meretz in 1996. But whatever the result, Kadima, Labor and Meretz are unlikely to exceed by much their combined total of 44 seats. Any combined total less than fifty seats leaves them too far behind the total for the parties of the Right.

In the 32 years from 1977 to 2009 the Right has only been behind the Left twice in the interbloc balance: in 1992 by two seats and in 2006 by 20 seats (with Kadima from the Right being counted with the Left). Twice the two blocs have been tied: in 1984 and in 1999. In 1984 the two main parties formed a government of national unity, which is always a recipe for the preservation of the territorial status quo.[44] In 1999 a rather unstable Labor-led coalition resulted that shed all the religious parties that gave it a majority before the crucial negotiations at Camp David.[45]

Israel's multiparty system, which normally has between ten and twelve parties represented in the Knesset, is similar to those that existed in Weimar Germany in the 1920s and early 1930s, in the French Fourth Republic from 1946 to 1958, and in Italy in the second half of the twentieth century.

The most relevant of these for our purposes is the French Fourth Republic, which began its decolonization in the 1950s. It was able to decolonize from French Indochina in 1954 only after suffering a major military defeat at the Battle of Dien Bien Phu. Not having suffered such a defeat in Algeria, it was necessary for the French settlers in Algeria, the army and the Gaullists to conspire in a coup d'état in May 1958 that put de Gaulle in power as almost a proconsul. He wrote a new constitution and changed France from the parliamentary Fourth Republic to the semi-presidential Fifth Republic. Once this was completed he spent the next three years getting out of Algeria.[46]

A coup d'état was necessary because the "Algerian lobby" or settler lobby of those in favor of *Algerie française* knew how to exploit the party system of the Fourth Republic to preserve the status quo. They had representatives in all of the main parties from the socialists to the Gaullists.[47] Likewise, today the Israeli settlers have representatives in the main parties of the Right and in the past in Labor as well. During the Begin-Shamir era of 1977–1992 there were three main settler parties: the Likud, the National Religious Party (NRP), and Tehiya. The NRP has traditionally held control of key ministries that were crucial to the settlement enterprise. The *Gush Emunim* (bloc of believers) settlement movement took over control of the NRP in the 1970s through its Young Guard. They changed it from a rather accommodationist Orthodox party that was a reliable coalition partner for Labor to a settler party that was a reliable coalition partner for the Likud. Tehiya, which was created in 1979, went out of business in 1992 after bringing down the Likud-led coalition and then failing to meet the entry barrier to the Knesset. It had four framed portraits hanging on the wall of its main office in Jerusalem: Ze'ev Jabotinsky, Avraham Stern, Rav Zvi Yehuda Kook and Yitzhak Tabenkin. These were meant to appeal to its various electorates: former Likud voters, former NRP voters and Land of Israel Movement members.[48]

Hendrik Spruyt, a political scientist who wrote a book on decolonization in the British and French empires during the twentieth century,[49] argues that not only is Israel's electoral system very similar to that of the French Fourth Republic but that multiparty systems do not behave like two-party systems on territorial issues. This is both because the settler lobby is better organized than the proponents of change and because the diffuseness of power makes effecting change more difficult. Settlers almost uniformly and universally object to the status quo being changed. Party discipline can prevent political outbidding from occurring in multiparty democracies, but Israel has very weak party discipline with members of the Knesset (MKs) often switching parties within the same bloc, sometimes multiple times during a single Knesset. This is most common in the religious and Jewish Right blocs and among Center parties because they are often so ad hoc and unstable. Only one Knesset finished with the same number of parties that it began with and one MK switched party affiliations five times in one month. In sixty years Israel has only managed to make two reforms to its electoral system: raising the entry barrier from one to two percent (in two increments), and the disastrous double-vote system that was soon undone.[50]

It would take a very important, authoritative dynamic politician to change Israel's electoral system because most of the smaller parties, particularly the religious parties, have a vested interest in the status quo. In the past at least two significant attempts were made and failed. Ben-Gurion, Israel's first and third prime minister, had nearly fifteen years in office to effect change, and he failed to do so despite an expressed interest in change. In 1977 former Chief of Staff and world-famous archaeologist Prof. Yigael Yadin ran explicitly on the platform of electoral reform. But because the Democratic Movement for Change received only fifteen seats and the NRP received ten, Begin and the Likud were able to form a government without Dash. The only politician in the recent past likely to have been able to effect electoral change was Ariel Sharon. But instead he spent his political capital on disengagement. Until Israel develops another Sharon, electoral change will be impossible without the combined consent of the two largest parties and a few other MKs. Mofaz went into government with the Likud in the spring of 2012 in order to effect such reform but ended up leaving two months later when there was no electoral reform and no reform of the law that allowed the ultra–Orthodox to avoid military service. Netanyahu had caved to pressure from the religious parties.

Since the mid–1990s the Jewish immigrants from the former Soviet Union began to move to the Right, with most voting either directly for the Right or for two Russian ethnic parties, *Israel B'Aliya* and *Israel Beitenu*, which either merged with the Likud (the former) or emerged out of it (the latter). These immigrants — 850,000 between 1990 and 2000 — came from the largest country in the world to one that is quite small in both absolute and relative terms. So it is not surprising that many do not feel inclined to surrender more territory to Arabs, whom they compare to the anti–Semites in the former Soviet Union. Their protest vote in 1992 against the Right for mismanaging their absorption had given way to the feeling that they had to manage their own destiny by voting for ethnic Russian Jewish politicians in their own parties. Although they are not uniform in their voting patterns — no solid ethnic bloc: about 12–15 percent are on the Left, 25 percent on the Right, and the rest (60 percent) are floating voters — the majority vote Right of Center. In 1999 a large bloc of defectors left Israel B'Aliya and joined the newly formed Israel Beitenu. In 2003 after receiving only two seats, Israel B'Aliya joined the Likud. Israel Beitenu formed the National Union with two other rightist parties in 2003 and then a year later became a "Russian party with an Israeli accent."[51]

Starting in the 1980s the ultra–Orthodox or *haredi* religious parties have started to move towards the National Religious Party's brand of modern Orthodoxy or religious Zionism. These are known as *haredim leumim* or nationalist ultra–Orthodox. The singular abbreviation for this is *hardal*, or the Hebrew word for mustard.[52] And the religious Zionists have started to become more like the ultra–Orthodox. In the 1980s Shas leader Arye Deri was quite close to both Haim Ramon and Yossi Beilin in the Labor Party. But he was unable to sway his spiritual mentor, Rav. Ovadia Yosef, to support the formation of a Labor coalition in 1990.[53] Today this would probably not even be considered. In a few decades the two groups may have few differences between them. Some Israeli political scientists have referred to Russian Jews and ultra–Orthodox as the "soft right."[54] This is in addition to the Likud and the NRP, which was renamed Beit Yehudi ("Jewish home").

Competition from Israel Beitenu and Beit Yehudi keeps the Likud from growing too moderate on territorial issues. But the Likud remains the most powerful party on the Israeli Right and the one whose ideology and history we must focus on in determining the limits of Israeli concessions. We must now look at the history of Revisionist Zionism.

CHAPTER TWO

Revisionist History
and Ideology

In 1922 British Colonial Secretary Winston Churchill unilaterally partitioned the east bank of the Jordan River — what is today the country of Jordan — to give to Abdullah I, the son of Feisal, who had been been kicked out of Damascus by the French. The British had established two branches of the Hashemite dynasty of the Hejaz in Arabia in their mandatory territories of Iraq and Palestine, the partitioned portion to be known as Transjordan. This caused Vladimir "Ze'ev" Jabotinsky, the founder of the Jewish Legion, which had fought for the British in its Palestine campaign during World War I, to resign from the executive of the World Zionist Organization the following year because he did not think that its reaction was sufficiently vigorous.[1]

Over the next fifteen years Jabotinsky, a Russian Jewish bon vivant and polyglot intellectual journalist from Odessa, was to create an alternate ideology and organizational infrastructure that was the basis of the Israeli Right after independence. The Revisionist Movement consisted of three parts: the Revisionist Party, or HaTzohar, founded in a Paris café in 1925; the Betar youth movement, founded in Riga in 1923; and the Irgun Zvai Leumi (National Military Organization), or Etzel (the Hebrew acronym for IZL), founded in Palestine in 1937. Jabotinsky was not a politician and considered himself to be more a prophet or seer, that is an ideologue, than a practical politician. Jabotinsky had been arrested in 1920 for his role in founding the Hagana as a self-defense organization to protect Jews during Arab communal rioting. He was eventually released after a few months despite having been sentenced to years in prison. In late 1929 he was permanently exiled from Palestine for the role of some of his followers in provoking the Arab pogroms that roiled the territory in August. And after 1917 he was exiled from Russia by the Russian Revolution, so that he faced a double exile from the land of his birth and his ideological homeland.[2]

A decade after he founded the Revisionist Party, Jabotinsky withdrew from the World Zionist Organization (WZO) to form the New Zionist Organization (NZO), after he made paying the annual dues to the WZO voluntary for his followers. So the WZO retaliated by suspending the Revisionist Party's participation and funding and he withdrew. The Revisionists were always much stronger in the Eastern European diaspora than they were in the Jewish Yishuv (colony) in Palestine. Betar was strongest in Poland, where it had some 60,000 members. It also had branches in Czechoslovakia, the Baltic States, Romania, Hungary, Italy, France, and the United States — twenty six countries in all, with a total membership of 78,000 in 1938.[3]

Jabotinsky saw himself as the natural successor to Theodor Herzl, who had founded political Zionism in 1896. He was in competition with both Chaim Weizmann, who had procured the Balfour Declaration from Britain in 1917 and was the leader of the World Zionist Organization, and with David Ben-Gurion, who headed the Jewish Agency in Palestine that dealt with the British mandatory authorities. Jabotinsky's Revisionist ideology had three main ideas: *hadar* (dignity and pride), *monism,* and *territorial maximism.* Jabotinsky's personal authority united the three branches of the movement. *Hadar* meant that Jews should be well groomed, polite, and full of ethnic pride. He believed in the outward trappings of power: a flag, an army, a government, and so forth. He also believed in political realism — the combination of one's own strength plus that of political allies in order to achieve one's goals. *Monism,* or oneness, meant that the Zionist movement should only have a single goal — national independence in its homeland. He used the Orthodox religious prohibition against mixing different types of fabrics to illustrate his belief that Zionism could not be mixed with other non–Jewish universalistic creeds such as communism, socialism, or fascism.[4]

Of course, he was himself a nineteenth century liberal (today a conservative), and he did not consider this mixing an alien belief system with Zionism. During the 1930s he was in competition with a trio of ideologues within Palestine who had joined the movement followed the Arab pogrom of 1929. These three, Abba Achimeir, Y.H. Yevin, and Uri Zvi Greenberg, all came from the Left and were admirers of both Lenin and Mussolini.

Achimeir formed a group called *Brit haBiryonim* ("union of thugs") and considered himself a fascist. The three urged Jabotinsky to transform himself into a fascist-style dictator of the Radical Right but he resisted.[5]

Jabotinsky was not an admirer of Mussolini but toyed with the idea of letting Italy inherit the Palestine mandate from Britain as a means of keeping pressure on London to fulfill the mandate's terms. Jabotinsky, who had studied in Italy at the turn of the century, was an Italophile. In 1933 the Polish Betar leaders signed a petition advocating "a closing of the English chapter," that is, the end of the British mandate in Palestine. Menachem Begin was one of the signators.[6]

In 1923, the same year he resigned from the Zionist executive, Jabotinsky published two articles entitled "The Iron Wall." He prefaced one by stating that he was indifferent to Arabs but the attitude of Arabs to Zionism was of great importance. Jabotinsky was morally opposed to expelling the Arabs from Palestine. He believed that at present and for the foreseeable future it would be impossible to arrive at a peace agreement with the Arabs. Therefore it was necessary for the Zionists to build up an "iron wall" of bayonets behind which they could protect themselves from Arab hostility until such time as the Arabs were ready to come to an accommodation with them. Professor Avi Shlaim of the London School of Economics claims that the labor Zionist leadership of Israel in Mapai and the Labor Party later adopted this doctrine without attribution. In truth, they probably came to the same conclusion a few decades after Jabotinsky, following the Arab Revolt and the War of Independence. But Shlaim notes that Jabotinsky thought that the Zionists should come to an accommodation with the Arabs whereas today's Likud leaders believe that such an accommodation is impossible.[7] In defense of today's Likud leaders, Jabotinsky never gave up his belief that Israel should occupy, not only all of Western Palestine — Israel, Gaza and the West Bank — but Transjordan as well.

In 1931 Avraham Tahomei, an officer in the Hagana, quit the organization and formed his own breakaway faction, Hagana B, over a number of policy questions. Hagana B was joined by a number of Revisionists and yeshiva students in Palestine. When Tahomei returned to the Hagana in 1937, the Revisionists founded the Irgun Zvai Leumi.[8]

In April 1936 the Mufti of Jerusalem, Haj Amin al-Husseini, the Arab leader that the British dealt with, declared a general strike that soon turned into an armed revolt against both the British and the Zionists. The Hagana instituted a policy of *havlaga,* or restraint, in the face of the Arab Revolt. The Maximalists called for a more vigorous policy of resistance. The Etzel began advocating reprisal attacks for attacks on Jews.

In 1937 the British appointed a commission led by Lord Peel to investigate the situation in Palestine and the viability of the British commitment to a Jewish national home under the League of Nations mandate. Both Weizmann and Jabotinsky gave evidence before the commission. On February 11, 1937, Jabotinsky told the Peel Commission, "If Great Britain really is unable to do it [carry out the Mandate], we will bow to her decision, but we then shall expect Great Britain to act as any Mandatory who feels he cannot carry out the Mandate: give back the Mandate."[9]

The commission came up with a partition plan, the Peel Plan, that divided Palestine into three areas: an Arab state in Judea, Samaria, and the Negev, a Jewish state in the coastal plain, Jezreel Valley, and Galilee, and a neutral mandatory corridor that ran from Bethlehem, Jerusalem and Ramallah in the East to just south of Jaffa. The British press began hinting that partition would be the recommended solution in April, and the official recommendation came in July. The mainstream Zionists accepted the partition; the Revisionists and the Arabs rejected it. Jabotinsky went on a speaking tour of South Africa in 1937 in opposition to the partition plan and to promote an evacuation of Jews from Eastern Europe in light of the danger from Hitler. In a speech on July 7, 1937, that was telephoned to supporters in the Yishuv, Jabotinsky predicted that Britain would never try to implement the partition scheme. He compared it to the Latin verb form *aio*: "It is present, it is imperfect, and it has no future." In November 1938 a second British commission, the Woodhead Commission, told parliament that partition was not practicable. After this, Jabotinsky gave up any talk of replacing Britain as the mandatory power.[10]

During July 1938 the Etzel carried out a reprisal bombing in the Arab market in Haifa and Jabotinsky condemned it. The month before an illegal immigrant from America, Shlomo Ben-Yosef, was hanged for attacking an Arab bus as part of a reprisal attack. He is considered a nationalist hero by the Israeli Education Ministry today. Jabotinsky's protests were ridiculed by the Etzel leadership.[11]

At the Third World Conference of Betar in Warsaw in September 1938, Begin made a speech attacking Jabotinsky's policies of restraint. Begin was under pressure to keep Avraham Stern, a leading Irgunist, from recruiting Betar members into the Etzel. Jabotinsky interrupted him several times with pertinent questions, and then at the end made a realist attack on Begin's speech and compared it to the noise of a squeaky door. In his speech, Begin proclaimed the start of the third period of Zionism — military Zionism — after practical Zionism, which began in 1882 with settlement in Palestine, and political Zionism, which Herzl founded in 1896. Jabotinsky told four of the Betar speakers that they should commit suicide, so in mock seriousness they drew up a suicide club agreement with an eighteen-point constitution and presented it to Jabotinsky, who then initialed it.[12]

The next decade was the period of military Zionism, and from September 1938 to February 1949 there was a transition from the leadership of Jabotinsky to that of Begin. Jabotinsky had little influence during the remaining two years of his life, before his death of a heart attack in New York in early August 1940, due to a de facto alliance between Betar and the Etzel against him and the Revisionist Party. Jabotinsky spent the last five months of his life in New York. In September 1939 Jabotinsky threw his support behind Britain in the Second World War.[13]

This led to a split in the Etzel in 1940 when Avraham Stern, a classics student at the Hebrew University who was not a Revisionist, left with his followers to form the *Irgun Zvai Leumi B' Eretz Israel* ("Etzel in the Land of Israel/Palestine"). It carried out an abortive terrorist campaign against the British in the winter of 1941–42 that resulted in Stern's murder by the British police and the arrest of most of its leaders. In 1943 Yitzhak Shamir, after escaping from a prison camp by tunneling, reformed the Stern Gang, as the British and its Zionist opponents dubbed it, as *Lohemei Herut Israel* (Fighters for the Freedom of Israel), or Lehi.[14]

Initially about a third of Etzel remained loyal to leader David Raziel, about a third defected to Stern, and about a third became inactive and dropped out rather than deciding between the two. Raziel was killed while serving on a secret mission for the British in Iraq in 1941. He was followed by Ya'akov Meridor, who served as an interim leader until Begin could get himself released from General Anders's Polish army.

Begin had become head of Polish Betar in 1939. In September 1939 he fled to Vilnius with his wife and Israel Eldad, later the ideologue of Lehi. In Vilnius he was arrested by the Soviet secret police, the NKVD, and imprisoned in Siberia for anti–Soviet activities — being a Zionist leader in Poland. Shortly after traveling across the Soviet Union in a prison train, he was released from prison to join General Anders's Polish army, which was being sent to fight the Axis in North Africa. After arriving in Palestine in 1942, Zionists managed to arrange a discharge for Begin from the army. Begin was appointed the head of Betar worldwide — although he had little communication with most Betar members in Eastern Europe. In 1943 he took command of the Etzel from Meridor. In February 1944 he declared an armed struggle against the British mandate in Palestine — after the Axis had been defeated in North Africa and Iraq.[15]

For the next four years, Begin ran the revolt from his Tel Aviv apartment. He was overall commander but in practice decided upon political strategy and wrote propaganda articles for the underground newspaper and wall posters that his poster boys put up at night. In the fall of 1944 the Hagana hunted down Irgun members and turned them over to the British in what became known as the *saison,* or hunting season. This was following the assassination by the Lehi of the British official in charge of the Middle East, Lord Moyne, in Cairo in November. During 1945–46 there was a United Resistance Movement consisting of Etzel, Lehi and the Hagana. After the Etzel blew up the wing of the King David Hotel in Jerusalem, which was serving as British military headquarters, in July 1946, the cooperation came to an end. Etzel and Lehi continued to cooperate so that one organization's operations would not interfere with the other's.[16]

In May 1948 Begin merged his men, except in Jerusalem, which remained separate under the partition plan, into the Israeli army. Before that, in April, his fighters and those of Lehi carried out a joint attack on the village of Deir Yassin, outside of Jerusalem, where Givat Shaul is today. The fighters took some casualties during the initial fighting that they were not used to, and so in revenge they massacred their captives after parading them through the streets of Jerusalem, figures given for the Arab dead in the massacre range from 90 to 250. The Arab leadership played up this massacre in their propaganda and it helped to set off a Palestinian refugee exodus.[17]

In June a surplus American landing ship full of weapons was donated by France to the Etzel command in Europe. They sailed the ship to Palestine and after unloading weapons near Haifa, the ship, dubbed the *Altalena* after one of Jabotinsky's pen names, sailed to Tel Aviv. Begin was willing to turn most of the arms over to the new IDF but wanted a small share to go to the Etzel in Jerusalem. Ben-Gurion refused and ordered one of the IDF's few cannons to open fire on the ship. The ship was sunk, but Begin resisted Eldad's advice to declare a revolt against the new Israeli government.[18]

In June 1948 Begin emerged from the underground and founded the Herut (Freedom) Party — named after the Etzel's underground newspaper — and positioned himself as Jabotinsky's natural successor. Begin simply converted the Etzel's ruling council into the party executive. Over time he would purge many Etzel figures who were too independent and rely mostly on Etzel's administrative staff, who were used to taking orders rather than using initiative.[19]

For Herut's first seventeen years it was in the political wilderness. Begin built his power on the Right on the basis of three myths that were not subject to argument or discussion. Anyone who questioned them was marginalized. The first was that Begin was Jabotinsky's natural successor. In this he was copying Edward Rydz Smigly, the Polish colonel who presented himself as Pilsudski's heir in 1935. The second was that the borders of mandatory Palestine were the same as the historical boundaries of Eretz Israel (the land of Israel/Palestine). The third was that Etzel's revolt was the main factor — in fact, the only important factor — in Britain's exit from Palestine.[20]

Jabotinsky never appointed a successor while he was alive but probably intended that his son Eri would become head of the Zionist movement. Begin coopted Eri Jabotinsky and a number of figures from the Etzel's European and American branches on to his Herut list for the elections to the First Knesset in February 1949. The Knesset then had an entry barrier of only one percent. Begin faced three competing lists from the secular Right: the official Revisionist Party, Meir Grossman's State List, and Lehi's Fighters List. The first two failed to cross the entry barrier and the Fighters List won only a single seat. But this was enough to keep its leaders out of prison following the murder of UN mediator Count Folke Bernadotte in September 1948. The Fighters List failed to run candidates for the Second Knesset in 1951 and it disbanded. Eldad wrote his memoir of the Lehi insurgency and then went into radical nationalist writing. Nathan Yellin-Mor, Lehi's political leader, later became pro–Palestinian and an advocate of peace. Yitzhak Shamir, Lehi's operations officer, went into business for seven years and then went to work for the Mossad for a decade in Europe. After he retired from the Mossad Begin recruited him into Herut.[21]

Begin started out calling for war against Jordan in order to conquer the east bank. Ben-Gurion contemptuously refused to refer to Begin by name in the Knesset and ridiculed his extreme nationalism. Ben-Gurion had a declared policy of forming coalitions with all parties except Herut and the Communists. In 1951 Herut went from 15 seats to only eight seats and Begin went into depression and considered retirement from politics. He was only brought back by the controversy over German reparations. He presided over a riot against the police outside the Knesset in downtown Jerusalem. In 1955 he called for the General Zionists to form a joint list with Herut. The General Zionists were the former supporters of Chaim Weizmann and consisted of small businessmen from Eastern Europe who supported capitalism. They rejected his overtures because of his extremist rhetoric and reputation.[22]

A decade later in 1965, before the elections for the Sixth Knesset, the Liberals (as the General Zionists were now called) negotiated a common voter's list with Herut, known as Gahal or *Gush Herut Liberalim* (Herut-Liberals bloc). In the first subsequent election in 1965 Gahal won only 26 seats, fifteen for Herut and eleven for the Liberals — fewer than what the two parties had won separately. Gahal repeated this total in 1969. At the same time the Left was going through a similar consolidation. In 1965 as Ben-Gurion defected from Mapai to form Rafi, Rafi and Ahdut Ha'Avoda joined together to form the first alignment. In 1968 Rafi would rejoin these two parties to form the Israel Labor Party and a year later Labor formed a common list with Mapam, known as the Alignment, that lasted for fifteen years.

The Gahal alliance worked by Begin deferring to Liberal leader Simha Erlich on all economic matters and Erlich deferring to Begin on all foreign policy and defense questions. This pattern would continue when Gahal became the Likud.[23]

In 1966 Shmuel Tamir, a prominent Jerusalem lawyer and former Etzel commander in Jerusalem, attacked Begin head-on at the annual Herut convention. He considered Begin to be a relic of the past. He wanted to democratize the party and bring in figures that were not part of "the fighting family," as Etzel veterans referred to each other. The party executive voted to discipline Tamir after an associate published an article critical of

Begin. Tamir refused to accept the punishment and resigned from Herut along with two other MKs and a number of the party's Young Guard, including Ehud Olmert, to form the Free Center. In the 1969 election the party gained two seats.[24]

But 26 seats was enough so that in late May 1967 Begin could initiate discussions with the National Religious Party and Rafi about forming a national unity government with Mapai and Ahdut Ha'Avoda and making David Ben-Gurion, who had retired as prime minister in June 1963, prime minister. Ben-Gurion did not want to return to government and Eshkol would not give up his place for him, but Rafi pushed to have Moshe Dayan appointed defense minister.

Together Rafi, the NRP, and Gahal went to prime minister Levi Eshkol and coerced or persuaded him to form a government of national unity that included Rafi and Gahal. Moshe Dayan was made defense minister instead of Yigal Allon, who was Eshkol's candidate. Historian Peter Medding considers the formation of this government, against Ben-Gurion's norm of excluding Herut, to signal the end of Israel's First Republic, or founding period, and the start of the second. Others have placed this point in 1977, when the Likud replaced Labor in power. I argue that a case can be made for dating it to 1974, when Yitzhak Rabin became the first prime minister who was not from Mapai and who was not from the generation that founded the state, but rather from the generation that defended it in 1948.[25]

Begin entered the government as minister without portfolio, which meant that he was responsible for whatever tasks Eshkol assigned to him or he could persuade Eshkol to give him. In February 1969 Eshkol died of a heart attack and was replaced by foreign minister Golda Meir as a compromise candidate between defense minister Moshe Dayan and labor minister Yigal Allon. Meir offered Gahal four additional ministries to remain in the government and said she would agree not to give back the West Bank. Most of Herut and the Liberals wished to remain in the government, which is what Begin feared. He feared that the love of power would replace ideology as the motivating force in his party.

But in December 1969 American secretary of state William Rogers came to the Middle East to negotiate a peace agreement. Begin suddenly decided that Gahal was needed in the government to prevent Meir from giving away the store. Begin negotiated five additional seats in the government for Gahal — two for Herut and three for the Liberals. He wanted to give the two additional Herut seats to Haim Landau and Ya'akov Meridor. Meridor wanted to retire and go into business, and he had already promised a seat to General Ezer Weizman, the deputy chief of staff, who was leaving the IDF. Reluctantly Begin relented and Weizman "parachuted" into the government as transportation minister. This later led to a mandatory "cooling-off" period for generals between retirement and entry into politics so that parties could not poach generals from the IDF.

In August 1970, after Meir decided that UN Security Council Resolution 242, which mandated that Israel withdraw from "territories captured in the recent conflict," applied to all of Israel's fronts with the Arabs, Begin decided to withdraw from the government. He narrowly won a vote over the objection of several Liberals and Meridor and Weizman. On August 6, 1970 Gahal pulled out of the government shortly before the Rogers Plan collapsed and was replaced by a ceasefire agreement on the Sinai front that ended the War of Attrition.[26] This decision angered Weizman, who then started actively recruiting his own supporters to replace members of the "fighting family." Weizman wanted a party that could capture power rather than a party of nostalgia for underground veterans.

In 1972 at the Herut annual convention, Weizman openly challenged Begin's leadership of the party. Begin easily slapped him down and replaced Weizman's supporters with his own in positions of power. Among these new people was Yitzhak Shamir.[27]

Ariel Sharon, a hero of the 1950s reprisal raids as well as a hero of the Six Day War, retired from the IDF in the summer of 1973. He decided that he wanted to pursue a political career as well as the life of a farmer on his ranch near Beersheba. But like Weizman, Sharon wanted to actually serve in government, so he decided to form a new opposition out of all of the secular parties of the Right. After holding a press conference following his retirement he began holding meetings with the leaders of the various opposition parties: Begin of Herut, Erlich of the Liberals, Shmuel Tamir of the Free Center, and Yigal Hurewitz of the State List (the remnant of Rafi after Rafi joined the Labor Party in 1968) and the Land of Israel Movement. When Begin appeared reluctant to cooperate, Sharon enlisted the help of Weizman and the two generals threatened to withdraw from politics unless there was union. In September 1973 the leaders of the four parties signed an agreement to form a common Knesset list. In the election held on December 31, 1973, while Israeli troops were still on alert on the Sinai and Golan fronts following the ceasefire that ended the Yom Kippur War on October 24, the Likud won 39 seats.[28]

Sharon initially joined the Liberals rather than Herut, his natural home in the Likud, so that he would not have to compete with Weizman for star billing. Sharon arranged a commission as the commander of a reserve armored division and spent most of his time on military matters and farming rather than participating in Knesset debates and party matters. Opponents in the Knesset passed a law prohibiting Knesset members from holding an active reserve commission at Sharon's rank, so he resigned his Knesset seat in December 1974. He was still hoping that he could eventually become chief of staff.[29]

In 1976 the Free Center and State List organized themselves into a common faction within the Likud, La'am ("to the people") along with members of the Land of Israel Movement. This was made easier by Free Center leader Shmuel Tamir exiting his own party to join Yigael Yadin's Democratic Movement for Change. In 1985 La'am joined Herut as the two parties had few differences on foreign policy — both parties were populated by hawks who were interested in defense and foreign affairs rather than social policy and economics.[30]

In May 1977 the combination of the shift of the mizrakhi vote to the Likud, the formation of the Democratic Movement for Change and a number of corruption scandals within the Labor Party made the situation ripe for the *ma'apach,* a Hebrew word related to the word for revolution and usually translated as "earthquake" or "upset." Ezer Weizman had been appointed by Begin as head of the Likud's election effort; Sharon had led it in 1973. Weizman downplayed ideology and portrayed Begin as a kind grandfather and family man, a safe leader in whom to entrust the future of the state. The Likud won 43 seats and Labor was reduced to only 32 seats. Notice that this is more than the Likud and Kadima have usually received since 2000. Sharon ran as head of his own party, *Shlomzion,* after both wings of the Likud failed to readmit him. He received only two seats — barely passing the entry barrier — and quickly joined Herut.[31]

Begin's first government of 1977–1980 can best be described as a transitional government rather than a real Herut or Likud government. Moshe Dayan served as foreign minister and Yigael Yadin as deputy prime minister. Begin wanted to make peace with Egypt and wanted as many former generals as possible in his cabinet in order to scare the Egyptians. He needed Dayan to reassure Washington. During Begin's first three years in power he carried out two major efforts: he made peace with Egypt (described in another chapter) and began a major settlement effort of the West Bank spearheaded by Agriculture Minister Sharon, who headed the government committee on settlement.

Moshe Dayan resigned after concluding a peace treaty with Egypt, after Yosef Burg of the NRP was placed in charge of the autonomy negotiations with Egypt. Weizman resigned as defense minister in March 1980 to protest the government's preference for settlement of the territories over consolidation of the peace process with Egypt. Dayan ran in the 1981 election and was elected to the Knesset before dying of cancer in October. Weizman went into business and made some money for his family before he set up his own party in 1984, Yahad, which then took him into the Labor Party. He would eventually be one of that party's leading doves. Begin replaced Weizman as defense minister in the pre–1967 pattern until the 1981 election.[32]

In 1981 Begin formed the first ideological Likud government with Yitzhak Shamir as foreign minister and Sharon as defense minister. Sharon began drawing up plans for an invasion of Lebanon in order to destroy the PLO's infrastructure in southern Lebanon and Beirut and to make Lebanon an overt ally of Israel. In December 1981 Israel annexed the Golan Heights in violation of the 1974 separation-of-forces agreement with Syria.

When Israel's ambassador to London was seriously wounded in an assassination attempt by a non–PLO Palestinian terrorist from the Abu Nidal faction, Sharon took advantage of the opportunity and shelled PLO positions, provoking a counter-bombardment of northern Israel. Two days later, on the fifteenth anniversary of the Six Day War, Israel invaded Lebanon. Sharon had the IDF push on to the outskirts of Beirut even though he had earlier assured the cabinet that the invasion would be basically a larger repeat of a 1978 invasion of southern Lebanon.[33]

Begin suffered from lifelong depression. In 1951 when Herut was reduced from 14 seats to only eight he went into depression. His wife, Aliza, died in November 1982. This, combined with the casualty reports from Lebanon and the condemnation of Israel due to the Sabra and Shatilla massacres (of Palestinians by Israel's Maronite Christian allies in Beirut), led to Begin going into depression. Finally, in September 1983, he told his cabinet that he could continue no longer and resigned as prime minister. Yitzhak Shamir was chosen by the Likud to take his place as party leader and prime minister.[34]

Begin's foreign policy was all aimed at ensuring the eventual annexation of the West Bank, either formal or de facto, by Israel. The invasion of Lebanon was in order to destroy the PLO as both a political and a military factor. The memorandum of understanding concluded with the United States in November 1981 was designed to assure American support or at least acquiescence in Israeli settlement on the West Bank. The Golan annexation was a test case. And the peace treaty with Egypt was envisioned by Begin as a de facto trade of the Sinai for the West Bank.

Ilan Peleg, an academic student of the Likud has argued, like Colin Shindler, that Begin basically redefined Revisionism. The two differ in their assessment of Jabotinsky, with Shindler seeing him as a classic nineteenth century liberal, or what we would call today a conservative, whereas Peleg sees him as a figure of the Radical Right combining conservative and protofascist beliefs. Peleg refers to the ideology of Herut and the Likud as Neo-Revisionism (Beginism). He argues that it consists of seven main traits:

• An emphasis on power, particularly military power, as the sole instrument in international relations;
• a tendency to romanticize the nation;
• seeing the outside world as anti–Semitic and dedicated to destroying Israel;
• an effort to dehumanize the enemy;
• an emphasis on territorial expansion and national rights;
• the equation of internal dissent with treason;
• and a continuous disrespect for international law.[35]

But Peleg argues that Neo-Revisionism is not fascism for a number of reasons:

• Neo-Revisionism does not demand a transfer of all power to the state;
• Neo-Revisionists are still committed to democracy and basic liberties;
• Neo-Revisionists do not glorify the past to the same degree as do fascists;

- Dreams of grandeur and glory are limited in Neo-Revisionism;
- Stylistic similarities with fascism are limited;
- Neo-Revisionism is a combination of secular realism and religious messianism and it looks to traditional values as a source of legitimacy.[36]

Shamir was a less flamboyant, articulate and more cautious copy of Begin. Like Begin he had been a senior figure in the underground, but in Lehi rather than the Etzel. Shamir, like Begin, was from Poland and was a member of Betar. After graduating with a law degree from Hebrew University, he joined Etzel in 1937 and then the Stern Group in 1941. He had an interrupted business career from 1948 to 1955 and from 1965 to 1970. He entered politics in 1970 after Begin recruited him to the executive of Herut. In 1977 after the Likud election victory, he was made speaker of the Knesset. He became foreign minister in March 1980, after Dayan's resignation. As foreign minister he oversaw the implementation of diplomatic relations with Egypt, after he abstained from voting on the peace treaty in the Knesset. He also oversaw the peace negotiations with Lebanon that resulted in a peace treaty that was never signed due to Syrian pressure on Beirut. He also oversaw the reestablishment of diplomatic relations with a number of African countries.[37]

Shamir was a long-term interim leader, presiding over his party during the era of national unity governments with Labor. As party leader he oversaw the merger with La'am in 1985, which essentially turned the Likud back into Gahal, and then the conversion of the Likud from a joint list to a full party in 1988.[38] The Liberals had lost out in the merger, and eventually even finance ministers like Benjamin Netanyahu would come from Herut.

Shamir's main task from 1984 to 1990 as first a co-equal and then as the prime minister was to prevent Shimon Peres and the Labor Party from introducing schemes for peace deals with Jordan or the Palestinians that would endanger Israel's control over the West Bank. From June 1984 to October 1986 Shamir was foreign minister and Peres was prime minister, and in October the two traded jobs as part of the rotation scheme. In 1987 Peres met with King Hussein in London and the two leaders decided upon an international conference on the Middle East. Shamir opposed the idea, and when Peres tried to enlist the support of secretary of state George Shultz to introduce the idea as an American plan, Shultz demurred.[39]

In December 1988 the United States recognized the Palestine Liberation Organization (PLO) as the representative of the Palestinians after the PLO recognized UN Security Council Resolution 242 and renounced terrorism. In 1989 Defense Minister Rabin came up with a plan for internal Palestinian elections in the territories that would elect representatives to negotiate peace with Israel. The plan was adopted by Shamir and became known as the Shamir-Rabin plan. But in order to outmaneuver him, three rivals in the Likud, Ariel Sharon, David Levy and Yitzhak Moda'I introduced resolutions putting restrictions on the plan that would keep the Palestinians from accepting it. Shamir officially promoted his own plan, but within the party he deferred to the "constraints ministers" and allowed his plan to die a slow death in the Knesset.[40]

When Ezer Weizman met with representatives of the PLO in Europe, Shamir moved to have him removed from the government. Peres and Rabin came to his defense and Weizman was reprimanded but remained in government.[41]

Herut during the 1980s consisted of three main camps: one loyal to Ariel Sharon, one of mizrakhi members from the development towns and urban slums loyal to David Levy, and a large central camp led by Shamir and Moshe Arens. Arens was a Latvian-American who graduated from the Massachusetts Institute of Technology and served in the American army before immigrating to Israel. He made his career as an aeronautical engineer designing jet aircraft for Israel's military industries before becoming ambassador to Washington during the First Lebanon War and then defense minister. During Shamir's Likud-led government of 1990–92 he was foreign minister during the Gulf War. Arens voted against the Egyptian-Israeli peace treaty. He was ideologically very similar to Shamir and was expected to be his successor as Likud leader. But when the Likud was defeated in the 1992 elections, Arens unexpectedly resigned from politics following Shamir's resignation as party leader. He had no desire to take on the task of rebuilding the party.[42]

A key faction in the Shamir-Arens camp was the "princes"—a group of second-generation Revisionists whose fathers had played major roles in either the Revisionist Party or the Etzel before going on to have careers in Herut and the Likud. They included: Benny Begin, son of the Etzel commander and Herut leader; Benjamin Netanyahu, son of a confidant of Jabotinsky's; Dan Meridor, nephew of Ya'akov Meridor, the former Etzel commander; Ron Milo; Uzi Landau, son of Herut minister Haim Landau; Tzahi Hanegbi, son of Lehi's radio announcer and the Likud and Tehiya MK Geula Cohen; and Tzipi Livni, daughter of an Etzel commander. The most prominent were Begin, Netanyahu and Meridor. Begin had trained as a geologist and went into politics rather late in his life. Meridor was a lawyer who had served as Menachem Begin's personal advisor at Camp David in 1978. Netanyahu, after serving as a commando in the Sayeret Matkal (Headquarters Reconnaissance) unit under Ehud Barak, embarked on a business career in the United States. Raised in both Israel and the United States, where his father Benzion was a professor of Jewish history, Netanyahu entered politics after Arens recruited him to serve in the Israeli embassy because of his fluent American English. He then went on to serve as Israel's ambassador to the United Nations during the early 1990s. In this role he became known to Israelis through his many television appearances on ABC's *Nightline*.[43]

It was the princes that provided the contestants in the Likud's leadership election in 1993. Uzi Baram had introduced American-style primary elections in Labor in 1988. Netanyahu urged that his party not give Labor the advantage and so should copy the innovation. Netanyahu defeated Begin and David Levy in March 1993 with 52 percent to half that for his nearest rival, Levy.[44]

Benjamin Netanyahu is one of three sons of Benzion Netanyahu, who was a senior literary figure in the Revisionist Party in Palestine close to Abba Achimeir and then in Herut before he was forced to move to the United States to seek employment. Benzion was a scholar of Jewish history specializing in medieval Spain. In his monumental work on the subject he contended that the marranos or conversos, Spanish Jews who converted to Christianity, were not persecuted by the Inquistion because they remained secretly loyal to Judaism but simply because they were Jews. He passed on to his three sons a love of Israel and a suspicion of Gentiles.

Benjamin, or "Bibi," as he is universally known in Israel, grew up in both Israel and the United States. After he completed his military duty in the *sayeret matkal* (headquarters reconnaissance) unit under his brother Yonatan and Ehud Barak, he returned to the United States to study business at the Massachusetts Institute of Technology and work for Boston Consulting. After two failed marriages due to womanizing, Netanyahu formed a lasting, if volatile, relationship with his third wife, Sara.

Netanyahu's rise through the ranks of the Likud was rapid due to his almost native English ability and his command of television, developed through methodical practice and analysis. Taking over the party just as the Oslo process was starting, he led its opposition to the process. This opposition was based both on mistrust of the Palestinians in general and Yasir Arafat in particular and an unwillingness to cede control of Judea and Samaria to Arab control. In June 1996 he defeated Peres in the first double-vote election in Israeli history. He had a solid victory among Jews, but the votes from Israeli Arabs made it a narrow victory, with Peres going to bed thinking that he had won.[45]

Netanyahu formed a narrow government based on the Right and the religious parties. He vowed to honor Israel's commitments under the Oslo agreements, but added that Israel was in trouble as Arafat used the opening of an ancient tunnel to give tourists a quicker access to tourist sites to exploit Palestinian suspicions of Israel. Riots followed and 37 Palestinian police and 29 civilians as well as 16 Israeli police and soldiers died in the gun battles that accompanied the riots.[46]

This, along with a bungled Mossad assassination attempt against Hamas leader Khalid Meshal in Amman in September 1997, earned Netanyahu a reputation as a clumsy operator in Washington.[47] In Dennis Ross's memoir, *The Missing Peace,* Netanyahu is the villain as well as Arafat. Ross blames Netanyahu for breaking the momentum of the peace process.[48] Netanyahu did sign two agreements while in office. First, he signed an agreement in 1997 leading to a separation between Jewish settlers and Palestinians in Hebron.[49]

Then, in October 1998, he signed the Wye River agreement, which ceded an additional 13 percent of territory to the Palestinian Authority after King Hussein left his sick bed at the Mayo clinic in Rochester, Minnesota, to plead for an agreement. Before the summit he appointed Ariel Sharon as his foreign minister, completing Sharon's rehabilitation within the party. But despite the cabinet and the Knesset approving the agreement, his party balked. In December many in his coalition voted in favor of an opposition no-confidence motion and his government collapsed, leading to new elections.[50]

In Israel's second double-vote election, Barak was elected by a wide margin over Netanyahu, 56 to 44 percent — much wider than the margin between the Left and Right.[51] Netanyahu promptly resigned from the Knesset and went into temporary political retirement. Sharon took over as party leader. Barak then proved to be too cautious with Syria and too bold with the Palestinians, which meant that he lost the prime ministerial contest with Sharon by an even wider margin than he had beaten Netanyahu by less than two years before.[52]

Sharon is usually described as coming from a Mapai background. This is only partially true. His father and mother were Jewish nationalists who were suspicious of socialism within a Mapai settlement. Sharon was taught by his father basic Jewish nationalism and a suspicion of Arabs. He then spent his formative years within labor Zionist institutions such as the Hagana and the IDF. During the 1950s he carried a Mapai membership card. During the Six Day War he began to move to the Right to a Rafi position close to that of Dayan and Peres (when the latter was a hawk). But he passed up a political career in the Labor Party in favor of one in the Right.[53]

Sharon had a nearly 33-year long political career from when he midwifed the birth of the Likud in September 1973 to his forced retirement from politics with a massive stroke in January 2006. During that time he created three political parties (the Likud, Shlomzion, and Kadima) but spent the vast majority of his career within the Herut portion of the Likud. His career can be divided into three portions: his rise and fall, September 1973 to February 1983; his exile and slow recovery, February 1983 to October 1998; and his triumph, October 1998 to January 2006. During the first period he was a mass of ambitious energy colliding with competitors as he careened from one office to the next on his rise to the top. He was not always sure how to get to the top, but he would go with all his might for the next rung up the ladder, bulldozing everyone in his path. In September 1982 two massacres and a Syrian bomb put an end to that sudden climb.

During his second phase, made without the protection of his admirer Begin, he took whatever ministry he could get in government while forming alliances of convenience with political rivals like David Levy and Yitzak Moda'i. Suspected by Shamir — who suspected everyone but Begin, of not being loyal enough because of his friendship with Ben-Gurion, he in turn then had to suffer as he was passed over in favor of Netanyahu. The settlers and his army veterans were his only consistent constituencies.

Sharon's tour of the Temple Mount on September 29, 2000, was an attempt to prove that he was steadfast in support of a united Jerusalem. It began the Al-Aksa Intifada, less as a cause than as an excuse, which in turn allowed him to beat Barak in February 2001. Sharon spent his first three years as prime minister attempting to break the Al-Aksa Intifada through three methods: targeted killings or assassinations of Palestinian terrorist and political leaders, an invasion of the West Bank by the IDF in the spring of 2002, and the construction of the separation barrier, a long combination fence and wall snaking along the edge of the settlement blocs in the West Bank and meant to prevent suicide bombers access to Jewish targets.[54] Sharon then spent his final two years planning and carrying out the disengagement from Gaza, which is covered in detail in a further chapter. During his time as prime minister he relied on a small "kitchen cabinet" of trusted advisors — his sons Omri and Gilad, his wife, and veteran journalist Uri Dan were his closest advisors.[55]

Netanyahu returned to politics in February 2003 when Sharon offered him the post of finance minister when Israel was at a low point economically. By liberalizing Israeli markets, Netanyahu turned the economy around and established his reputation as someone who understands economics. His campaign slogan in the 2009 election was, "Strong on security, strong in economics."

He resigned from the government in protest just before Sharon implemented his disengagement plan in August 2005.[56] He then suffered as the Likud suffered the nadir of its fortunes in the 2006 election, when half of its voters defected to Kadima. In the 2009 election his party came in with one seat less than Kadima, but President Peres tapped him to form the government based on the advice of most party leaders. Netanyahu built a coalition based on the Right but with Labor included, offering his former commander Barak the defense ministry that he had held under Olmert.

In mid–2009 Netanyahu faced a situation in some ways similar to that of Begin in 1977 — he was a new leader confronting a new liberal Democratic president in the White House. But from President Obama's perspective it was somewhat different. Where Carter was faced with an Israeli prime minister or prime ministers who were opposed to an overall settlement, he did at least face a prime minister who was eager to negotiate on the Egyptian front, and he had an Arab counterpart in Egypt who was also eager to negotiate. Obama soon discovered that he had both an Israeli prime minister and a Palestinian president who were not eager, if not actually afraid, to negotiate. But like Clinton in 1992, he had a constituency to which he had promised American engagement in a peace process.[57]

On his second day in office, Obama appointed George Mitchell, the successful mediator of the Good Friday Agreement in Northern Ireland, as his special negotiator for the Middle East, giving him the position held by Dennis Ross under George H.W. Bush and Clinton. Then on June 4, 2009, he made a speech in Cairo that was billed as an outreach to the Arab and Muslim worlds.[58] Some Israelis were offended because Obama seemed to imply that Israel owed its existence only to the Holocaust. In the zero-sum logic of the Israeli public if Obama was pro–Arab then he must be anti–Israel. Obama declined to make a similar visit to Israel to reassure the Israeli public. He then pressured Netanyahu to declare a settlement freeze as a means of establishing confidence among the Palestinians prior to negotiations.

Netanyahu stalled and new settlement construction was ordered. Then in November 2009, Netanyahu ordered a ten-month settlement freeze with several important exceptions. First, it did not apply to Jerusalem. Second, it did not apply to buildings already under construction. Third, it did not apply to buildings considered essential to the life of the settlement, namely, common buildings such as schools and synagogues. President Abbas then argued that he could not negotiate unless Netanyahu ordered a complete freeze. When the "freeze" expired in 2010 during the run-up to congressional elections, Obama could only attempt to bribe Netanyahu into extending the freeze. Despite very generous promises of military equipment Netanyahu refused to renew the freeze and risk the stability of his coalition. Conservatives blamed Obama for naively focusing on settlements instead of on an issue that they favored like terrorism. Except for a further speech on Middle East policy at the American Israel Public Affairs Committee (AIPAC), where Obama laid out a few parameters for Israeli-Palestinian negotiations, his peace effort was over for his first term. Netanyahu had shown that he could outmaneuver a distracted president with too many issues on his plate.[59]

Netanyahu's closest advisors until recently appear to have been his father, Benzion, who died on April 30, 2012, at age 102; his wife, Sara; and Barak. Some speculated that Netanyahu never felt free to make major territorial concessions while his father was still alive. But in 1993 he penned *Israel among the Nations,* which Likud watcher Ilan Peleg has dubbed "Revisionism for the Nineties." In it he discusses at length Israel's historical right to the West Bank and its need of the West Bank for security purposes. He reissued a slightly revised edition renamed *A Durable Peace* in 2000. Despite his call at Bar Illan University for a "two-state solution" in May 2009 he has never recanted what he wrote in 1993. It is doubtful that at this late point in his life his father's death will make much of a difference in his thinking. And his wife is said to be very hawkish.[60] Barak was trusted because as a member of a different party not on the Right, he is not seen as a rival.

The Israeli and Western press has recently dubbed Netanyahu "King Bibi" because of his widespread support both among the wider public and in his party. Since Sharon's exit from the Likud, Netanyahu has had no real rivals for the leadership. His biggest threat is Avigdor Leiberman, his foreign minister and the head of the Israel Beitenu "Russian" party. Many suspect that Leiberman has ambitions of taking over the Right from the Likud. But for now the Likud is nearly twice as large as Israel Beitenu.

Netanyahu and Sharon, the two post–Shamir leaders of the Likud, have a number of things in common. First, they have proven to be more flexible than Shamir or Begin when it comes to dealing with diplomatic overtures but just as committed to retaining Israeli control of the West Bank. Second, they both appeared flexible but put conditions on their offers that they know are unacceptable to all Palestinian leaders and go far beyond what the Left requires. Sharon spoke about offering the Palestinians a state that made up less than half the territory of the West Bank.[61] Netanyahu wanted the Palestinians to recognize Israel as a Jewish state, which would hurt efforts by Israeli Palestinians to have Israel redefined as "a state of all its citizens."[62] Third, both have been dedicated to expanding settlements on the West Bank even if they are willing to dismantle a few outpost settlers that were created without government authorization. Fourth, they have both been willing to use force to protect Israeli interests — a trait that they share with Labor and Kadima leaders.

How can we sum up ninety years of Revisionist actions? Neo-Revisionists will retreat under pressure but only on secondary or tertiary goals that appear beyond their ability to achieve. Begin eventually gave up his calls for Israel to go to war against Jordan to conquer the East and West

Banks. But once Israel had conquered the West Bank in 1967 Begin was unwilling or even unable to give it up. Sharon was willing to give up Gaza, but not Netanyahu. Sharon was also willing to give up the dream of Jordan as a Palestinian state. Netanyahu was willing to talk of a two-state solution but unwilling to take any real actions to implement that one speech.

We now must consider in detail how and why Likud coalitions and the ideologically similar National Party government in Pretoria were willing to give up conquered territory.

CHAPTER THREE

The Likud Retreats:
Sinai and Gaza

Israel has withdrawn from conquered territory on a number of occasions since 1948. Usually this has been due to foreign pressure from an important ally (the United States, 1957), due to foreign pressure from a regional power (Britain, 1949) or due to a peace agreement (Sinai —1974, 1975, 1982; Syria —1974). Thrice withdrawal came about for strategic reasons with no peace agreement (Lebanon —1985, 2000; Gaza — 2005). Most of these withdrawals took place under Labor governments, either as part of the post–Yom Kippur War peace process or as part of the Oslo process. But twice Israel under Likud governments withdrew: from Sinai in 1982 as part of the 1979 Egyptian-Israeli peace treaty during the premiership of Menachem Begin; and from Gaza in 2005 during the premiership of Ariel Sharon.

Before looking at the Egyptian-Israeli peace negotiations and the Gaza redeployment it would be helpful to examine Begin's strategic thinking. Begin's worldview was that of an optimistic late-nineteenth-century revolutionary. For Begin, the past dominated the present: his historical thinking was generalized, simplistic, and analogical. He believed in the existence of historical laws, which he regarded as being almost scientific laws in their validity. His historical outlook was heavily influenced by the cases of Poland in the early twentieth century, the Italian *risorgimento* or unification in the 1860s, and the Jewish Revolt of the 1940s. He was also heavily influenced by the appeasement of the 1930s and the Holocaust. His models of statesmen were Camile Cavour from the risorgimento and Winston Churchill. But according to fellow underground leader Natan Yellin-Mor, Begin saw history more as a slide show than as a movie — he tended to think in terms of discreet events rather than processes.[1]

Begin was a voracious reader of the classics of Judaism and Zionism and of nineteenth-century Western history. But his reading of general literature ended as a teenager. So he was much more influenced by *realpolitik* thinking sprinkled with romanticism than by humanism. Begin despised concepts such as self-restraint, partition, or withdrawal because they struck him as unheroic or even cowardly. Begin believed in unlimited territorial expansion. As a witness to the Holocaust who lost many relatives, including his parents, in it, he did not really believe in the existence of an international community. He rather believed in survival of the fittest. His worldview was not that different from that of the imperialist and totalitarian leaders of the interwar period.[2]

Unlike the Labor Zionist leaders who had been involved in the settlement enterprise during the prestate Yishuv, or the generals who fought in Israel's wars, Begin (and Yitzhak Shamir) lacked a firsthand knowledge of the geography of Israel outside of the main cities.[3] Begin had lived most of his live in either Jerusalem or Tel Aviv. Thus, during the negotiations with Egypt, Begin would have to rely on the opinions of generals who had fought and served in the Sinai in 1948, 1956, 1967, 1969–70, and 1973. In his government he had several such generals: former Chiefs of Staff Yigael Yadin and Moshe Dayan, former Deputy Chief of Staff Ezer Weizman, former Southern Command head Ariel Sharon and others. Begin did not believe in making territorial concessions for anything less than a peace treaty — they would invite more aggression. This is why he condemned the separation-of-forces agreements of 1974–75.[4]

Begin did not understand Arab culture. He did not know any Arabs — unlike Labor leaders such as Dayan and Allon who had grown up among Arabs. They were an abstraction for him. Begin tended to relate to Arabs as similar to European persecutors of Jews — Nazis or Polish anti–Semites.[5]

For Begin what was important was *Eretz Israel*—the land of Israel — whether defined in biblical or mandatory terms. He claimed that Eretz Israel "was divided in a war of aggression (1948), and was united in a war of self-defense (1967)." Begin's approach to Eretz Israel was based on three principles. First, that Israel had a historical right to all the land. Second, that the land could not be divided. And third, that Jerusalem was Israel's heart and eternal capital. He took the indivisibility of the land from religious thinking rather than from the writings of Jabotinsky. But, Ahdut Ha'Avoda, the faction in Labor led by Yigal Allon, had come to the same conclusion from a different premise. Begin would sometimes adjust his actions and perhaps even his beliefs, but normally not his rhetoric to accommodate political reality. Throughout his term as prime minister he refrained from annexing the West Bank. Initially this was due to a promise to Moshe Dayan not to do so if Dayan served as his foreign minister. Then he failed to do so in order to not jeopardize the Sinai peace negotiations. Finally, the Camp David accords prohibited him from doing so.[6]

In the mid–1970s, Israel seemed to face a choice between two countries and two Arab leaders to make peace with. The only two moderate Arab leaders willing to make peace with Israel in the 1970s were Egyptian President Muhammed Anwar Sadat and the Jordanian king, Hussein. Both insisted that the price for peace was a return of all of the land captured by Israel in June 1967 — or at least all of their countries' land. In June 1974, when he formed his first coalition government, Yitzhak Rabin promised the National Religious Party (NRP) that there would be a referendum before any of the West Bank would be returned to the Arabs. Because of this and because Jordan did not participate in the October 1973 war, Rabin did not enter into separation-of-forces talks with Jordan through U.S. Secretary of State Henry Kissinger in 1974. The Rabat Arab Summit in Morocco in October 1974 recognized the Palestine Liberation Organization (PLO) as the "sole legitimate representative of the Palestinian people."[7] This precluded Jordan from entering into peace negotiations with Israel to recover the West Bank without the express permission of the PLO — which it never gave. This removed King Hussein and Jordan from peace negotiations until the Oslo process of the 1990s.

Anwar Sadat became the leader of Egypt after the death of Gamal abd al-Nasser due to a heart attack in September 1970. Sadat offered Israel a non-belligerency agreement in 1971, but Golda Meir refused to enter secret talks even though defense minister Moshe Dayan wanted to explore the possibilities. In January 1974 Henry Kissinger negotiated a separation-of-forces agreement between Israel and Egypt with Israel pulling its forces back from the west bank of the Suez Canal and several kilometers back on the east bank. In September 1975 Egypt and Israel signed the Sinai Interim Agreement or Sinai II, in which Israel withdrew to the eastern side of the Giddi and Mitla Passes in the western Sinai in exchange for a non-belligerency agreement with Egypt. With this Sadat, the founder of the Free

Officers Movement in the Egyptian army following the 1948 war, established himself as the most pro–Western and boldest Arab leader. He became the obvious Arab leader for Begin to target for a contractual peace.

Begin's first coalition government in June 1977 was composed of the Likud, the NRP, the Democratic Movement for Change of Yigael Yadin, Ariel Sharon's *Shlomzion* and Moshe Dayan as an independent. Dayan and Yadin were mainly present to provide reassurance to Washington that this would not be a pure Revisionist/New Zionist government of the Right. Begin also wanted as many generals in his government because he personally admired them as the embodiement of Zionism and the "New Jew" and because he wanted to scare the Arabs.[8]

Shortly after forming his government, Begin went to the West Bank settlement of Elon Moreh, founded by the NRP settlement movement *Gush Emunim* (Bloc of Believers) in 1974, and proclaimed that "there will be many more Elon Morehs." Begin was announcing that ideological settlement as opposed to merely strategic settlements, as under the Labor governments from 1967–77, would have his government's full support.

Begin wanted a peace agreement with Egypt in order to secure Israel's southern flank while he set about settling and possibly annexing Israel's eastern flank. Begin traveled to Romania shortly after taking power so that he could put forward to a country that was on friendly terms with Egypt that he wanted peace. At this time President Carter was still focused on a comprehensive Middle East peace with Israel negotiating simultaneously with Egypt, Jordan, Lebanon, and Syria. Neither Labor nor the Likud wanted such a peace negotiation nor thought that such negotiations were likely to deliver peace. Jerusalem did not trust the Arabs and believed in engaging them separately and sequentially rather than all at once. That way Israel could only make territorial concessions to those leaders whom it trusted to keep the peace. Secretary of State Cyrus Vance proposed a joint Israeli-Jordanian administration over the West Bank in August 1977 but Begin rejected this.[9]

Romanian leader Nicolae Ceacescu invited Sadat to Bucharest in August and passed along Begin's interest in making peace and his own impression that he thought that Begin was a strong leader. Sadat decided to test the Israelis. Cairo contacted Jerusalem, probably through intelligence agencies that it wanted to hold a secret meeting to probe Israel's intentions. Foreign Minister Dayan went in disguise to Morocco, an Arab country with which Israel had good de facto relations, and there met with Egyptian deputy prime minister Muhammed Hassan al-Tuhami in two meetings in August and September 1977. Most sources claim that Dayan promised Tuhami a full Israeli withdrawal in exchange for peace. Dayan claims that he made no such promise but that he said that the withdrawal would match the quality of the peace offered. Begin biographers Sofer and Ned Temko accept this. Dayan's reply awakened the gambler's instinct within Sadat and he decided to invite himself to Israel without a promise. He later told Boutros Boutros-Ghali that he decided to invite himself to Jerusalem when he was flying to Iran to meet with the Shah and was flying over Turkey. Boutros-Ghali claimed that al-Tuhami was a Muslim mystic who believed that he had a personal mission to recover Jerusalem for Islam. He was Sadat's astrologer and court fool, but did not participate in cabinet meetings.[10]

Moshe Dayan was an Israeli war hero blessed with natural talent, bravery, and political fortune. He was promoted to chief of staff ahead of his time because his mentor, David Ben-Gurion, needed a general from Mapai rather than from Ahdut Ha'Avoda and the Palmakh.[11] Dayan together with Ben-Gurion developed the policy of retaliation raids for Arab infiltration in the 1950s. This led to the October 1956 Sinai War in which the IDF conquered the Sinai. In 1959 Dayan entered politics and became defense minister on June 1, 1967 on the eve of the Six Day War. Seen in the West as the personification of Israeli heroism, Dayan fell into disgrace in October 1973 when Israel suffered reversals in the opening days of the Yom Kippur War. After seven years as defense minister he resigned in May 1974 and went into political limbo. Three years later Begin rescued him to provide legitimacy for his government.

Dayan was the author of the Dayan Plan or "functional compromise," a concept under which the West Bank would be part of Jordan for representation but part of Israel's defensive perimeter. Opposing this was the Allon Plan or "territorial compromise," which envisaged a partition of the West Bank with Israel getting a third to forty percent and Jordan the remainder. Israel would annex the Jordan Valley and the Etzion bloc of settlements near Bethlehem. Jordan rejected both these versions of the Jordanian Option and both became unofficial Israeli government policy. Settlement was carried out in terms of the Allon Plan but Israel remained in control of the West Bank and Gaza. In 1971 Dayan famously declared that he would rather have "Sharm al-Sheikh without peace, than peace without Sharm al-Sheikh." This was an easy declaration to make in 1971 as no Arab leader was then offering Israel peace. It is the equivalent of telling a girl that she couldn't be your girlfriend when she has not made the offer.[12]

The other main foreign policy actor in Begin's first government was Defense Minister Ezer Weizman. Unlike America, Britain or France where the most important cabinet position is foreign minister, or Ireland, where it is finance minister, in Israel it is defense minister. This is because the foreign minister is usually seen largely as a public relations agent for the government, but the defense minister is involved whether there is war or peace.

Weizman, like Sharon, came from a combined Labor and Herut background. He was the nephew of Israel's first president, Chaim Weizmann, the former head of the World Zionist Organization and force behind the Balfour Declaration of 1917. Both Dayan and Weizman came from the closest thing that Israel had to an aristocracy. Dayan's father Shmuel, was a member of Mapai and a member of the Knesset for Israel's first decade until 1969. He had founded Israel's first moshav or cooperative settlement, Nahalal, after having left Israel's first kibbutz, Degania, where Moshe was born.

Weizman was secretly a member of both the Hagana and the Etzel. Impressed by the boldness of the Etzel, he secretly took the oath, and carried out at least one mission for it. But because he was a pilot and the Etzel lacked an air force he served in the Hagana's air arm after World War II. He spent the 20 years after the War of Independence in the IDF climbing quickly through the ranks. This was easier than in the ground forces because most of Israel's pilots and mechanics in the 1948 war were foreign volunteers, both Jews and Gentiles, who left by 1950. Weizman was one of three Israeli pilots to serve as fighter pilots during the war. The best of the three, Motti Alon, was killed in a crash due to a bad engine. After serving as head of the Israeli Air Force from 1958–64, Weizman became deputy chief of staff under Rabin. In 1969, convinced that he would never make chief of staff because of his Herut views, he quit and joined the government as the Herut minister of transport. Less than a year later he was out of government when Begin pulled Gahal out of the government.

Weizman, like Dayan and Rabin, had developed a respect for some Arab officers that he encountered in foreign officers courses. During the peace process he would befriend the Egyptian defense minister, Field Marshal Abd al-Ghani al-Gamassy. Weizman's oldest son had been severely wounded by a sniper along the Suez Canal during the War of Attrition while doing his mandatory army service. This brought home personally to Weizman the cost of continued war and conflict.[13]

On October 1, 1977, there was a joint Soviet-American communique issued that called for the reconvening of the Geneva Conference on the Middle East, which last met before Christmas 1973, before the end of the year. There was no reference to Security Council Resolution 242 but there was mention of a solution to the conflict being based on the "legitimate rights of the Palestinians." The communiqué was really intended to sideline the Syrians and the PLO as Kissinger had done in 1973. This set off alarms in Jerusalem as it is often used as code language in Arab diplomatic language for the replacement of Israel with a Palestinian state.[14]

Three days later Foreign Minister Dayan met with Carter and Vance in New York. Dayan said he would be willing to attend the summit on the basis of Resolution 242 but not on the basis of the communique. After attempting to get Carter to reaffirm all previous American commitments to Israel, Dayan began to lobby the president for American support for a separate Egyptian-Israeli peace. He argued that the Arabs would be like a "one-wheel cart" after a peace agreement and could not drive to war. Vance proposed instead that the two sides each issue their own statements. After Dayan objected, the two sides spent several hours drafting a joint communique restricted to Geneva.[15]

Sadat distrusted both Syrian President Hafiz al-Asad and the Soviets. He did not want to give either a veto over his diplomatic strategy by tying him to a comprehensive peace strategy. Knowing that Israel was open to returning much of the Sinai to Egypt in exchange for peace, Sadat announced on November 9 in the Egyptian parliament that he was willing to travel to the ends of the earth, even to the Israeli Knesset in Jerusalem, for the sake of peace. Yasir Arafat who was in the audience clapped along with everyone else because he mistook this statement for empty Arab rhetoric. The speech, broadcast on Egyptian radio, was picked up by the Arab affairs correspondent of the *Jerusalem Post*. He passed on word of the speech to the government and asked for a reaction. The Israeli response was through the American embassy to accept the offer and formally invite Sadat to visit Israel and speak at the Knesset.[16]

This author was in Jerusalem when Sadat came and vividly remembers all the Egyptian flags lining the streets along the path that Sadat's motorcade would take to the Knesset along with the special editions of the Hebrew and English newspapers in Israel with their welcome to Sadat in Arabic. This was in great contrast to the welcome that the Israeli delegation received at Ismailiya little over a month afterwards. Sadat in his Knesset speech laid out the entire list of Arab demands except for recognizing the PLO as the only legitimate representative of the Palestinians. Sadat constantly claimed that he had taken all the risks for peace and now it was time for Begin and the Knesset to reciprocate by meeting his demands. Dayan, Weizman, Chief of Staff Mordechai "Motta" Gur, and Begin were all worried by Sadat's speech and saw it as an ultimatum.[17] But the scene at the airport where Israeli leaders past and present greeted Sadat was very moving. When Sadat mentioned the destruction that war had brought to Egypt, someone pointed out that Dayan and Yadin had both lost brothers in Israel's War of Independence.

Sadat then reciprocated by inviting Begin to Ismailiya for Christmas. Before then Begin traveled to Washington to present his autonomy plan to Carter at the White House. The plan, based on something out of Ze'ev Jabotinsky's final book, called for personal autonomy for the inhabitants of the West Bank and Gaza but left Israel in control of the territory. It was similar to the way the Austro-Hungarian Empire worked. Begin then mistook Carter's politeness for support.[18]

In Egypt the Israeli delegation noted the Stalinist cult of personality with the huge murals of Sadat in all types of uniforms along with the lack of any type of welcome for the Israelis. Sadat and Begin held a private meeting at the summit that was a failure, their last until the Camp David summit in September 1978. The two agreed to the creation of separate military and political committees to meet in Jerusalem in January. At the opening banquet for the two committees, Begin addressed to the head of the Egyptian delegation as "young man," a term he used with anyone who was younger than him. The leader feigned being insulted and Sadat withdrew the delegation the following day.[19]

In February Sadat and Carter met at Camp David and plotted a joint American-Egyptian strategy to corner Begin and get him to deliver on the West Bank. The Carter-Sadat friendship was one of the great historical partnerships between national leaders. Both regarded the other as his closest foreign political friend. Carter had little background in the Middle East. Carter knew no Arabs before being elected president. He visited Israel in May 1973 and came away sympathetic to both Israel and Zionism. But he also had some sympathy for the Palestinians. Sadat liked Carter when they first met in 1977 for three reasons. First, he was from the country rather than the city. Second, Carter was personally and openly religious. And third, Carter was a former career military officer (in the U.S. Navy). In other words, Sadat saw in him a reflection of himself.[20]

Carter soon realized that Sadat did not really care about the West Bank and just needed cover for a separate peace with Israel. At this point Carter began reorienting his Middle East peace strategy away from a comprehensive approach to a separate Israeli-Egyptian peace. At this point his objective was to ensure that Israel gave enough so that Sadat could live with it. Throughout the first half of 1978 the peace process was becoming unraveled as Sadat attacked Begin in the Egyptian press and Carter declared Israeli settlements to be illegal and leaked to the press contents of a memorandum comparing Begin's version of Resolution 242 and that of previous Labor governments. Sadat had a problem sticking to the script worked out at the meeting in his statements.[21]

In July there was a meeting of the American, Egyptian and Israeli foreign ministers at Leeds Castle in England. The meeting did not substantially advance the peace process, although Egypt offered its own peace plan for the first time, but Dayan came out of it thinking that there was real room for peace with Egypt and joined Weizman in trying to convert Begin. Dayan became convinced that Egypt wanted peace because he threatened to withdraw Israel's offer and end the process unless Egypt softened its stance and the Egyptians backed down. That same month Labor leader Shimon Peres met with Sadat in Vienna, beginning his transformation from hawk to dove. This led the Socialist International to issue the Vienna Document, which called on Israel to withdraw on all fronts and for Palestinians to be included in peace talks. This was the start of European involvement in the Middle East peace process, which culminated in observer status for the European Union (EU) Middle East ambassador at the Taba talks in January 2001.[22]

On July 20 Carter discussed with his top advisors the idea of inviting Begin and Sadat to a high-profile summit at Camp David as a means of pressuring them into reaching an agreement. Most of his advisors opposed the idea as too risky for his presidency — Carter himself described it as "an all or nothing gamble," and Vice President Walter Mondale said he was betting his presidency on it. Vance was sent to the region in August to invite Begin and Sadat to Washington in September. Both accepted with pleasure, although Dayan suspected an Egyptian-American trap.[23]

The Camp David summit was the most prepared summit on the American side in American history. The only other summits or major negotiations that come close are the Dayton Peace Talks in September 1995 and the Camp David Summit of 2000. Carter had a thick briefing book on the foreign delegations and the issues to be discussed prepared for him by the State Department. The State Department concentrated on the linkage between Sinai and the West Bank, which Carter felt instinctively was much less important for Begin. "Sadat cannot afford a failure and he knows it; both Sadat and Begin think that you cannot afford failure; but Begin probably believes that a failure at Camp David will hurt you and Sadat, but not him," Zbigniew Brzezinski shrewdly wrote in a memo to Carter before the summit.[24]

The American goal for the summit was to get the two countries' leaders to begin thinking more flexibly and concretely about peace rather than just repeating their nationalist dogmas. The State Department saw the two national leaders as somewhat similar. "Both men are master manipulators, utilizing basically two different personality styles in order to achieve power and control." The State Dept. wanted Carter to use Dayan to influence Begin while limiting Foreign Minister Muhammed Ibrahim Kemal's cautious influence on Sadat. This was because Begin was the hawk in his delegation and Sadat was the dove in his.[25]

Boutros-Ghali wrote that Egypt did not know how to prepare for Camp David properly. Sadat's strategy at the summit was to stress his own personal flexibility as opposed to the rest of the Egyptian delegation and to trust in Carter. Sadat was unpredictable and, at least according to Boutros-Ghali, al-Tuhami was crazy and Boutros-Ghali's job was to keep him occupied by theological discussions on sharia and the like, so he would not cause problems. Sadat was only concerned with the return of Sinai and was willing to give Gaza as a "gift" to King Hussein of Jordan in return for Jordan joining the process. Sadat wanted a separate peace with Israel and had no intention of going to Geneva for an international peace conference.[26]

President Franklin D. Roosevelt had established Camp David, Maryland as a presidential retreat during his presidency and Dwight Eisenhower renamed it after his grandson. It briefly attained fame for the "spirit of Camp David" following a summit with Soviet leader Nikita Khrushchev in 1958. Its main advantage was that it was isolated in the hills and could be closed to the press to maintain secrecy.[27] The Camp David Summit of 1978 lasted for thirteen days — the same length of time as the Cuban Missile Crisis of 1962 — from September 5 through September 17. Originally Carter only set aside four days for the summit — no one dreamed that it would last thirteen days.

The Camp David Summit of 1978 was simpler than that of 2000 because there were fewer issues to discuss. The main issues were: the Israeli settlements in the Rafieh salient in northeastern Sinai, the two Israeli airbases in Sinai, the timing of the Israeli withdrawal, the establishment of diplomatic relations between Egypt and Israel, and the autonomy framework for the West Bank and Gaza. By contrast in 2000 the Israelis and Palestinians had to discuss borders, security, settlements, refugees, and Jerusalem — all very complex issues.

Except for two meetings between the three leaders at the start of the summit that did not go well, the summit quickly began to work on the basis of separate bilateral meetings between the Americans and the Egyptians and Israelis. Sadat's first presentation was very nationalist or pan-Arabist and Begin was in fact relieved that it was so uncompromising. He spent three hours the next day picking apart the Egyptian proposal point by point for Carter. The American ambassadors to Egypt and Israel had warned Carter by telegrams to keep the two leaders apart during the summit. Sadat was an actor *manqué* who loved the big dramatic gesture, whereas Begin had trained as a lawyer and was legalistic. "Sadat was a real amateur. He often moved hastily and predictably," said his former acting foreign minister Boutros Boutros-Ghali years later. "You cannot imagine how difficult, how agonizing, it was to deal with Begin," said American diplomat Harold Saunders after the summit. Cyrus Vance saw him as "a combination of Old Testament prophet and courtly European ... an odd mixture of iron will and emotionalism ... harsh and acerbic at one moment and warm and gracious the next."[28]

Carter came up with the idea of keeping an authoritative American negotiating record that the two other sides used. The Israelis hated this but gave in. The Egyptians also wanted to keep their own record. Clinton's failure to imitate this practice was a contributing factor to the failure at Camp David 2000.

Dayan did most of the formulating or generating of ideas for the Israeli delegation — as he had done for Kissinger's shuttle diplomacy in 1974, which also consisted of Begin, Defense Minister Weizman, Attorney General Aharon Barak (later chief justice of the Israeli Supreme Court) as the legal advisor, and Avraham Tamir as Weizman's military aide. Barak would put them into treaty language. Dayan would sell his ideas to the Egyptians through either Weizman or the Americans. In turn, the Americans would sell their ideas to Begin through his senior advisors. The American delegation consisted of President Carter, Vice President Mondale, secretary of state Cyrus Vance, national security advisor Zbigniew Brzezinski and Middle East advisor William Quandt. Sadat was accompanied by foreign minister Muhammed Ibrahim Kamel, future acting foreign minister Boutros Boutros-Ghali, defense minister Abd al-Ghani al-Gamassy, Hassan al-Tuhami and others. The limit for each of the foreign delegations was eight people. The people doing most of the work for those thirteen days were Carter, Vance, Dayan and Barak. Vance, who actively negotiated, was not seen by the Israelis as being hostile towards them; Brzezinski, who only advised Carter, was seen as hostile. Brzezinski reminded Begin of the Polish aristocracy — his father was a Polish diplomat — and Dayan of Begin. Begin and Brzezinski, who both spoke Polish, communicated only in English, possibly out of consideration of the others or because Brzezinski's Polish was rather rusty.[29]

Sadat since his Knesset speech had become more rigid. Much of the summit consisted of Begin's advisors coming up with ways of convincing Begin to make concessions on the Rafieh settlements and the airfields. The Americans, on the last day of the summit, agreed to finance the reconstruction of the Israeli airfields in the Negev desert within Israel — $3 billion, with $800 million as a grant and the rest as a long-term loan. Begin was convinced to allow the Knesset to vote on the settlements and to make it a non-binding vote so that party members would not be required to vote a certain way. This salved his conscience. Israeli withdrawal from the Sinai would be in two stages with the second stage being completed three years after the signing of a peace agreement. This gave time for the Israeli military to adjust to the loss of Sinai and reconstruct the airfields.

Begin strategically used time by keeping the talks focused on minor issues to "eat up the clock" while the major issues were left undecided until Begin was ready to make a concession. Sadat, like Arafat in 2000, refused to negotiate on those issues of most importance to him. Sadat twice threatened to walk out, on Days 10 and 11, and Carter had to plead with him to stay. Carter made some threats to Sadat about what effect his sudden departure would have on Middle East peace, Egypt's relationship with the United States and their personal friendship. Sadat told his aides simply, "I shall sign anything proposed by President Carter without reading it." On Day 13 two agreements were concluded: the preliminary outline for an Egyptian-Israeli peace treaty and an agreement for self-rule for the Arabs of the West Bank and Gaza. Begin had successfully worn down the Americans, who in turn wore down Sadat. The agreements were translated into Hebrew and Arabic, with the West Bank being translated into Yehuda va Shomron (Judea and Samaria) in the Hebrew version, where the Palestinian Arabs became the Arabs of Yehuda and Shomron.[30]

Already at Ismailiya Sadat had decided that Weizman was the only Israeli that he wanted to deal with. Weizman prevailed on Sadat to hold a private meeting with Dayan, which did not go well as Dayan did not defer to Sadat. Although Sadat liked Weizman, Boutros-Ghali seemed to prefer his counterpart, Dayan. He respected Dayan's problem-solving abilities and his future orientation and creativity. But he feared Dayan's moodiness and unpredictability — "one minute arrogant and bitter and the next creative." After Camp David he urged Sadat to deal with Dayan because "he had intellectual courage, imagination, and Begin's confidence." And was much less rigid than Begin.[31]

Originally the three parties gave themselves 90 days to complete a peace treaty and Begin agreed to a settlement freeze during this time period. The Americans were convinced that he had agreed to a settlement freeze until the autonomy negotiations were completed — but it is extremely unlikely that Begin would have agreed to such an open commitment. As Sol Linowitz later said it seemed to have been a genuine misunderstanding. The linkage between the Egyptian-Israeli peace treaty and the West Bank and Gaza was fudged, at Barak's suggestion, by language that the Americans and Sadat could interpret one way and Begin a different way.[32]

In reality the negotiations on the peace treaty took another seven months. This is partially because Begin received much criticism from his own party and supporters for the agreement. Although the government agreed to accept the accords by a vote of 11–2, Begin had to rely on the opposition Labor Party to approve the accords and the Egyptian-Israeli peace treaty in the Knesset. Several key figures in the Likud, including future prime minister Yitzhak Shamir and future foreign and defense minister Moshe Arens, either voted against or abstained during the votes. Of his former colleagues in the underground former Lehi leader Natan Yellin-Mor praised the accords, but Lehi ideologue Israel Eldad and Shmuel Katz, Eitan Livny, Haim Landau, and Ya'akov Meridor of Etzel were very critical. Brzezinski wrote Carter another memo in November saying that he had lost control of the peace process. Begin now feared Israeli public opinion and Sadat Arab public opinion more than either feared the United States or wished to please it.[33]

Begin, like Sadat, kept his negotiators on a short leash. They were forced to refer back to him for every concession that they made. This also slowed down the negotiations. After his death it was revealed that Begin suffered from clinical depression throughout his life. Dealing with the disapproval of his former colleagues from Betar, the underground and Herut may have put Begin into a depression and this could have contributed to the length of the negotiations. Historian David Reynolds thinks that Begin was purposely prolonging the negotiations in order to reduce American leverage as Carter got closer to an election. Dayan and Weizman both complained of carping by their ministerial colleagues whenever they returned home to report after Camp David. In the end, Carter and Vance were forced to come to the Middle East in March 1979 and engage in shuttle diplomacy between Cairo and Jerusalem before the remaining issues were wrapped up and a peace treaty between Egypt and Israel was signed in Washington at the end of March.[34]

Sadat replaced al-Gamassy as defense minister with another war hero, Kamal Hassan Ali, thereby weakening Weizman's ties with the Egyptian establishment. The post–Camp David Israeli negotiating team consisted of Dayan, Weizman, Barak and Meir Rosenne, a Likud academic close to Begin. The Egyptian team consisted of Kamal Hassan Ali, Boutros-Ghali, Ashraf Ghorbal and Osama al-Baz. Al-Baz was anti–Israel and Boutros-Ghali had built his diplomatic career specializing in the Palestine problem. Both wanted a peace process that was much more focused on the West Bank, whereas Dayan resisted any leakage between the two separate Camp

David accords — the outline for autonomy and the outline of a bilateral peace treaty. As a result of the Iranian revolution, Israeli demands for a guaranteed supply of Egyptian oil increased. This and the question of the relationship of the treaty to Egypt's other defense obligations were the main issues holding up an agreement.[35]

President Carter flew to Cairo on March 6. He left for Israel on March 10. A few days later he returned to Cairo, and the treaty text was ready on March 14. The peace treaty was signed on the White House lawn on March 26, 1979. American ambassador to Egypt Hermann Eilts told Boutros-Ghali that "the Camp David agreements are a catastrophe." Kissinger told Eilts that he could have gotten a better deal for Egypt.[36]

When the autonomy negotiations convened in Israel that spring, both Dayan and Weizman were absent. Dayan was recovering from cancer surgery. He resigned from the government in October 1979. Weizman was embarrassed by Israel's positions on autonomy and resigned as defense minister in late May 1980. The autonomy negotiations soon bogged down until Egypt pulled out of them completely. Yosef Burg, the head Israeli negotiator "knew nothing about Arabs" according to Boutros-Ghali. But Boutros-Ghali looked down on Israeli politicians like Dayan and Allon because they spoke colloquial peasant Arabic rather than educated classical Arabic.[37]

Shibley Telhami, an American academic of Israeli Palestinian origin, has written an analysis of Camp David. He claims that the Israeli delegation came the closest to optimal bargaining behavior, the Egyptians were the worst and the Americans somewhere in between. He credits this both to Israel's democratic system and to Begin's personality. Begin allowed his negotiator subordinates to gain advantage for him by bargaining while retaining the option of rejecting their concessions. Begin was not approachable by the Egyptians, whereas Sadat could be approached by any of the Israelis or Americans. Sadat took pleasure in demonstrating his power by overruling his subordinates. Whereas Begin could be persuaded by his subordinates, especially Dayan, they had to argue with him and convince him. Telhami faults Egypt with not getting more linkage on the West Bank with regard to settlements and the implementation of autonomy.[38]

But in reality I believe this is unfair — Begin was as determined to have a free hand in the West Bank as Sadat was to be rid of the Palestinian problem. The only way that both could be satisfied was by Begin making concessions on the Sinai settlements and airfields and Sadat basically agreeing to give Israel a free hand in the West Bank as long as Jordan refused to enter the negotiations. Both got what they needed and conceded the rest.

In 1999 the author predicted (by email) to George W. Bush advisor Condolezza Rice that President Clinton would make a major push for a peace agreement in the Middle East in order to repair his tattered reputation. I also predicted that he would fail. I did not need a crystal ball — I knew that he lacked sufficient time to deal with the complexity of the issues involved even if he were as smart a negotiator as Carter, which he was not. The failure in 2000–2001 involved a moderate Israeli coalition led by the Labor Party and Meretz, which was much more forthcoming than the Likud would ever be. If one takes the earlier Brzezinski quote above and replaces Sadat with Barak, Carter with Clinton, and Begin with Arafat one sees the situation that Clinton was dealing with in 2000.

Due to the ravages of time, Benyamin Netanyahu or his successor would not face Etzel or Lehi volunteers vigorously opposing them. But the Likud in the decade of 2000 was infiltrated by Moshe Feiglin and his followers from the Jewish Leadership faction. This is based on Jewish settlers from the West Bank. Feiglin is capable of providing as vigorous an opposition to a peace agreement that sacrifices the West Bank as Shmuel Katz provided to Begin in 1978. Remember that Netanyahu was the disciple of Moshe Arens who voted against Camp David and Begin refused to allow any references to UN Resolution 242 in the Camp David Accords precisely because he did not want to agree to withdrawing from the West Bank.[39]

Remember the issues that Arafat raised because of his terrorist past. Any viable peace agreement between the Israelis and Palestinians would probably involve at least some Hamas leaders in addition to those from Fatah's armed factions. Sadat was a professional military officer without a real terrorist past (although he collaborated with the Germans in 1941–42 as a spy).[40] Sinai was largely an empty desert adjoining another desert, the Negev. The return of the Sinai to Egypt did not significantly degrade Israel's strategic posture. If Israel were to give up the West Bank, a Palestinian state would be very close to several major Israeli cities including its capital. While it might be quite possible for Israel to safely give up its control of the West Bank if the territory remain demilitarized, public perception could easily be that this would be quite dangerous. Such was the perception on the Right in Israel during the Oslo process of the 1990s. Such perceptions were too much for Israel to overcome in 2000. Since the reality of the Al-Aksa Intifada and the rocketing of southern Israel by the Islamists in Gaza in the aftermath of our next case have only served to strengthen such impressions.

Ariel Sharon was the second former general, four years after the first, Ezer Weizman, to join the Israeli Right. Like Weizman he came from a mixed political background. His parents were independent thinkers and Sharon suffered as a child from the isolation of being a political leper in the small Labor village. But in the 1950s as the protégé of both Moshe Dayan and David Ben-Gurion he led Israel's first commando unit that carried out the Ben-Gurion-Dayan activist defense policy before October 1956. He demonstrated tactical genius on the battlefield in 1967 and 1973, but his inability to follow orders or to get along with both superiors and subordinates kept him from being named chief of staff.

In the summer of 1973 he was forcibly retired from the army as he was deemed unsuitable for promotion from major general. Upon retirement he became a private farmer, founded the Likud party from four right-wing parties, and managed to become the leading hero of the October 1973 Yom Kippur War when he lead an armored invasion of the west bank of the Suez Canal. For the next three years he had a flawed start in politics as he attempted to juggle his political ambition and his frustrated ambition to be named chief of staff. After having quit the Liberal Party he formed his own party that won only two seats in 1977 and then he rejoined the Likud, this time as part of Herut. In June 1982 he invaded Lebanon in a bid to remake the country's politics and after the Sabra and Shatilla massacre he was fired as defense minister. He spent the next fifteen years in a series of secondary cabinet positions until Benyamin Netanyahu rescued him by making him foreign minister in October 1998. In February 2001 he finally reached his goal as prime minister. He spent nearly the next five years as a Likud prime minister. His term was spent fighting the Palestinian intifada and then carrying out the disengagement from Gaza. His entire political career was spent championing Jewish settlement: in Sinai, in Gaza, and in the West Bank.[41]

Likud Prime Minister Ariel Sharon invited anyone who thought they could do better with the Palestinians than through his strategy of repression and separation to go ahead. He was taken up on this by Yossi Sarid, leader of the liberal Meretz and Yossi Beilin, the architect of the Oslo diplomacy who paired with a number of leading Palestinians including Yasir Abd Rabbu, a leading figure in the Palestinian Authority under Arafat. Bankrolled by the Swiss government with $6 million in funding the two sides met in the Movenpick Hotel on the Dead Sea to see if they could negotiate an unofficial peace treaty starting where the Taba negotiation and Clinton parameters had left off. The Israeli delegation included four former ministers including former Labor leader Avram Mitzna, former Chief of Staff Amnon Lipkin-Shahak, former head of police Alik Ron, another reserve general, and leading liberal writer Amos Oz. The Palestinian delegation was made up of leading Fatah figures and independents. On October 12 the negotiations were completed and the "treaty" signed with much fanfare in Geneva on December 1. Seven hundred guests attended the ceremony including 58 first-tier politicians from all over the world. Among these were: former President Jimmy Carter, former Soviet leader Mikhail Gorbachev, former South African President F. W. de Klerk, and Nelson Mandela participated via video linkup.[42]

The agreement called for an Israeli withdrawal from all of Gaza and 98 percent of the West Bank, with a sovereign corridor connecting the two territories. Undivided Jerusalem was to be the capital of both states. The Palestinians would control the Arab quarters of the Old City and the surface of the Temple Mount, with Israel controlling the Jewish Quarter and the Western Wall. There was to be compensation for Palestinian refugees but no refugees would be allowed into Israel without its consent.

The Geneva Initiative, as the project was labeled in acknowledgement of its funding, was branded "a mortal danger" by Sharon. The plan was endorsed, however, by both Secretary of State Colin Powell, who invited the signers to Washington to brief him, and by Prime Minister Tony Blair of Britain. The initiative was also well received throughout Europe. In Israel, public opinion divided sharply over it. Some 39 percent supported it while 70 percent thought no one outside the government should negotiate on Israel's behalf. Clearly at least nine percent of the population was confused.[43]

The Geneva Initiative bears some resemblance to the KwaZulu-Natal Indaba, a negotiation conducted between the Natal Provincial Government and the Zulu homeland of KwaZulu in South Africa with the participation of a number of political parties and churches. The Indaba (a Zulu word meaning roughly *parley*) took place over eight months and resulted in an agreement to merge the two territories and eliminate apartheid within them. As with Geneva, the parties had no authority to implement the agreement by themselves. The ruling National Party in Pretoria rejected the Indaba as too radical, a form of majority rule (which it was not). This caused the South African ambassador to London, Denis Worrall, to resign and run in the May 1987 election as an independent along with a former National Party MP, Wynand Malan, and a prominent Afrikaner business-woman. Of the three independents, only one, Malan, won a seat, but Worrall lost his election to a sitting minister by only 39 votes out of thousands cast. This shook up the South African parliamentary opposition and had an effect on the decision by President F.W. de Klerk to negotiate with the African National Congress in 1990.[44] I expected that the Geneva Initiative would have a similar major impact on Israeli politics, and I was not disappointed.

Even before the Geneva signing ceremony, Sharon was contemplating an alternative to Geneva. In November he flew to Rome and met secretly with Assistant Secretary of State for Near Eastern Affairs Elliott Abrams. Abrams was shocked when Sharon revealed his plan for a unilateral Israeli withdrawal from Gaza. As an American Jew of the neo-conservative persuasion Abrams was a Likud supporter. Having believed that retention of the territories were important to Israel's security, he was startled to find that Sharon anticipated leaving them. But as an American official he had little choice but to go along. On November 21, Israel's Channel 2 reported that Sharon planned to withdraw from a number of settlements in both Gaza and the West Bank.[45]

On December 9, 2003 Sharon spoke on Israeli television and after praising the Road Map as a fair plan, he stated that if the Palestinians did not fulfill their responsibilities under the plan in the next few months, Israel would take the initiative and unilaterally disengage from them. Sharon defended his decision in terms of both security and economy: it would lower Israel's exposure to terrorism and reduce the costs of maintaining Israeli security. Israel was then in the midst of a deep recession caused by the Intifada. "I remain confident that as long as we remain united in our convictions, we will succeed, whatever path we choose to follow."

The speech was very light on details — offering neither a where nor a when.[46]

Initially most Israeli commentators discounted the importance of the speech. Sharon was mired in legal problems resulting from campaign-finance scandals involving his sons. Many saw the speech as merely a temporary distraction, a political sleight-of-hand trick. Foreign governments in the West and in the Arab world also discounted the speech as they saw Sharon's character as an expansionist hawk as being fixed and a given. The press wasted little newsprint on analysis of the speech over the coming weeks as it concentrated on accounts of his legal troubles. But the settlers, who had supporters within the prime minister's office, took Sharon at his word. They organized a demonstration attended by 120,000 in Rabin Square in Tel Aviv on January 12. They carried a huge banner that read "Arik, Don't Fold." But polls showed that most Israelis supported unilateral withdrawal.[47]

On February 2, 2004 Sharon gave an exclusive interview to *Ha'Aretz* diplomatic correspondent Yoel Marcus. *Ha'Aretz* is not normally a paper read by the Likud rank-and-file, rather it is a cross between the *New York Times* and the *Guardian,* read by Israel's professional, business, and political (particularly those from Labor and Meretz) elite. Sharon told Marcus that he intended to withdraw from all 17 Israeli settlements in Gaza and four in the northern West Bank. Marcus immediately put the details of the interview on the paper's websites, where they could be read in English and Hebrew. Sharon surprised not only his own party but ministers within his own government.[48]

The reaction to the interview, whose details were of course announced in the electronic media, was very negative within the Likud. Sharon attempted to build support in his party and ensure Israel's security by stepping up the program of targeted killings of terrorist leaders. On March 22, 2004, Sheikh Ahmed Yassin, the spiritual leader of Hamas, was assassinated by guided missiles launched from a helicopter. A previous attempt to kill him, when the house in which he was meeting was hit by missiles, failed as the wrong floor was targeted. Over 150,000 attended his funeral in Gaza and Muslims around the world condemned the murder. His deputy, Rantisi, declared war on Israel. Three weeks later Yassin's successor, Abdel Aziz Rantisi, who had already survived one Israeli assassination attempt, was killed. National Security Advisor Condi Rice defended Israel's right to use assassination in response to terrorism. After this Hamas kept the identity of its leaders confidential and its leadership went into hiding.[49]

On August 31 two Hamas suicide bombers detonated themselves on two neighboring buses in Beersheva killing sixteen and wounding over a hundred. This was claimed by Hamas as vengeance for the assassinations of Rantisi and Yassin. A week later Israeli helicopters fired missiles into a Hamas training camp in Gaza killing fourteen and wounding thirty. At least eleven of the victims were positively identified as belonging to Hamas. In an interview with journalist friend Uri Dan, Sharon said, "We eliminated the leaders of Hamas ... and other terrorist heads when the time was right. The same principle goes for Yasser Arafat. We will treat him like the others. I see no difference between him and Yassin." It was a clear warning to Arafat. In April 2004 Sharon during a visit to the White House managed to get Bush to tacitly agree that Arafat was no longer off limits.

In the same interview, Sharon said that he preferred to concentrate on a single track of the peace process at one time and that because Assad supported terrorism, he was not a suitable partner for peace. To the question of "What after Gaza?," Sharon replied: "It is therefore very possible that after our retreat from Gaza, there will be nothing else for a very long time."[50]

So Sharon's strategy for dealing with the Palestinians was basically a two-track approach of targeted killings, construction of the defensive barrier, limited raids against suspected terrorist infrastructure, and heightened security on one hand combined with unilateral withdrawal on the other. Before I examine Sharon's fight to implement disengagement, it might be worthwhile to examine his motivation. Sharon initially argued for disengagement in security and economic terms as a withdrawal to a more easily defended perimeter.

Later in an interview with Uri Dan he argued that if Israel had done nothing it would eventually have come under American pressure to do something, so better an Israeli plan than an American one. This can be labeled "preventative diplomacy."[51] But did Sharon really fear pressure from Bush or the international community? Like most Israeli leaders, Sharon only cared about the bilateral relationship with Washington. Of Israel's prime ministers, only Moshe Sharett in the 1950s and Shimon Peres cared much about the reaction of the "international community." Ben-Gurion was famous for saying "uum, shmuum" in a derogatory reference to the UN.[52] Peres really cared only about the opinions of the great powers, as Ben-Gurion had taught him. This meant during the Cold War initially Bonn, London, Moscow, Paris, and Washington. After the Europeans ceased to be major weapons suppliers to Israel, their importance lessened considerably. Only Moscow and Washington remained — although Peres liked to use the opinions of Europeans to back up his own opinions in Israeli political arguments. Sharon was a political disciple of both Ben-Gurion, who mentored him when he was a young officer, and Menachem Begin, who had a close relationship with Sharon during his early political career. Neither cared much for international opinion. And Sharon was probably Bush's closest foreign political friend, so he had little worry about pressure from Washington.

Another possible motive was Sharon's legal difficulties. Sharon and his family were involved in three major political financial scandals from 2002 to 2006: the Annex Research Affair, the Cyril Kern Affair, and the Greek Island Affair. The three involved illegal campaign contributions, bribery and influence peddling. Sharon was never indicted before he suffered his coma in January 2006, but his son Omri was found guilty and sentenced to nine months in prison, nine months suspended, and a fine of 300,000 Israeli shekels.[53] In 2007–8 many Israeli political analysts, especially those in the press, were convinced that prime minister Ehud Olmert, Sharon's successor, was vigorously pursuing negotiations with Mahmoud Abbas as a means of political survival in the belief that as long as an agreement with the Palestinians appears likely he would be spared prosecution. Sharon may have believed that making peace or at least withdrawing from the territories would end his prosecution. But it is unlikely. Israeli prosecutors, like American prosecutors, decide on whether or not to prosecute based on how likely they are to win a conviction. If the evidence had been there to ensure a conviction he would have been prosecuted. And if he wanted to avoid prosecution, he would have been more likely to engage in negotiations with the Palestinians over disengagement rather than one-sided cooperation discussions.

The other explanation was that Gaza had little historical or religious sentiment for most Israelis — it had been ruled in ancient times by the Philistines rather than by the Israelites, whereas the West Bank had a great deal of importance. Even though Sharon was always motivated by security considerations rather than ethno-religious sentiment (Sharon was an agnostic),[54] he considered the West Bank to be of much greater security importance for Israel than Gaza. Gaza bordered the Israeli Negev Desert, which is scarcely populated with the only Israeli town of any size bordering Gaza being Sderot. The West Bank, in contrast, borders Israel's Sharon Plain (after which Sharon was named) where the bulk of Israel's population is located as well as Israel's capital and largest city, Jerusalem. The idea behind Sharon's disengagement was that Israel would preempt demands to withdraw from the West Bank by sacrificing Gaza. The Palestinians could then either demonstrate that they were ready for independence, or more likely, not ready. Chaos in Gaza would continue to reduce the demand in the United States for Israel to withdraw from the West Bank.

National Security Advisor Major General Uzi Dayan attributed Sharon's decision to withdraw from Gaza to a conversation he had with Sharon about demographics. Dayan warned Sharon that by 2020 there would be 15 million people living between the Jordan River and the Mediterranean and only 45 percent of them would be Jews.[55] By withdrawing from Gaza, Israel eliminates at least a third of the Arab population from Israeli control, thereby significantly delaying the day when the Jews would be a minority within the area under Israeli control. Dayan, the nephew of former Defense Minister Moshe Dayan, was denied the top job in the IDF because he was considered to be too moderate. Gilad Sharon credits this as having been his father's primary motivation.[56]

Sharon claimed that he weighed four possible options. First, to eliminate the Palestinian Authority and return to the status quo ante before 1994. Sharon ruled this out because he did not want Israel to once again resume responsibility for over a million Palestinians. Second, was to negotiate a Geneva-style final agreement. Sharon deemed this to be too dangerous. Third, was to do nothing — which Sharon also considered to be dangerous. Last, was to implement a unilateral strategy. This is what Sharon decided upon.[57]

A biographer of Secretary of State Condoleeza Rice gives her the credit for the idea. He claims that when Sharon told Rice that he wanted to withdrew from five settlements in Gaza, she urged him to instead withdrew from all the settlements there. He then agreed. She told Sharon's advisor Dov Weissglas that the Road Map was "at best a marginal plan." So she was looking for something to replace it with.[58]

The first hurdle Sharon tried to get over in implementing his disengagement strategy was winning approval within the Likud. Sharon could have gone for a national referendum on disengagement — which polls indicate he would have won handily — but to call a referendum he would have needed a majority in the Knesset, so he opted first to try for approval in his own party.[59]

On January 29, 2004, Sharon traded hundreds of live Lebanese and Palestinian prisoners in exchange for the bodies of three dead Israelis and a live Israeli colonel who was also a drug dealer, kidnapped in Lebanon when a drug deal went bad. Sharon looked weak. Sharon then ordered the assassination of Yassin so he could look strong again. On April 14, 2004 in a meeting at the White House, President Bush made major concessions to Israel in the official American approach to the conflict. Bush announced that the final borders in a settlement would have to conform somewhat to reality on the ground and that a return to the June 4, 1967, border would probably not be possible. He also committed the U.S. to the idea that Palestinian refugees would be resettled within the Palestinian state rather than in Israel. Both Crown Prince Abdallah of Saudi Arabia and President Mubarak of Egypt had lobbied against making any such concessions as did Palestinian Finance Minister Salam Fayad, an independent who made three trips to Washington.[60] The second was not a major change in America's position, but the first was. This was a major gain for Sharon and Israel.

But even this was not enough to win a referendum in the Likud. When he returned to Jerusalem he found that three Likud ministers including Foreign Minister Silvan Shalom and Finance Minister Benyamin Netanyahu were openly opposing the disengagement plan. Sharon agreed to a party referendum on his plan. Ten days before the vote, Netanyahu — ever the political opportunist — switched his position and came out in favor of disengagement. But the anti-disengagement campaigners with thousands of volunteers from the settlements mounted an effective door-to-door canvas. Three days before the vote all newspaper polls put the "no" campaign ahead. On May 2, 2004, the Likud rejected by a 60 to 40 margin or 3 to 2 Sharon's plan. It was a humiliating defeat for a man who was not used to defeat. He would either have to give up on disengagement or find a way to maneuver around his opponents within the party.[61]

On May 15, 150,000 supporters of withdrawal — mostly from Labor and Meretz, who had attended Peace Now rallies in the past — held a pro-disengagement rally in Tel Aviv. A year before a rally by these individuals on behalf of Sharon would have been unthinkable. Sharon decided to resubmit the disengagement plan to a government vote once again. He first dismissed two members of the far-right National Union from the coalition. He won a 2:1 margin of 14 to 7 in the vote on June 4 — the 37th anniversary of the beginning of the Six Day War, although he was forced to commit himself to a second vote before withdrawal. Two days later two members of the National Religious Party resigned from the government. Labor had committed itself since April 14 to supporting the government on withdrawal from outside. On June 9 the government published a timetable for withdrawal: it would begin on August 15 and be completed by the end of September 2005. Sharon considered six weeks to be adequate time.[62]

On June 30, the Israeli Supreme Court rendered a decision on Israel's defensive barrier — allowing it in theory but requiring the government to reroute some 30 to 40 kilometers along its length to take the needs of local residents into account. On July 10 the International Court of Justice ruled that the wall, the ICJ decided to use the loaded terminology used by the General Assembly, was illegal in its entirety as it was constructed on Palestinian territory. This decision was completely ignored by Israel. Only the United States representative voted against the decision.[63]

On June 15, Attorney General Mazuz held a press conference and announced that there was insufficient evidence to indict Sharon in the Greek Island Affair. Labor was able to join the coalition, but a motion to invite Labor in failed within the Likud. Shinui was threatening to leave the coalition, which it did in September, arguing that Sharon was not taking enough steps for peace. Sharon was left with a minority government that could be toppled at any moment if the right and left could agree to combine in a vote of no confidence.

Nationalist rabbis began issuing opinions that religious soldiers should reject military orders to evacuate soldiers as settlement of *Eretz Israel,* the land of Israel or Palestine, was more important than secular law. A demonstration was held in which a human chain of 125,000 people stretched from the gates of the Gush Katif settlement bloc in Gaza to the Western Wall in Jerusalem.[64]

At the beginning of October, Sharon's political advisor, attorney and liaison to the left Dov Weinglass granted an interview to *Ha'Aretz*. In it he claimed that thanks to Sharon and disengagement, the project for a Palestinian state had been shelved indefinitely. It was part of Sharon's PR campaign of selling disengagement. On October 25, Sharon took the disengagement plan before the Knesset for a vote. He won by a huge margin of 67 to 44, with both Labor and Meretz voting for it. It was like the Camp David Accords in September 1978 — a quarter century before — that had passed with the support of Labor while many Likud members either abstained or voted no.

Two days later Yasir Arafat was suddenly evacuated to France for medical treatment after a mysterious blood condition that had plagued him since April suddenly grew worse. Three weeks later he died on November 11, 2004. Palestinians blamed his death on Israeli poisoning. Israelis said it was due to AIDS as Arafat was rumored to be bisexual. No samples of his blood were made available for testing to disprove either contention. His funeral a few days later became the occasion for hysterical demonstrations of grief. In January 2005 the PLO elected Mahmoud Abbas as the new chairman of the organization and president of the Palestinian Authority. Abbas's only competition came from a cousin of Marwan Barghouti after Marwan dropped out of the race. Israel had said that if Marwan Barghouti were elected he would have to serve out his term in his prison cell.[65]

In early December, Shinui voted against Sharon's budget. Sharon dismissed Shinui's ministers from the government provoking a crisis as he had lost his parliamentary majority. Sharon went to the Likud and requested permission to bring Labor into the government. He said that if they did not approve he would be happy to call new elections. While Sharon was likely to again end up with the largest party, the Likud was unlikely to replicate its 40 seats and many of the MKs would be out of a job. It was granted by a 62 to 38 percent margin. Labor came into the government and vowed to remain until the disengagement was complete. Sharon now had a stable coalition to work with. Labor joined the government in January with seven ministries, with Shimon Peres serving as deputy prime minister.[66]

On January 15, Abbas was sworn in as the new Palestinian president, some 16 months after he resigned as prime minister. On January 22 a new *hudna* was concluded with all major Palestinian terrorist groups except

Islamic Jihad participating. Israel responded to this by ending its targeted killings of all but Islamic Jihad figures. On February 8 Sharon and Abbas met in Sharm al-Skeikh at a summit hosted by President Mubarak and King Abdullah of Jordan. As a result of a request from Abbas, Sharon released hundreds of Palestinian prisoners.[67]

Sharon began to prepare the way for disengagement in earnest. In February it was announced that the term of Chief of Staff Lt. Gen. Moshe "Boogy" Ya'alon would not be extended for a fourth year, as was customary. IAF Commander Major General Dan Halutz would be his replacement and the first IAF "blue beret" to become chief of staff in IDF history. Traditionally, most IDF chiefs of staff after the Yom Kippur War came from a special forces background of either the paratroopers or the *sayeret matkal*. Ezer Weizman had come close to being the first IDF chief of staff from the IAF in the late sixties, serving in the number two position, but quit the army after he was passed over for promotion in 1969. Weizman and most commentators thought he was rejected because he was known to be a supporter of Begin's Herut (the forerunner of the Likud) at the time. Ya'alon was passed over for renewal because he was not known to be a supporter of disengagement and was outspoken. A new head of the General Security Service, Shabak, was also appointed in May.[68]

In February the Knesset passed a law allowing compensation for those settlers in the territories who would be evacuated. On February 20 Sharon signed the evacuation orders for the 24 settlements — all of those in Gaza and four in Samaria, the northern West Bank. The orders called on them to be evacuated by July 15. But a few weeks later the date was changed to August 15 because the earlier date fell during the Tisha Ba'Av religious festival commemorating the worst tragedies in Jewish history before the Holocaust. The IDF and border police began a six-month training period for the evacuation mission. The troops designated to evacuate would be unarmed. Sharon and the IDF had learned lessons from the evacuation of the Yamit settlements in northeastern Sinai in April 1982, which Sharon had supervised as defense minister.

The Bush administration also began to run interference on behalf of Sharon and disengagement. When Shinui threatened to vote against the budget in March 2005, Bush had Democratic Congressman Tom Lantos, who had grown up together with Shinui leader Tommy Lapid in Budapest, contact him. Lantos proposed that they both fly to London to meet and discuss the matter. Lapid said the trip was not necessary but listened to his argument over the phone. Lapid later received a second phone call from an American official who lobbied him with arguments about the importance of the disengagement. Realizing his bargaining power, Lapid imitated the religious leaders he loved to attack and negotiated with Sharon for an additional $167 million for his pet projects in the budget.[69]

The majority of settlers were convinced that Sharon would drop his evacuation plans either for political reasons or reasons of divine intervention. The religious settlers had interpreted Arafat's death as divine intervention. They would now pray for divine intervention against Sharon. Their prayers, if they were answered, were answered five months too late. Few took up Sharon's offers of compensation to leave early.[70]

On June 21, Israel carried out its first assassination since the Sharm al-Sheikh summit against an Islamic Jihad leader. The organization had taken credit for a suicide bombing of a Tel Aviv disco on February 25 that killed five and wounded fifty. Because Abbas had kept the territories quiet, Sharon turned over responsibility for security in Bethlehem and Kalkilya to the Palestinian Authority. Abbas promised to deploy 5,000 policemen around the Gush Katif settlement bloc in Gaza during the evacuation and requested that they be permitted to carry weapons for protection.[71]

James Wolfensohn, the former World Bank chairman who was appointed special negotiator in the Middle East for the Quartet, concentrated on getting the Israelis and Palestinians to coordinate in six areas prior to disengagement: border crossings; connecting Gaza with the West Bank; rebuilding the Gaza airport (destroyed by Israel in 2002) and building a new seaport; demolition and disposal of homes in settlements to be evacuated; and preserving the settlers' greenhouses. Wolfensohn secured international funding from a group of rich philanthropists to purchase the greenhouses from the settlers — so that the settlers would not be tempted to simply vandalize them.[72]

The Bush administration led by Secretary of State Condolezza Rice centered its Middle East policy in 2005 around the disengagement. Rice was forced to explain to the Palestinians that because Sharon had sold the move as a unilateral one for domestic political reasons, there would be no real coordination beyond security and arranging for removal of the rubble. The Palestinians had decided not to preserve the settlers' homes because the space was more valuable for building either housing projects with apartment complexes or industry. The Palestinian Authority was upset because Abbas and Fatah needed to demonstrate that negotiation was a more effective strategy than terrorism. Wolfensohn testified before the Senate Foreign Relations Committee six weeks before the scheduled disengagement that still much had yet left to be done.[73]

On August 7 the Israeli government met and approved the withdrawal from the first three settlements. On August 15 Sharon went on Israeli television to sell the disengagement to the Israeli public. "This operation is essential for Israel," argued Sharon. "We cannot keep Gaza forever. More than a million Palestinians live there in overpopulated refugee camps, in poverty, without hope," explained Sharon. Mahmoud Abbas issued his own statement. "The Israeli withdrawal is a very important step in our history. But it is only a beginning. Such a withdrawal must take place not only in Gaza, but also in the West Bank and in East Jerusalem."[74]

The actual evacuation began on August 17. The first day seven Gaza settlements were evacuated with Israeli soldiers carrying settlers out of their homes and loading them on buses. The next day a further four settlements were evacuated. On the third day only a single settlement was evacuated. The IDF then rested a day and on the fifth day evacuated another five settlements. By August 22 the IDF had finished evacuating the settlers from Gaza. Bulldozers then moved in and flattened the 2,800 houses, various community buildings and 26 synagogues. All this had been done under the eyes of about 500 Israeli and foreign journalists and broadcast live over Israel's three main television channels. Two of the four settlements in Samaria on the West Bank were evacuated on August 23 and the settlers from the other two settlements left on their own. The entire evacuation had taken only six days. Sharon considered the operation to have been a great success. Like his great victories in the 1967 war, the secret had been meticulous planning and preparation and training.

The settlers filed a motion in Israel's High Court of Justice in Jerusalem to prevent the state from destroying the synagogues in Gaza. The Court granted the state permission to go ahead and demolish the synagogues, but Sharon decided not to. He informed Saeb Erekat, the head Palestinian negotiator, that the synagogues would stay intact and asked him to protect them as holy places. When the last Israeli soldiers pulled out of Gaza on September 12, crowds of Palestinians poured into the former settlements. The most radical among them desecrated four of the synagogues before the cameras of the world. Sharon had demonstrated that he also knew something about public relations.[75]

In Gaza Hamas took credit for the Israeli withdrawal. A large Hamas banner read in Arabic, "Four years of resistance beat ten years of negotiation." A survey by the Palestinian Center for Policy and Survey Research had 40 percent of the Palestinian public attributing the withdrawal to the actions of Hamas and Islamic Jihad, 21 percent to the resistance of Fatah, and only 11 percent to the actions of Abbas. The unilateral withdrawal so strengthened Hamas that it was able to take over control of Gaza from Fatah and the Palestinian Authority in a violent coup in the summer of 2007. The disengagement combined with the notorious corruption of the Fatah-led Palestinian Authority under both Arafat and Abbas allowed Hamas to triumph in elections held in the Palestinian territories in January 2006. This allowed Sharon to once again argue that Israel had no one to talk to. He had cannily survived one year of a moderate Palestinian leader.[76]

On September 15, 2005 Sharon spoke before the UN General Assembly in New York. He was treated like a hero by the Europeans and even by some of the Arabs. He spoke in front of some 160 world leaders at the opening session. Sharon hinted at future withdrawals from the West Bank if the Arabs ended terror. Qatar said that the Arabs should reciprocate the disengagement with some appropriate action of their own. He received a public handshake from embattled Pakistani leader General Pervez Musharraf and had a good meeting with King Abdallah of Jordan. Sharon had finally become popular with Jewish communities in both America and Europe. Sharon was popular at a time when both President Bush and President Chirac of France were down in the polls. He could serve out the rest of his term without having to worry about outside pressure for further concessions.[77]

Sharon returned to Israel and discovered that he was the proverbial prophet who was an outcast in his own country, or at least his own party. He was threatened by Benjamin Netanyahu on the right who would constrain him and could possibly unseat him. So Sharon began sending out feelers within the Likud about building a new centrist party, a design first broached by Haim Ramon of Labor. Thirteen, or a third of the Likud's forty MKs were willing to follow Sharon into this new party. If he won commitment from at least one MK in Labor he would have the one-third he needed to be recognized as a new faction until elections could be held.

On November 12 and 19 Sharon's "kitchen cabinet" or "ranch forum" of close political advisors met at his Sycamores farm. On November 21, Sharon announced at a press conference that he was forming a new centrist party and calling new elections. He immediately went to President Moshe Katzav and requested that the Knesset be dissolved and that new elections be called for March 28, 2006. On December 18 Sharon was hospitalized after suffering a minor stroke. He was put on blood thinner to prevent clotting. On January 4 he was rushed to the hospital in Jerusalem by ambulance from his farm after suffering a severe headache. During the trip he suffered a massive stroke, and he went into a coma shortly after arrival. Sharon's political life was over even if his physical life still had some time left. The next day Ehud Olmert was named interim prime minister. Olmert led his new party, Kadima into elections in March. The disengagement was Sharon's last major policy act as prime minister. Condi Rice failed to follow through and see that the Karni Crossing agreement of 2005 that she had mediated between Israel and the Palestinian authority on allowing Palestinian produce into Israel was implemented. Palestinian produce was soon rotting at the crossing, while trucks were waiting for clearance to pass through.[78]

It is not yet clear how history will judge the disengagement. The settler community, part of Sharon's core constituency since he entered politics in 1973, instantly reviled him as a traitor. Anyone who doubts this has only to read the feedback columns in the *Jerusalem Post* and *Ha'Aretz* and the Hebrew press. He is seen by them as an Israeli Benedict Arnold or Shabbtai Tzvi (the false prophet of the Greek Jewish community who proclaimed himself the messiah in the seventeenth century and ended up converting to Islam). What is clear is that any future peace agreement between Israel and the Palestinians will require evacuation of at least some of Israel's West Bank settlements — those located in the interior away from Israel's borders — if not all of them. The hold that the national religious community had over Israeli politics has been broken. A precedent has been set for forcible evacuation of settlements on a large scale. And there is just about no one else who could or would have done so. Those on the right had lacked the desire to do so and those on the left lacked the leverage to do so.[79]

Sharon's disengagement was like Nixon's opening to China, arms control agreements with the Soviet Union, and withdrawal from Vietnam, de Gaulle's withdrawal from Algeria, F.W. de Klerk's peace deal with the ANC, and David Trimble's signing of the Good Friday Agreement in Northern Ireland. He demonstrated the old truism that it takes a hero of the right to make peace with the enemy.

But because of a lack of negotiation with Mahmoud Abbas, Hamas was allowed to gain credit for the withdrawal. This is similar to what happened when Barak withdrew from Lebanon in 2000 and Hezbollah took credit. Hamas is fast eclipsing Fatah in Palestine and the conflict is returning to its Islamist religious roots that it had during the British mandate before the rise of Arafat. This may lead to another generation of conflict between the Israelis and the Palestinians until Hamas is ready to make peace with Israel and Israel is ready to withdraw to the 1967 borders. Since 2005 southern Israel has been bombarded with thousands of rockets from Gaza and forced to reinvade Gaza in late December 2008 to put an end to the threat. There is little likelihood of a repeat of unilateralism on the West Bank, according to academic Itamar Rabinovich.[80]

Hamas won the Palestinian elections in January 2006. Foreign Minister Tzipi Livni begged Secretary of State Condi Rice to prohibit Hamas from participating on the grounds that Hamas failed to meet the conditions of the international community. Everyone in the Bush administration was confident that Fatah would win and told her not to worry. Bush told Abbas not to hold an election if he thought he would lose, but Abbas was convinced that Hamas would win less than 35 percent of the vote. He was wrong.[81] In the summer of 2007 Hamas forcibly took power in Gaza and expelled many Fatah activists and killed others.

In December 2008 and January 2009 Israel carried out a three-week war against Hamas in Gaza in response to years of Palestinian rocket attacks against Israeli settlements. Hamas claimed that 1200 Palestinians were killed. The war led to a wave of anti–Semitism in Europe and Israel came under increased diplomatic pressure. In the election that followed in February 2009 Kadima came in first with 28 seats to 27 for the Likud, but Benjamin Netanyahu was invited by President Shimon Peres to form the government as the right had 65 seats compared to 55 for the left and center parties. Whatever diplomatic gains that may have occurred as a result of the disengagement seem to have been lost as a result of the war.

The feature that these two withdrawals had in common was that they were from territory that was not unambiguously part of core *Eretz Israel*.

Northeastern Sinai fell within the biblical borders of ancient Israel as given to the children of Israel. But there is very little evidence of Jewish settlement there in ancient times. In the modern period it was not part of the British League of Nations mandate. Likewise Gaza was not part of ancient Israel, but rather inhabited by the Philistines, a Greek-speaking Mediterranean people. And the Jews did not settle it during the mandate. Both Begin and Sharon were willing to give up territory elsewhere in order to strengthen Israel's hold on the West Bank.

Today there are two main occupied territories left: the Golan Heights and the West Bank/Judea and Samaria. The former was part of *Eretz Israel* but was not a significant part of Jewish history. Ancient synagogues have been found on the Golan, but no major battles took place there for Israel before 1967. By contrast the West Bank was more important to Jewish history before the twentieth century than was the Plain of Sharon or the Negev desert or even parts of Galilee. Jerusalem is the heart of Jewish history and it is surrounded by the West Bank on three sides. The western edge of the West Bank borders the most densely-inhabited portion of Israel. This is the area between Ashkelon and Haifa. By contrast the Golan is much further away from Israeli cities. The eastern Galilee is thinly populated by Jews. No major Jewish population centers are reached from the Golan until the Mediterranean coast.

Politically the negotiations over both the Golan and the West Bank will be very difficult. But Israel successfully negotiated the separation-of-forces agreement of May 1974 with the father of the current Syrian ruler. And it came close to reaching a peace agreement with Hafiz al-Asad in 2000. But Ehud Barak lost his nerve and would not agree to a complete Israeli withdrawal without some sort of gesture from Asad. Asad refused to make any such gesture. And the settlements on the Golan are Labor settlements, inhabited by settlers willing to resettle for financial compensation. The Likud does not have a real stake in the Golan settlements.

By contrast the Palestinians have been divided since 2007 between the Hamas-controlled Gaza and the Fatah-controlled West Bank. Neither set of leaders is especially well entrenched to where it can afford to make major concessions to Israel in exchange for peace. Neither seems capable of giving up its demand to a "right of return" for Palestinian refugees to Israel — a deal breaker for Israel. And even if the Likud should decide that it wanted to give up the West Bank, it does not control the settlers living there. Although many of the settlers on the West Bank vote for the Likud, others vote for the Jewish Home (Beit Yehudi) party or Avigdor Lieberman's Israel Beitenu, or Shas. Labor could deliver its own settlers on the Golan in the event of a peace deal much easier than the Likud could deliver the settlers on the West Bank.[82]

So far there have been four Israeli prime ministers from the Likud. When it came to withdrawing from the West Bank, the most recent of these, Benjamin Netanyahu has proved to be the most flexible. Begin shrewdly traded the Sinai for the West Bank at Camp David. Shamir refused to negotiate seriously about the West Bank in his over six years as prime minister from 1983 to 1992. Netanyahu negotiated an agreement on Hebron in 1997 and then a further redeployment of the IDF on the West Bank in 1998 at the Wye Plantation but his coalition never carried out the latter agreement. Sharon as Likud leader and prime minister spoke of an independent Palestinian state but on less than half the territory of the West Bank — something that would not be acceptable to any Palestinian leader or to international opinion.

Part of Martin Mansergh's secret in his negotiations with the Republicans of Sinn Fein was to be able to point to republican history in the Republic of Ireland and the Free State before it. He could use Eamon de Valera and Sean Lemass as examples as republican taoisigh operating successfully within a partitionist settlement. The Likud yet lacks a prime minister who has negotiated to withdraw from a key portion of *Eretz Israel*. Sharon made rhetorical history when he spoke of the occupation. Netanyahu spoke of a demilitarized Palestinian state if it was willing to accept Israel as a Jewish state. But the example of a Likud prime minister withdrawing successfully from the Golan would be a much more concrete and useful precedent. So for the above reasons, President Obama or one of his successors should use his energy and political capital involved in Middle East peacemaking on an attempt to mediate a Golan settlement rather than a West Bank/Gaza settlement.

CHAPTER FOUR

South Africa
Leaves Namibia

For forty-three years South Africa was involved in a dispute with the international community over the control of South-West Africa/Namibia, which in many respects resembles Israel's dispute over the occupation of the Palestinian territories. The main differences are that Israel has had a staunch ally, the United States, whereas after 1960 South Africa lacked such an ally, and that in the case of Namibia it had a liberation movement, SWAPO, which was separate from the African National Congress (ANC), where as the Palestinians have the same liberation movements for both the territories and Israel itself as all were once part of mandatory Palestine.

What is today Namibia was first colonized by Germany in 1890 — one of the last parts of Africa to be colonized by Europe. The Germans were particularly ruthless and carried out an extermination campaign against two of Namibia's indigenous peoples, the Herero and the Nama, driving them into the desert and poisoning water holes. By the end of 1905 the Herero had been reduced to between a fifth and a quarter of their previous population — reduced from between 60,000 and 80,000 to 16,000, of whom all but 2,000 were in German concentration camps. The Nama were lowered in number by between 35 and 50 percent. By 1911 there were only some 9,800 Nama compared with between 15,000 and 20,000 in 1892.[1] This had the effect of shifting the center of population in the territory from the south to the north. German South-West Africa was Germany's main settler colony in Africa, with German settlers established in the capital, Windhoek, and in smaller settlements such as Luderitz and Swakopmund. In the winter of 1915 the Union Defence Force of South Africa, under the command of prime minister Louis Botha and defense minister Jan Smuts, invaded South-West Africa as part of the Allied effort in World War I. Germany had only minor colonial forces in the territory, and the conquest, which was completed in July, was mostly a matter of logistics.[2]

After the war Great Britain requested from the new League of Nations that South Africa be allowed to exercise a "C" class mandate over the territory. Such a mandate was the type assigned to African colonies of Germany that had been conquered and meant that they could be administered as part of the territory or possessions of the mandatory power with independence not being contemplated for decades if ever. In 1939 the League of Nations stopped meeting due to the outbreak of World War II and held one last meeting in 1946 to wrap up unfinished business by turning it over to the United Nations, which had been founded in San Francisco in the spring of the previous year.

The white-only assembly of South-West Africa passed resolutions in 1934, 1943, and 1946 requesting that South Africa annex the territory. During World War II British Prime Minister Winston Churchill, an arch-imperialist himself, twice urged Prime Minister Jan Smuts, who was serving in the Imperial War Cabinet in London, to annex the territory.[3] Smuts, preoccupied with Imperial business, put this off until 1946, which proved to be too late. In 1946 a number of countries on the Trusteeship Council objected to the annexation and Pretoria was left with continuing the administration under the terms of the League of Nations mandate while proclaiming that the United Nations had no standing in the territory.[4]

In 1950 South-West Africa began electing four members of parliament to the South African parliament in Cape Town. While this continued for the next quarter century, all of its members of parliament would be from the National Party. By the mid–1970s the whites in Namibia numbered some 100,000—the largest ethnic group after the Ovambo and about 10 percent of the population. According to South African Namibia specialist Andre du Pisani, the breakdown among the three white ethnic groups was: Afrikaners, 62 percent; Germans, 25 percent; and English-speakers, 12–13 percent. The latter are mostly businessmen as compared with the Afrikaners, who are mostly civil servants or farmers. Most of the Afrikaner civil servants were expected to return home to South Africa upon independence.[5]

For the next quarter century the conflict or dispute was a legal one carried out in the World Court at the Hague, with cases against the South African administration of Namibia being heard in 1954, 1959, 1962, 1966, and 1971. As South Africa ruled South-West Africa under the mandate as if it were part of its own territory — a fifth province — it applied apartheid and in the early 1970s organized the territory into a series of ethnic homelands as in South Africa. In the 1966 case the South African legal team was led by future Foreign Minister Roelef F. "Pik" Botha, who won the case for South Africa. At this point it became political, with the South-West Africa People's Organization (SWAPO) led by Sam Nujoma starting a guerrilla insurgency from Portuguese Angola and organizing with the independent African countries in the UN to oppose South Africa's continued occupation of the territory in the UN Security Council and General Assembly. In 1966 the General Assembly passed a resolution (2145) calling for the termination of the mandate, and in 1970 the United Nations Security Council passed a resolution voiding the League of Nations mandate and declaring the continued occupation illegal. This was upheld by the World Court in 1971.[6]

Because of the continued Portuguese colonial rule in Angola, SWAPO's armed wing, the People's Liberation Army of Namibia (PLAN), was forced to rely on Zambia, which gained independence in 1964, to provide it access to Namibia through the Caprivi Strip, a long finger of territory that ran between Botswana to the south and Angola and Zambia to the north. SWAPO was then an ally of the Union for the Total Independence of Angola (UNITA), one of three liberation movements operating in Portuguese Angola, which had struck a ceasefire agreement with the Portuguese in 1971. In 1973 the South African Defense Force (SADF) assumed responsibility for the counterinsurgency effort in South-West Africa against PLAN from the South Africa Police, which were stretched thin policing in South Africa and carrying out counterinsurgency duties in Rhodesia.[7]

South Africa was relatively sheltered from the decolonization wave that swept Africa in the late 1950s and 1960s. Prime Minister Harold Macmillan made his "winds of change" anti-colonial speech in front of the South African parliament in Cape Town in 1960, putting Pretoria on notice that London was siding with the forces of anti-colonialism. In March 1961 there was the Sharpeville massacre that led to the banning of the African National Congress (ANC), the Pan-Africanist Congress (PAC), and the South African Communist Party. In December 1961 the ANC's armed wing, MK, undertook a sabotage campaign that was largely crushed by mid–1963 when the movement's headquarters was discovered in a

Johannesburg suburb. In 1964 MK's leadership was sentenced to lengthy terms in prison, including life terms for Nelson Mandela and others at the treason trial. From 1964 to 1974 South Africa was largely shielded from developments in the rest of sub–Saharan Africa by a belt of white-ruled countries to the north: Portuguese West Africa or Angola, Rhodesia, and Portuguese East Africa or Mozambique. These territories acted like the territories did for Israel after 1967, providing it with buffer zones.

Then, in April 1974, the Portuguese army carried out a coup d'état led by junior officers tired of fighting in Portugal's African wars in Guinea-Bissau, Angola, and Mozambique. Guinea-Bissau and Mozambique were given independence rather quickly and easily as in each there was only a single liberation movement. But in Angola interference by outside forces on behalf of the three competing liberation movements led to a civil war that broke out in mid–1975. Pretoria at Washington's request intervened in October 1975 on behalf of UNITA. Pretoria was also acting on behalf of a number of African countries, including Zambia and Zaire, which were alarmed at the prospect of the Soviet-aligned MPLA seizing power. Initially the South African invasion, Operation Savannah, was disguised as an effort by Portuguese mercenaries to seize control. The SADF used Portuguese mercenaries and forces originally part of the MPLA and then of the FNLA led by Daniel Chipenda to carry out its invasion. Pretoria eventually poured in 3,000 of its own troops. When the American Congress prohibited American intervention, Pretoria decided to pull the plug on the operation and its last forces returned to Namibia in February 1976. South Africa suffered a total of 35 killed in Angola in 1975–76: eighteen national servicemen and seventeen permanent army. Its forces were better trained than its opponents but were at a firepower disadvantage.[8]

During the last two decades of white rule in South Africa, when the Border War in Namibia was at its height, South Africa had three different heads of governments: Prime Minister John Vorster (1966–1978), Prime Minister and later State President Pieter Willem Botha (1978–1989) and State President Frederik Willem de Klerk (1989–1994). As de Klerk was basically a transitional figure after South Africa had ended its occupation of Namibia, we are concerned only with the first two. Vorster was politically conservative but interested in South Africa maintaining friendly relations with other African countries. In 1974 he undertook his détente initiative to bring about good relations with other countries in Southern Africa. As part of this he co-sponsored with Zambian President Kenneth Kaunda a ceasefire in Rhodesia and peace talks that broke down after a single day in August 1975. But the initiative led to the creation of the Frontline States (FLS), an organization of all the countries bordering the white ruled countries of Southern Africa or that had military camps for the liberation movements (Tanzania) on their territory. Originally the FLS consisted of Botswana, Mozambique, Tanzania, and Zambia, in November 1974. A year later these were joined by Angola.

Due to ill health Vorster was forced to step down as prime minister in September 1978; he then became president of South Africa but revelations from the Infogate scandal forced him to step down from this ceremonial job in 1979.[9] He was replaced by his defense minister, P.W. Botha. Botha was known as Piet Wapen ("Piet the Gun") for his militaristic disposition and as the Groot Krokodil (big crocodile) for his temper. He had been behind Pretoria's intervention in Angola. He then used his remaining time as defense minister to correct the deficiencies in the SADF's armament that Operation Savannah exposed — mostly the lack of long-range artillery. Where Vorster was passive on internal affairs because of the negative effects from a 1969 split in the ruling National Party, Botha was eager to carry out a number of reforms designed to make apartheid more viable over the long run. But where Vorster was conciliatory in international relations, Botha was combative and saw a "total onslaught" against South Africa directed by the Soviet Union that could only be countered by a "total strategy."[10]

As a result of the Angolan civil war several changes occurred in SWAPO's insurgency in Namibia. PLAN suddenly had access to northern Namibia from Angola. South Africa allied itself to UNITA in 1975 and became its main patron over the next decade. This caused SWAPO to switch its alliance from UNITA to the MPLA. And many of the soldiers of Daniel Chipenda's Eastern Front became part of the 32 "Buffalo" Battalion based at Kutima Lima in the Caprivi Strip and officered by Portuguese-speaking white South African officers. The Buffalo soldiers became the only remnant of the FNLA (Angolan National Liberation Front) as the Angolan civil war became a two-way struggle between the MPLA, based in Luanda on the coast, and supported mainly by mixed-race Angolans and Mbundu blacks in the north and west against UNITA, which was based in Jamba and supported by the Ovimbundu in the southeast.[11]

SWAPO was mostly a liberation movement that drew for its support from those located in the north of the territory: the Ovambo, who made up roughly half the population of the country, along with the Kavongo and the Kaoko. In the mid–1980s South African intelligence estimated that SWAPO had roughly the support of two-thirds of the population because of its overwhelming support among the Ovambo and its significant levels of support among the Kavongo and Kaoko peoples.[12]

South African counterinsurgency strategy was based on four policies during the Botha period: first, heavy investment in medical and educational resources in the border area to keep the populations along the border quiet, and even providing some intelligence to the SADF; second, cross-border operations into southern Angola to destroy PLAN's infrastructure and large concentrations of guerrillas; third, developing support among the other peoples of Namibia as a political counterweight to SWAPO; fourth, relying on UNITA to protect the eastern third of the border from infiltration by PLAN guerrillas in exchange for military aid.

In January 1976 the UN Security Council passed Resolution 385, which set out in general terms the conditions necessary for independence. In 1973 Vorster had committed South Africa to eventually granting independence to Namibia, a dramatic change in policy. In April 1976 Secretary of State Henry Kissinger undertook a peace initiative in Southern Africa to attempt to limit the damage from the Cuban-Soviet victory in Angola by negotiating independence in Rhodesia and Namibia. Kissinger's main effort was on Rhodesia, where he pressured (with South African assistance) Rhodesian Prime Minister Ian Smith to concede majority rule in September. The Rhodesian part of the effort failed because the black liberation forces were politically divided and unready for a settlement or to even negotiate with Kissinger as mediator. But Kissinger did manage to negotiate terms for Namibian independence with Vorster in September, but SWAPO rejected these because it wanted power handed to it without internationally-supervised elections.[13]

In September 1978 the Security Council passed Resolution 435, which filled in many of the blanks of 385 and became for the Namibian issue what Resolution 242 was for the Arab-Israeli conflict. President Jimmy Carter had come into office in January 1977 with a foreign policy committed to human rights and he was in favor of supporting a peaceful transition to black rule in Rhodesia and Namibia. When Germany began a two-year membership on the Security Council in January 1977, the leading Western powers decided that this would be a good opportunity to deal with Southern African issues — Namibia, Rhodesia, and apartheid. The five Western powers (Britain, Canada, France, Germany, United States) decided to concentrate on Namibia as this was the "easiest" of the three issues to resolve. The UN ambassadors of the five powers formed the Contact Group and set about negotiating a resolution of all of the outstanding issues standing in the way of the implementation of Resolutions 385 and 435 in Namibia by engaging with the Frontline States, Nigeria, Scandinavian countries, and Nigeria. SWAPO, like the PLO, was suspicious of many of the countries negotiating on its behalf.[14]

Negotiations were held on a regular systematic basis from 1977 to 1979 and fitfully from 1979 to 1981, until all issues had been resolved by the end of 1982. The Contact Group deliberately refused to deal with the status of Walvis Bay, a South African enclave that since colonial times had been administered as part of the Cape Colony and had never been part of the German territory, but was claimed by SWAPO for geographic reasons.[15] Pretoria was carrying out a double-track strategy of simultaneously negotiating with the Contact Group and preparing an internal settlement through what became the Democratic Turnhalle Alliance (DTA). The DTA was an alliance of traditional African ethnic parties, mostly from central and southern Namibia, that had first met in the German Turnhalle (gymnasium) in Windhoek in 1975. The leader of the South-West Africa National Party, Dirk Mudge, became its chairman but was forced to withdraw from the National Party, which was dominated by apartheid supporters. He formed the Republican Party as the new white component of the DTA.[16]

Mudge later complained that until 1973 the internal parties were completely ignored by Pretoria, and after that they were ignored by the Contact Group and the UN. Despite threats of sanctions, Pretoria went ahead and held internal elections in Namibia in December 1978 to elect a constituent assembly. Although Carter had once had the cabinet discuss possible symbolic sanctions against Pretoria, the other four countries in the Contact Group were adamant that sanctions were a stick with which to threaten but never to actually enact — London was opposed to them. When sanctions did not materialize after the elections, Pretoria knew that it was a bluff.[17]

In January 1981 the Reagan administration came into office with an anti–Soviet orientation. Reagan appointed as his assistant secretary of state for Africa Chester Crocker, a young academic from Georgetown University married to a Rhodesian woman. Shortly after coming to power Crocker persuaded Secretary of State Al Haig, who had refused to endorse Resolution 435 during his Senate confirmation hearing, in March 1981 to link implementation of 435 to the Cuban presence in Angola. This greatly upset SWAPO, the Frontline States, most of Africa, and the other members of the Contact Group because it linked an issue for which there was no legal mandate to one for which there was. It brought the diplomacy of the Contact Group to an end. But this actually gave Pretoria an incentive to implement 435 because it addressed one of their main fixations: the large Cuban presence that Pretoria saw as being aimed at itself.[18]

Namibia was largely a hostage to internal South African politics. Afrikaner politics in South Africa was divided between the *verkrampte* ("narrow ones") and the *verligte* ("enlightened ones"). The verkrampte were conservatives who wanted apartheid administered on very rigid lines and were opposed to mixed sports competitions. The verligte wanted to reform apartheid to make it more flexible. P.W. Botha was a verlig in internal terms, but a verkramp in external policy who supported a policy of *kragdigdiheid* ("forcefulness"). Pik Botha, who was P.W. Botha's main rival (they were not related, Botha is a common South African name with another Botha in the cabinet who was not related to either), as both a verlig and a believer in diplomacy. P.W. Botha's main political aim upon coming to power was to enact a number of internal reforms to apartheid such as allowing certain categories of urban blacks permanent residence in South Africa as opposed to the homelands, which in theory all blacks were assigned to, and allowing organized bargaining labor rights for black unions. He passed these reforms in his first two years in office.

His major remaining reforms were the creation of a tricameral parliament with houses for mixed-race coloreds and Indians and a deal with township councilors. A referendum in the fall of 1983 paved the way for the new constitution that made Botha a "state president" with enhanced executive powers and elections to the two black houses of parliament. These elections were held in August 1984 and resulted in very low turnouts that basically robbed the newly-elected representatives of legitimacy. They also led to substantial internal unrest in the African townships. By mid–

1985 substantial sections of the country's urban areas were under martial law that the following year became a national state of emergency.[19]

The Soweto uprising of June–December 1976 led thousands of black youths to flee into exile with many of them subsequently undergoing guerrilla training. An attack on a SASOL coal-to-oil conversion plant in June 1980 signaled the start of a serious military capability by the MK. Over the next few years MK carried out a number of attacks on high-visibility targets such as Air Force headquarters in Pretoria in 1983. These attacks amounted to "armed graffiti" meant to boost the political efforts of the ANC in organizing internally but not a serious military threat to the regime. But combined with the internal black unrest carried out by the ANC's internal wing, the United Democratic Front, and strikes and work stoppages organized by the Congress of South African Trade Unions (COSATU), these constituted a major economic threat to the South African economy.[20]

PLAN guerrillas were well-trained, motivated and brave. A large presence of South African national servicemen and permanent force troops were necessary to patrol along the border and pursue those guerrillas who managed to infiltrate into Namibia. These troops were expensive to maintain so as a result the SADF resorted to cross-border raids and invasions in order to keep the momentum on its side and to keep expenses lower.[21]

PLAN activity increased along the border in 1981, leading to a series of successful cross-border operations from July 1981 to January 1984 starting with Operation Protea. South Africa's first major raid into Angola against SWAPO was Operation Reindeer against the Cassinga camp. It consisted of an attack by the South African Air Force followed by a parachute drop by South African paratroopers and a sweep through the camp. Critics charged that it was an attack on innocent refugees, a charge that had often been made about Rhodesian external operations in Mozambique and Zambia from 1976 to 1979 on which the early South African operations seem to have been modeled. During these raids Cuban troops did not interfere unless South Africa attacked them or a facility that they were sharing in common with PLAN. But by 1983 Angolan army units, FAPLA (People's Liberation Armed Forces of Angola), were starting to protect PLAN much more than previously and the Cubans were becoming a factor.[22]

In the mid–1980s Pretoria seemed to be in a good position. On March 16, 1984 Mozambique President Somora Machel and President P.W. Botha signed the Nkomati Accord in a ceremony in Koomatiport, South Africa on the border. The accord pledged both parties not to support internal opponents of the other. South Africa pledged to stop arming RENAMO (Mozambique National Resistance) guerrillas and Mozambique agreed to stop supporting the ANC. Mozambique carried out its end of the agreement but SADF elements continued to supply RENAMO. In September 1984 the United States mediated the Lusaka Accords between Angola and South Africa. South Africa withdrew its forces from southern Angola and Angola committed itself to keeping PLAN from infiltrating into the evacuated area. A Joint Monitoring Commission was created by Angola and South Africa to monitor the ceasefire, but neither side nor SWAPO was really committed to the long-term maintenance of the agreement. In between these two agreements, P.W. Botha and Pik Botha took a diplomatic tour of Western Europe in May 1984 that included Britain, Portugal and Germany among other countries. Pretoria seemed to have broken out of its diplomatic isolation.[23]

A combination of anger at the limited nature of the apartheid reforms and the deliberate exclusion of Africans from the Tricameral Parliament combined with the underlying "timber" of poor schools with the purpose of raising servants, rising unemployment, inflation, and poor municipal services quickly turned a protest against rent increases in the Vaal Triangle area of the Transvaal into a national uprising in September 1984. By mid–1985 every major urban township except Soweto was going through violent unrest. This resulted in municipal states of emergency throughout magisterial districts in South Africa, which were then replaced by a national state of emergency in June 1986. By June 1987 incidents of violent activity had been reduced about 85 percent. But the unrest was not completely extinguished for about another year.[24]

But two years after P.W. Botha's triumphal tour of Europe the situation was very different. In 1985 under Congressional pressure President Ronald Reagan enacted a number of largely symbolic economic sanctions against Pretoria in response to the internal unrest. The following year Congress voted a set of much stiffer sanctions by a vote of 84–14 in the Senate in August. Reagan vetoed the sanctions and the Senate overrode the veto by a vote of 78 to 21, the first time a presidential veto had been overridden on a foreign policy issue since 1973. The European Economic Community, the forerunner of the European Union, voted similar sanctions that same year.[25]

By the mid–1980s there were about 30,000 Cuban troops in Angola. The number peaked in early 1988 at 52,000. In September 1985 a major FAPLA offensive against the UNITA capital of Jamba was halted by the SADF and UNITA north of Mavinga with heavy losses. Soviet General Konstantin Shaganovich arrived in Angola in December 1985 to take charge of Angolan war planning. Shaganovich had some thousand Soviet officers in command and training posts and some 2,000 East Germans working in intelligence and signal units within Angola. General Arnaldo Ochoa Sanchez was put in charge of all the Cubans in the country.[26]

In 1986 a raid by the South African Navy and Special Forces on the Angolan port of Namibe and a UNITA offensive disrupted preparations for a new FAPLA offensive against Mavinga-Jamba. But a two-pronged offensive against Mavinga began in April–May 1987 with an attack from Lucusse southwards. UNITA managed to repulse this feinting attack on its own but, as in 1985, turned to Pretoria for assistance in dealing with the main offensive aimed at Mavinga from Cuito Cuanavale. This began with an offensive by five brigades for a total of between fifty and sixty thousand men armed with modern Soviet weapons and supported by air cover on August 14, 1987.[27]

The SADF was given the mission of stopping the offensive, inflicting heavy losses, recovering captured enemy equipment and training UNITA in its use. The Cuito River in southeastern Angola was to be Pretoria's defensive perimeter. The SADF never had more than three thousand men on the ground at any one time and these consisted of artillery units, mechanized infantry battalions, and special-forces reconnaissance units all dubbed the 20th Brigade. South Africa fired its first shots in the offensive on August 13, 1987 — mortar rounds. In mid–March 1988 these units swapped with fresh units and the task force was redesignated 82nd Brigade. In their attacks that took place over the next seven months the South Africans used UNITA as their infantry troops. UNITA soldiers rode into battle on South African infantry fighting vehicles and also fought dismounted. Except for the recon troops, the South African soldiers fought mounted in their Ratel infantry fighting vehicles, tanks or remained firing artillery from the rear.[28]

Due to the intense heat to which the South African soldiers were not acclimatized, and tropical diseases such as cerebral malaria, as well as dust, many of the soldiers later suffered from post-traumatic stress disorder and some had to be evacuated due to either malaria or dehydration during combat. Most South African casualties were caused by mines and by anti-tank weapons fired at Ratels. The Soviets had developed an integrated missile and radar-directed gun air-defense artillery system comparable to those that operated in Hanoi from 1970 to 1973 and along the Suez Canal in 1970 and 1973 and in Syria in 1982. The Angolan air force also had regular air cover from bases near Cuito Cuanavale. South Africa was forced to fly sorties from northern Namibia and from the Western Transvaal.[29]

The South African Air Force adopted a NATO technique designed for nuclear war of "bomb tossing" in which the aircraft would release the bomb while climbing from low altitude to high altitude in a reverse dive, causing the bomb to be projected forward of the aircraft. Through practice the pilots had become quite proficient at this technique. They would fly missions at either twilight in the evening or in the predawn first light of the morning so that they would have enough light to see but could still escape aerial detection. Because of these techniques and the discipline of their pilots, the SAAF lost only three aircraft during the period of combat in Angola in 1987–88: two Mirage F1-AZ jets and a Bosbok prop-driven artillery-spotting aircraft. Only one of the Mirages was lost to ground fire; the other was lost to pilot error when the pilot lost orientation while correcting a minor technical error. South Africa never used its air superiority Cheetah fighters — Mirages upgraded with Israeli kits to resemble Israel's Kfir fighters. These were retained for air defense over South Africa.[30]

South African pilots did not have a high opinion of Angolan pilots — they considered them among the worst in Africa. The Cubans were better. Pilots of the two sides first clashed in the air in late January 1988 but neither side claimed any aerial victories. "Air-to-air combat was now completely out of the question for us," said Brigadier General Dick Lord. This was because of the lack of fuel for it after arriving over the battlefield. "One thing that worked for us was that FAPA despite the high quality of its MiG-21s, MiG-23s and SU-22s was among the worst trained air forces in Africa. And it operated according to rigid Soviet doctrine," added Lord. One South African pilot had downed two MiGs a year apart in the early 1980s. During the fighting the South African artillery once "captured" the

Angolan air force by firing smoke rounds among the Angolan positions causing the Angolan planes to attack their own men thinking that they were the enemy.[31]

After the third Battle of Tumpo east of Cuito Cuanavale in which the South Africans lost three Olifant tanks to mines, Castro began making propaganda claims that Angola had defeated the South Africans with Cuban assistance because South Africa had failed to capture Cuito Cuanavale. The Angolans showed the three captured Olifants to the international media with great fanfare. But after the war was over he was more honest in a speech that he gave in Havana on July 9, 1989.[32]

In order to investigate this claim I read every South African account of the war that I could get a hold of. These varied from the memoirs of Defense Minister Magnus Malan and Chief of Staff General Jannie Geldenhuys to those by ordinary national servicemen who wanted to simply tell their stories of the fighting for therapeutic benefit. Only in one account did I find a claim that South Africa had a war aim of capturing the town. This was in an account by the battalion sergeant major of the 32 Battalion, Piet Nortje. And according to the book flap he left the battalion and returned to South Africa in January 1988, before the thickest fighting.[33] British journalist Fred Bridgland writes that several unit commanders urged the SADF command to capture the town, but because P.W. Botha and Magnus Malan did not want to escalate the fighting this was not approved. If South Africa had captured the town it would have been like Stalingrad for the Wehrmacht — a vulnerable bridgehead in enemy territory. Lieutenant General Kat Liebenberg said that taking Cuito Cuanavale would be "like the dog that finally caught the bus."[34]

South Africa's only defeat was at Tumpo where an Angolan bridgehead across the Cuito River was left, but following the third battle, South African engineers sowed minefields around the town leaving it useless as the starting point for a further offensive against Mavinga.[35] I find accounts written by retired South African generals and soldiers at the end of apartheid or under majority rule to be more credible than claims by Angolans and Cubans while those regimes, with their lack of freedom of speech, are still intact.

The fighting in November 1987 and February and March 1988 was South Africa's first conventional combined arms campaign since 1945 and the first time South African tanks had seen combat since 1945. The fighting from 1985–88 was the first time that the South African-designed G5 artillery gun was used in combat. Only sixteen G5's were deployed in Angola and were used throughout the campaign. The Olifant tank and Ratel Infantry Fighting Vehicle both proved themselves during the fighting.[36] But the 90mm HEAT (high-explosive anti-tank) round was inadequate against the Soviet T-55 tanks and the Ratel-90s often had to fire five rounds before they found the "sweet spot" where the rounds could penetrate between the turret and the hull. Logistics proved to be a major challenge due to the ad hoc nature of most of the units deployed.[37]

Angola lost probably a billion dollars' worth of equipment in the fighting. Estimates put the number of FAPLA and Cubans killed in Angola in 1987–88 at 4,768 — although how such a figure was arrived at is beyond the knowledge of this writer. The SADF lost 31 killed and 90 wounded in combat. The munitions used by the SADF in combat in 1987–88 cost Rand 328.7 million or about $100–$125 million dollars. In addition to the aircraft mentioned-above lost the SADF lost five tanks damaged of which two were recovered, and five Ratel IFVs. South Africa did not lose a single gun in Angola. The SADF claimed that the Angolans lost: 94 tanks, 100 combat vehicles, 34 multiple rocket launchers, seven mobile bridges, nine guns, 389 trucks and other vehicles, five radars, twenty-two 23 mm anti-aircraft guns, nine jet aircraft and nine helicopters. The final campaign involved some 40,000 troops on all sides of whom only 3,000 were South Africans or South-West African territorials.[38]

After the fighting in southeastern Angola, South Africa and the Cubans clashed in southwestern Angola in late June 1988. In early 1988 Cuba began redeploying its troops including newly-arrived troops in south-western Angola near the border. In April the Cubans began interfering with SADF cross-border operations against SWAPO with clashes on April 18 and again on May 4. Major concentrations were at Xangongo, about 100 kilometers north of the border and at Techipa. The Cubans began upgrading airfields at Cahama and Xangongo and building a 300 meter bridge across the Cunene River at Xangongo. In May a reconnaissance patrol spotted Cubans south of Techipa. Castro seemed to be bluffing as negotiations began in London on May 3–4 over a solution to the Border War. He wanted to raise the stakes for Pretoria and be able to claim a victory for political purposes before he pulled Cuban forces out of Angola.

General Del Piño, who had defected in 1987 to the United States from Cuba, sent word to the SADF from his American safe house that the Cubans lacked the training, logistics, and communications to carry out a full-scale offensive along the border. He also warned that Castro was an adventurer by nature and therefore unpredictable. On June 8 General Geldenhuys ordered another general mobilization of Citizen Force soldiers to deal with the Cuban threat. There had been an earlier mobilization in January for the fighting in southeastern Angola.

On June 26 a 32 Battalion platoon was saved from Cuban troops just south of Techipa by SADF artillery support. The SAAF had been banned from engaging in air combat over Angola out of fear of an escalation. On June 27 a SADF force of 32 Ratel IFVs of different variants clashed with a Cuban mechanized force consisting of three tank companies equipped with T-54 tanks. The Cubans lost at least two tanks, two ZSU anti-aircraft guns, and several trucks and about sixty men. The SADF lost two Ratels, one killed and several wounded. Later that day in an effort to trap the South African force Cuban MiG-23s dropped bombs on the Calueque Dam, which contained a bridge over the border to Namibia, and hit a squad of SADF infantrymen around a water tanker killing eleven. Two MiG-21s were downed by SADF air defenses.

Pretoria had been delinquent about informing the South African public about the nature of the fighting in Angola. Questions were first raised in parliament in late January 1988 by the opposition leader, Colin Eglin of the Progressive Federal Party.[39] When the casualties from the bombing were announced they were front-page news and hit the public hard. The international press misinterpreted this as a shift in the balance-of-power in Angola. Only 23 days later in New York City on July 20, South African, Cuban and Angolan negotiators agreed on fourteen principles as a basis for peace in Angola and Namibia. Both superpowers had put pressure on the two sides to back down and negotiate. The basic deal was implementation of Resolution 435 in exchange for a staged Cuban withdrawal from Angola.[40]

In April 1988 General Geldenhuys received orders to join the South African peace delegation in London the following month for peace negotiations. In January the Cuban government had agreed to withdraw from Angola in exchange for implementation of Resolution 435, allowing peace talks to take place. The Cairo Round of negotiations in late June, as the final fighting in southern Angola was taking place, was the start of a step-by-step approach. The South African delegation was a mixture of generals and diplomats led by Foreign Minister Pik Botha and Defense Minister Magnus Malan. The next round in July at Sal Island off the coast of Africa was also quite productive. But for Geldenhuys the Geneva Round from August 2–5 was the turning point of the negotiations. A basic problem common to many peace negotiations was a lack of trust: the UN and Moscow did not trust Pretoria to implement its end of the agreement in Namibia and Pretoria did not trust SWAPO.[41]

The last South African troops pulled out of Angola on August 29, 1988 and were so tired that they barely noticed all the dignitaries lined up to greet them including President Botha. The pullout had begun on August 10. In the Geneva Round earlier that month Cuba had agreed to pull its troops back to an agreed upon line away from the border in exchange for South Africa withdrawing completely.[42]

Although the November 1, 1988, deadline for wrapping up the negotiations specified in the Geneva Protocol was missed, a final agreement in which Cuba agreed to pull its troops out of Angola by July 1, 1991 in exchange for implementation of Resolution 435 in Namibia was signed in New York at the United Nations on December 22, 1988. The South African delegation was almost wiped out in the terrorist bombing that blew up a plane over Lockerbie, Scotland but one official scheduled a later flight then Pik Botha wanted so that he could spend time with his fiancé at Heathrow. Secretary of State George Shultz wanted Crocker to sign the agreement, but Crocker pointed out that protocol required the American equivalent of foreign minister to sign the document.[43] Pretoria and Luanda also agreed not to support internal opposition movements against each other. This meant that Pretoria ended its aid to UNITA in exchange for Luanda expelling the African National Congress from Angola. This meant that in the future South African guerrillas would have to find their way from camps in Tanzania to South Africa. This paved the way for the unbanning of the liberation movements by President F.W. de Klerk in February 1990 and the negotiated end to apartheid and minority rule.[44]

Why did Pretoria suddenly agree to leave Angola in 1988, a decade after first trying for an internal solution in December 1978? There are several simple answers to this — all wrong. The first is that Pretoria was defeated at Cuito Cuanavale and forced out of Namibia. This was first tried by Castro in a major address on June 2, 1988 in which he spoke of the history of Africa being divided into "before Cuito Cuanavale and after." The more sophisticated version of this was that the military balance had tilted against Pretoria because it lacked the modern aircraft to be able to deal with the latest Soviet SAMs and MiGs. The truth is that in a year of combat South Africa lost only two jets and only one was due to combat. Serious countries do not change major foreign policies over the loss of a single aircraft.

The South African version is that Castro made a few demonstrations along the border in the spring and early summer (northern hemisphere) of 1988 to cover up their defeat. Although this does come closer to the truth, it fails to explain why Pretoria was suddenly eager to leave Namibia. Even if Havana decided to unilaterally withdraw from Angola, Pretoria without an agreement would have been faced with an expensive deployment in Namibia to what end? Namibia was serving as a buffer zone protecting the Karoo Desert of the Cape Colony, while the major urban centers of South Africa had been in flames from late 1984 to 1988 for internal reasons that had nothing to do with the Cubans or Namibia. Pretoria was facing economic sanctions and banks in Europe were refusing to rollover South African loans at low rates due to the unrest.

In 1985 American South African-watcher Robert S. Jaster predicted that South Africa would leave Namibia when it was politically convenient for P.W. Botha to do so. The 1983–84 revamping of the DTA into the Multiparty Conference (by the addition of SWAPO-Democrats under Andreas Shipanga and part of the rival South West African National Union (SWANU) to the old DTA) to give it a nationalist veneer had failed to create an internal opposition that could compete politically against SWAPO and win elections. The National Party had split in 1983 over the tricameral parliament and granting the vote to non-whites. The Conservative Party had replaced the Progressive Federal Party as the official opposition in the 1987 general election. But now Botha had a chance to bring peace and eliminate both SWAPO and the ANC as threats.[45]

Theodor Hanf, a German academic specialist on South Africa, explained:

For what was the reason for South Africa to try to remain in Namibia? To some extent, at least, it was the fear of giving up a part of Southern Africa, which was once supposed to become a fifth province, to majority rule. South Africa wanted to stay in what they called South-West Africa because they wanted to prevent it becoming an example for South Africa proper.

It was very costly; and for many it had already become a lost operation. So from the very moment that the real action, the first emergency, was taking place inside South Africa, there was no longer any political benefit of holding on to Namibia: it had become a total liability.[46]

The general feeling among realist analysts of South Africa was that the pullout from Namibia occurred not because of a military defeat, but because the SADF was overstretched and the deployment made little sense. One author noted that Rhodesia had been more important strategically as a buffer state than Namibia, because it was closer to the country's industrial centers in the Transvaal. But there were two emotional factors involved concerning white politics. Rhodesia was where the Jameson Raid was launched from in December 1895 that contributed to the Second Anglo-Boer War of 1899–1902 that resulted in the loss of independence for the Afrikaner Boer republics. The percentage of Afrikaners within the white population of Rhodesia was roughly the same as the percentage of English-speakers in Namibia. So conservative English-speaking whites tended to support Ian Smith of Rhodesia, where as the Afrikaner securocrats thought that he was a *verkramp* who was preventing South Africa from installing a moderate multiracial regime.[47]

CHAPTER FIVE

Fianna Fail and the Claim to Northern Ireland

Ireland has been historically, along with Spain and Portugal, the poorest country in Western Europe. It has also been one of the most religious, with higher rates of weekly and even daily mass attendance among ordinary Catholics than any other country in Europe, except for the province of Northern Ireland. Until recently there was no divorce in Ireland, and abortion is still strictly prohibited, so annually many young Irish women travel to Britain for abortions — "an Irish solution to an Irish problem" as the late Charles Haughey termed it. It was until the twenty-first century, the Vatican's favorite European country because both the population and clergy were subservient.

Ireland has also been one of the more corrupt First World countries since gaining independence from Britain in 1922. This corruption has become more visible in recent decades with taoiseach (prime minister) Charles Haughey openly flaunting a lifestyle that was far beyond the means of his salary during the 1980s. A decade later he was found out lying to an official investigation into corruption. Questions are now being raised about the finances of his protégé, Taoiseach Bertie Ahern, who gained a reputation as a peacemaker for his role in the Northern Ireland peace process. There were three taoisigh (prime ministers) involved in the Northern Ireland peace process of the 1990s: Charles Haughey, Albert Reynolds, and Bertie Ahern. I will now review the corruption during their terms in office and in general in Ireland during the late twentieth century, before looking at the history of Fianna Fail and its attitude towards Northern Ireland.

Since independence there has always been a certain level of corruption in Ireland because the Irish, after having lived for centuries under foreign British rule, regarded the government as fundamentally foreign. Thus payment to the government was to be avoided as much as possible. In Ireland politics has always been much more local than national, with members of the Dail (TDs) being elected on the basis of what benefits they could provide for local constituents first, the constituency as a whole second, and the nation third. Irish voters would often reward politicians who had been exposed as corrupt with record-high first-preference votes. Such was the case with Haughey, Michael Lowry of Fine Gael, and Bertie Ahern.[1]

Corruption within Fianna Fail began on a large scale in the mid– to late–1960s when Haughey was finance minister through the Taca organization. Taca was a fundraising scheme in which prominent businessmen would pay a substantial fee to attend a dinner with Fianna Fail ministers and other party TDs at one of Dublin's finer hotels on a semi-annual basis. It was an introduction service between those seeking favors and politicians seeking bribes.[2]

During the 1970s and his time as Fianna Fail leader from December 1979 to February 1992, Haughey cultivated an image as a member of the noveau riche aristocracy by living in expensive homes, having his own island, dining at expensive French restaurants, and wearing fine French silk and linen shirts. No one in the press questioned how Haughey could afford this lifestyle on his official government salary. Some assumed that he had made very shrewd investments while he was an accountant in a private firm before becoming a government minister. But most were "sneaking regarders" who secretly admired Haughey's ability to beat the system and prided themselves on their ability to ignore the lifestyles and sexual mores of the political class, much as the American press did in Kennedy's day.[3]

"When Haughey was in power the money flowed in and when he was out the money dried up," wrote investigative journalist Colm Keena. This made him desirous to stay in power whatever the cost, which led to the coalition with the Progressive Democrats in 1989 and the break with Albert Reynolds. His finances began to spiral downwards as soon as Taoiseach Jack Lynch sacked him during the arms crisis in 1970. Haughey had bought his first estate, Abbeville, in north County Dublin, in 1969, along with 250 acres. Haughey's official income was insufficient to pay for the upkeep of the property let alone the mortgage. Anglo-Irish Bank (AB), Haughey's personal bank in the 1970s, continued to fund Haughey's overdrawn accounts throughout the 1970s in the belief that one day he would pay them back as a senior minister or taoiseach. It also did not hurt that AIB's general manager was the brother of Fianna Fail's leading fundraiser during that time. In April 1973 Haughey owed AIB 230,000 Irish pounds. By February 1974 he had reduced this to 120,000 by selling off land and borrowing from another bank. Throughout the decade AIB kept pressing Haughey to pay off his debt but kept cashing his checks. In June 1977 Lynch brought Haughey back into the cabinet as health and social welfare minister. Haughey's spending began swelling again and his total debt with AIB soon shot up to 580,000 Irish pounds. Haughey offered AIB to get an Iraqi bank to deposit 10 million pounds as partial settlement of his debt. When he became taoiseach in December 1979 he owed AIB over one million pounds.[4]

During the early 1980s Haughey had nearly 1.8 million in total in four different accounts — at Northern Bank Finance Corp., Guinness Mahon Cayman Trust (GMCT) and others. During the 1980s he was allowed to maintain an overdraft of up to 200,000 Irish pounds at GMCT. He closed out his last account there in June 1987 and he made no major withdrawals after January 1984.

During the late 1980s and early 1990s Haughey benefited from "loans" from supermarket owner Ben Dunne, who took charge of his father's company's finances after the latter's death in 1983. Dunne was kidnapped by the IRA in 1981 and cruelly treated, which may have led to his subsequent cocaine addiction later on. Dunne was introduced to Haughey in 1986. He subsequently offered to pay off all of Haughey's debt to the various banks by himself. From 1987 to 1992 Haughey received 1.8 million Irish pounds from Dunne.[5]

The government had a special fund for party leaders to help finance certain working expenses such as dinners for the party and so on. For eight months in 1991 Haughey used his party leader's account to pay for shirts from a Paris tailor and to pay for meals at an expensive French restaurant for the cabinet following cabinet meetings.[6]

A close political friend of Haughey's was Brian Lenihan, who served as his foreign minister and was later the party candidate for president in 1990, until he was publicly caught in a major lie. In 1989 Lenihan developed liver problems not related to drinking. Paul Kavanagh raised funds from businessmen to finance Lenihan's operation at the Mayo Clinic in Rochester, MN, and to finance his family's travel and stay in Minnesota. Haughey took an active role in soliciting funds from businessmen both for the party's 1989 election fund and for the Lenihan fund. But Haughey had those contributing to the Lenihan fund make the checks out to himself rather than to the fund.[7]

On the morning of the 1989 election, property developer Mark Kavanagh donated 100,00 Irish pounds — 25,000 in a check made out to the party and 75,000 in three 25,000 bank drafts that went directly to Haughey. Between contributions from Kavanagh and Michael Smurfit the party received 75,000 out of a total of 160,000, with the remainder going directly to Haughey.[8]

In 1988 Haughey bought a yacht for 120,000 Irish pounds in Spain. He later had the yacht renovated at a cost of 75,546 Irish pounds that was paid for by a company called Dedeir.[9]

Altogether Haughey received some 9.1 million Irish pounds in "contributions" between 1979 and 1996, or 45 million Euros in 2012 Euros. In 1997 Ben Dunne was in Miami, Florida. High on cocaine, he became irrational and suicidal and the police were called. He managed to avoid jail time, but the story of his contributions to Haughey was revealed when his siblings took him to court in a fight over management of the family fortune following the incident. As a result the McCracken Tribunal was set up in 1997 to investigate Dunne's contributions to various Irish politicians. Haughey was compelled to testify and was caught in a web of lies and forced to admit that he had perjured himself. From 1997 to 2005, when he died, Haughey was in disgrace and his party disowned him. The McCracken Tribunal was followed by the Moriarty Tribunal (1997–2011) and the Flood/Mahon Tribunal (1997–2011), which investigated different aspects of political corruption in Ireland.[10]

Haughey was followed as taoiseach by Albert Reynolds, who had been minister of industry in the late 1980s during the period covered by the Beef Tribunal (1992–94), the first of the major Irish corruption tribunals of the 1990s. Larry Goodman, a self-made businessman, was owner of Goodman Industries and Europe's largest beef exporter in the 1980s. Under a scheme subsidized by the European Union, Irish (and British) beef was exported to Iraq and guaranteed by the Irish taxpayer. More cattle were exported under the scheme than there were in all of Ireland at the time, which meant that the Irish government was subsidizing the export of foreign beef as well. When the facts became known, the Progressive Democrats threatened to leave the coalition unless an official tribunal was set up to investigate the matter. The Beef Tribunal established that the fraud cost the Irish taxpayer 8.6 million Irish pounds in lost income tax. Goodman over declared the amount of beef exported in order to collect unearned EU subsidy payments. The Beef Tribunal's report blamed the over reporting on two junior female office workers who had nothing to gain from the fraud. Finally two other, low-ranking Goodman executives, who also did not make any financial gain from the fraud, were charged and prosecuted for the offense.[11]

Reynolds was only mildly censured in the report and Haughey escaped any censure whatsoever. As is related here, the Beef Tribunal led to the fall of Reynold's two governments. The first was after he publicly called Progressive Democrat leader Desmond O'Malley's testimony to the tribunal "dishonest." The second was after Reynolds's spin on the report's findings led to major stress in the relationship between himself and Tanaiste (deputy prime minister) Dick Spring in the summer of 1994. Reynolds was also tainted by a scandal involving a scheme by which major foreign investors could receive Irish passports in exchange for their investments. This scheme benefited a major Palestinian investor named Masri who invested in Reynolds's pet food company. The investment was perfectly legal, but it was Reynolds who had proposed the scheme.[12]

After Reynolds came Bertie Ahern, who served as party leader from December 1994 to 2008, when he resigned after being caught in a web of lies to the Tribunal. Ahern was the first Fianna Fail leader to win three consecutive elections since De Valera and the most successful leader since De Valera. He was, at 43, the youngest party leader in Fianna Fail's history.[13]

From 1986, when he separated from his wife, until late 1993, Ahern did not use a bank account but merely cashed his checks. This way there was no paper trail. On December 23, 1993, Ahern took out a loan of over 19,000 Irish pounds to pay for his legal separation. Ahern claimed that his friends raised cash to pay off his separation loan and gave him 22,000 Irish pounds on December 27, 1993. But one of those contacted said that he paid the money to help run Ahern's constituency. In 1994 Ahern was paid some 8,000 pounds Sterling for speaking to an Irish émigré group of businessmen in Manchester. This was an average of 400 pounds Sterling per attendee. Fourteen witnesses gave testimony to the planning tribunal that investigated Ahern's finances in 2007–8. But there are no records to back up Ahern's account of his finances. Tim Collins, one of Ahern's close political associates — known as the Drumcondra Mafia after his constituency — lied to a planning tribunal in 2008 about a deal in which he made 600,000 Irish pounds in the purchase of the Battle of the Boyne site by the Irish government in 2000.[14]

By 1994 Ahern was living in an apartment in the first floor of his constituency office, St. Mark's, instead of in one of Haughey's palacial mansions. Unlike Haughey, Ahern's tastes and hobbies are inexpensive and ordinary. So, as a result, he did not draw attention to his finances and projected an aura of being uninterested in money. "Bertie was the meal ticket," said one of his friends — implying that their friendship was not totally disinterested. Five of the twelve men whom Ahern identified as donors for his "dig outs" (bail outs) in 1993–94 were appointed to serve on state boards.[15]

In September 2002 the Flood Tribunal outlined the record of corruption of former Foreign Minister Ray Burke, who was forced to resign in October 1997 and replaced by David Andrews — who had earlier served as foreign minister at the start of the peace process — and eighteen witnesses were implicated in the findings. Ahern had Dermot Ahern (no relation), a senior party figure, investigate Burke after rumors of his corruption circulated. Dermot Ahern cleared him. In October Ahern praised the Flood Tribunal report in the Dail. As a result of the Tribunal, 35 million Irish pounds in unpaid taxes were recovered and Burke was sent to prison for six months for tax evasion. In September 2003 Judge Flood retired and was replaced by Alan Mahon, and the tribunal became the Mahon Tribunal. The two tribunals were estimated to have cost 194 million Euros, of which 50 million was recouped in discoveries by the Criminal Assets Bureau and the Revenue Commissioners.[16]

During Ahern's second term he created a culture of celebrity in Ireland, in which he linked his government and party to both the national business elite and international celebrities. His daughter had an expensive wedding in Paris in 2003, bringing back memories of Haughey's life style. Ahern himself seemed to have only two issues that he personally cared about: building a sports stadium in Dublin — which he did — and the Northern Ireland peace process. Like Blair, he devoted much time after 1998 to keeping the peace process on track, until it was finally bedded down in 2007.[17]

On September 13, 2006, justice minister Michael McDowell was elected leader of the Progressive Democrats (PDs). The following month the coalition government between Fianna Fail and the PDs came close to breaking up over the rumors about Ahern's corruption. But because Ahern was the most popular party leader in Ireland, with an approval rating of 53 percent, the coalition held together.

On April 29, 2007, Ahern dissolved the Dail and called his third election as party leader. Ahern was personally endorsed by former president Bill Clinton, former mediator George Mitchell, and British prime minister Tony Blair because of his role in the peace process. His opponent, Enda Kenney of Fine Gael, had a total government experience of 2.5 years as tourism minister. Fianna Fail had more first preference votes than in 2002, but three fewer seats (probably as a result of fewer lower preference votes).[18]

After two days of examination by the Mahon Tribunal, Ahern's story of his personal finances was in tatters. In October 2007 he agreed to pay taxes and penalties on 70,000 Irish pounds of unreported income. Both the cabinet and party were solidly behind the taoiseach, as no faction saw any advantage in his fall from grace or power. And journalists now feel free to accuse him of having committed perjury with impunity. But in late March 2008, the party began to abandon Ahern after he let his secretary take the Tribunal's aggressive interrogation with no support. In June 2008, after he resigned from office, Ahern claimed that he had made the unaccounted for money at the racetrack. In June 2009, Ahern's older brother, Max, came in fifth place in a by-election in Dublin Central for his brother's old seat. The Ahern name was now a burden rather than an asset. After the economy crashed in 2008, Ahern's reputation suffered drastically and Fianna Fail lost power in 2010, coming in behind Fine Gael and Labour. By then Irish citizens rated Ireland last out of 27 European countries surveyed in levels of public trust.[19]

In the 1980s the party was closely identified with the beef industry. In the 1990s and 2000s, during the Celtic Tiger economy, it was identified with property developers, the construction industry, and realtors. The party's in-house magazine, *The Nation*, was so full of property development ads that it looked like an industry brochure. Academic political scientist Elaine Bryne concluded that Ireland suffered from over-regulation, which caused the business community to look for rent seekers in government in order to avoid and exploit this regulation. By the 1980s the situation was one of state-capture, in which the business community had gained control of the government.[20]

She also attributes the problems largely to cultural factors: the lack of an anti-clerical political tradition as in mainland Europe, the focus of Irish Catholicism on sexual morality rather than on other aspects of Catholic and Christian teaching, and the fact that Irish Catholicism, unlike Protestantism, did not emphasize the good opinion of others but rather relied on a relationship with God mediated by the Church. Homosexuality was considered to be much worse than corruption, or as one wag put it, "it's okay to be bent as long as you're straight."[21] This was supported by public opinion that secretly admired those able to steal from the state and looked down on those who were honest, as evidenced by the derogatory terms of "Honest Jack" for Jack Lynch and "Garret the Good" for Garret FitzGerald.[22]

In these two features, religiosity and corruption, Ireland is very similar to the Palestinian Authority. The main difference is that these traits are typical for the Middle East but not typical for Western Europe. Another similarity is the way in which the dominant religion has become so much of the national culture. Traditionally, during the twentieth century Irish national identity was identified with both the Celtic-Gaelic culture and Catholicism. One author referred to the common perception in the early twenty-first century that being Irish consists of "being white, Catholic and settled."[23] Many Catholics have defined Irishness in terms of cultural artifacts, like Irish music, Irish dance, Irish sports, and the Irish language, that have left many Protestants feeling left out. Many Catholics have tended to conflate religion with nationality and so identify Protestants with the English, and because of history education in Irish schools many Irish equate all Protestants with the Anglo-Irish ascendancy that ruled the country in the nineteenth and early twentieth centuries. This feeling of exclusion has in turn caused many Irish Protestants to emigrate to either England or Northern Ireland. This has resulted in Protestants being reduced from about a tenth of the population at independence to about 3.5 percent today.[24]

Likewise, a similar situation exists in Palestine, where Arab culture and Arab nationalism have been defined in terms of Islam. There has been a high rate of emigration of Christians from Palestine during the twentieth century to the United States, Western Europe, and Latin America. Christians are now a minority in Bethlehem, where they used to be a majority.[25]

Ireland has the most electorally successful and dominant party in Western Europe. For nearly eight decades, from 1932 to 2010, the Fianna Fail ("Warriors of Destiny" in Irish) party has been the main party in Irish politics, with two sixteen-year periods in power and one thirteen-year period.[26] Its closest rival in European politics is the Social Democratic Party in Sweden. But the Swedish Social Democrats had a shorter reign at the top, from the 1940s to the 1990s. Fianna Fail has created a winning brand from a competition of populist nationalism, economic pragmatism, influence peddling, and the talents of its leaders. Fianna Fail was founded in 1926 in the Scala Theater in Dublin by a splinter group from Sinn Fein, the political wing of the Irish Republican Army (IRA). Its leaders included the leading figures from the losing side of the Irish Civil War of June 1922 to May 1923. Its first leader and dominant personality through its first decades was Eamon de Valera, or Dev, who was the president of the rebel Irish republic during the Irish War of Independence and before that one of the leaders in the Dublin Easter Rising of 1916.[27]

In January 1922 the Irish Republican Army split into rival wings over the peace treaty that Michael Collins and Arthur Griffith had signed with Britain in December 1921. The treaty left the six counties of northeastern Ireland — all in Ulster province — as a province, Northern Ireland, in the United Kingdom, under home rule. It also left Ireland as a Free State in the British Commonwealth, with members of the Dail and Seanad (parliament) required to take an oath of loyalty to the British monarch as sovereign. It was over the oath rather than over partition that De Valera led the anti-treaty forces into a civil war. Three years after the war ended, De Valera was tired of being excluded from politics and so proposed an end to Sinn Fein's policy of abstention, which over the following decades would be a fundamental dogma. After losing the vote, De Valera took his followers and formed a new party. In the 1926 general election they became the opposition.[28]

In 1932 Fianna Fail assumed power for the first time and remained in government without any coalition partners for the next sixteen years. After a break of only a few years they were back in power for another sixteen-year stretch. Ireland's main opposition party through the decades was Fine Gael, which was formed from Cumann na nGaedheal, the ruling party from 1922 to 1932; the National Centre Party; and the National Guard (Blueshirts) veterans paramilitary organization in September 1933.[29] From the mid–1960s until the late 1980s Ireland had a "two-and-a-half party system" consisting of Fianna Fail, Fine Gael, and the much smaller Irish Labour Party, which predated the War of Independence but was only about half as large as Fine Gael. In the late 1980s two smaller parties emerged, the Workers' Party and the Progressive Democrats.[30] Starting in 1989 Fianna Fail under Charles Haughey was also forced to abandon the party's cherished policy of governing alone as either a majority or minority government with the support of independents.

De Valera had a vision of Ireland as a pure autarkic, agrarian republic. He envisaged most Irish as being Irish-speaking Catholic peasants engaged in either farming or fishing for a living, with few major industries in the country. In 1937 he wrote a new constitution that reflected that vision and the Oireachtas (Dail and Seanad combined, or parliament) adopted it. Article Two claimed the entire island of Ireland and the small outlaying islands as the territory of the state. But Article Three said that until reunification was possible the constitution would only be in force in the area of the previous Free State constitution. The country was renamed Ireland, or Eire in Irish. He was then pursuing an economic war with Britain, refusing to make certain payments called for in the 1921 peace treaty and insisting that Britain would not have wartime access to the treaty ports. And he abolished the loyalty oath. James McElligott, the secretary of the Department of Finance when the constitution was drafted, was very critical of Articles 2 and 3 and thought that they were impeding unification and might result in London taking Dublin to the World Court in the Hague over its territorial claim. In 1948, when the opposition came to power, Ireland was officially made a republic, although it had been so de facto since 1937.[31]

Fianna Fail was officially known as the Republican Party in English, although the press and public referred to it by its Irish name. Two of Fianna Fail's five basic planks referred to unification and the Irish language. All civil servants were required to be bilingual, although few Irish spoke Irish as a daily language outside of the Gaeltacht or Irish-speaking area in the northwest in Connaught province. This over time largely became limited to the Aran Islands and Galway area. But Irish remained a required subject in school, and many a pupil hated it and dreaded the final exams in the language.[32] In practice the language was used mainly in politics, as reflected in the names of the major parties and the titles of several offices such as the prime minister (taoiseach, pronounced "tee shuck"), deputy prime minister (tanaiste), and speaker (ceann comhairle). But such usage appeals to the national feeling of the population and enhances the brand name of Fianna Fail.

Under Taoiseach Eamon de Valera Ireland had no truck with Northern Ireland, which had an autonomous status within the United Kingdom, with its own parliament and prime minister and government. De Valera finally retired as taoiseach in 1959 at age 77, following his election to the ceremonial post of president. He remained president until 1973, when he retired at age 90. His immediate successor as taoiseach was Sean Lemass, who also took part in the Easter Rising. Lemass immediately began opening up Ireland to the outside world by ending De Valera's policy of autarky and establishing open trade relations with many Western countries. He encouraged industrialization and foreign investment in the Irish economy. Lemass also changed his party's and country's policy towards Northern Ireland by exchanging visits with the then Northern Ireland prime minister Terence O'Neill in 1965 and 1966. Lemass traveled north to Belfast in 1965 and O'Neill traveled south the following year to Dublin. They worked out an understanding that Northern Ireland would end discrimination against Catholics and Dublin would stop challenging the legitimacy of Northern Ireland. De Valera had pursued a complicated policy of non-recognition of partition by not allowing the IRA to mount attacks on Northern Ireland from Ireland and by interning IRA members both during World War II and during the Border Campaign of 1956–62. He hanged six members of the IRA during World War II and 26 died between April 1939 and May 1946, when they were released from prison.[33]

Jack Lynch, a former nationally famous athlete at cricket and Gaelic football, became taoiseach in 1966. He was a compromise candidate between the rival Charles Haughey, who was then finance minister, and George Colley. But he, like Golda Meir, another compromise leader, soon became very popular in his own right.

The following year the Northern Ireland Civil Rights Association (NICRA) was founded by a number of leading Catholics and Protestants who wanted to protest against discrimination in employment, housing allocation, and the franchise to make Northern Ireland like the rest of the

United Kingdom and less like a conquered province ruled as a settler colony. NICRA decided to imitate the American civil rights movement as it saw Northern Ireland as analogous with the American South. Journalist Conor Cruise O'Brien described the much tougher situation of Catholics in Northern Ireland compared to Protestants in the Republic as being due to the fact that some of the former attempted to subvert the state whereas the latter never did.[34]

They began a series of protest marches across the province similar to the famous Selma-to-Birmingham march in the South in 1965. Protestant loyalists backed by the police began attacking the protesters with clubs, stones, bricks, and so on. in October 1968. In April 1969 O'Neill resigned after a series of sabotage attacks by the Ulster Volunteer Force (UVF) and an election challenge by Ian Paisley.

By August 1969 the province was torn by ethnic strife and the British government in London called in the British army to keep order. Troops were flown in from the mainland and initially welcomed by the Catholic nationalist population. The British army would remain in Northern Ireland on deployment for the next thirty plus years — the longest combat deployment in British history.

Ireland was quite affected by events in Northern Ireland, which quickly became known as the Troubles, a euphemism recalling an earlier period from 1912 to 1923. Neil Blaney called for intervention. The army leadership warned Lynch that intervention against the British army would be a catastrophe. The Irish foreign minister tried to get the UN Security Council to debate the situation, but Britain prevented this. Lynch authorized the creation of a government relief fund to aid refugees fleeing the strife and coming to the border. Finance minister Charles Haughey was put in charge of the fund. Three field hospitals were set up along the border. And in late 1969 the Anglo-Irish Division of the Department of Foreign Affairs was created to deal specifically with Northern Ireland.[35]

Haughey abused his position in order to purchase arms from an international arms dealer through a captain in the Irish army. These were to be used to help create a more traditional Republican Movement to replace the socialist-inspired Republican Movement, which had sold off the last of its arms from the Border Campaign to Welsh separatists and adopted a purely political approach. With this guarantee of backing, the traditionalists broke away from the IRA and Sinn Fein in December 1969 and January 1970, after Sinn Fein ended its policy of abstention from the Dail. The new movement became known as the Provisionals — the British would use the acronym PIRA to refer to them throughout The Troubles. The older movement styled itself the Official IRA and Official Sinn Fein. Lynch was finally informed of the plot and on May 5, 1970, sacked finance minister Charles Haughey and Neil Blaney. George Colley became the new finance minister. Kevin Boland then resigned voluntarily. This was the worst scandal in the party's history until the revelations about Haughey's corruption emerged in the late 1990s.[36]

Haughey took another decade to fight back from disgrace back to power. He began by speaking at party functions all over the Republic. In 1972 he was elected to one of the five largely honorary party vice-presidential positions. In 1973 he was elected to the Dail, party stalwart Frank Aiken then stopped attending party functions in protest. The other two ministers became marginal figures in Irish politics with one, Neil Blaney, becoming an independent closely aligned with Fianna Fail, Independent Fianna Fail — his former party branch, and the other, Kevin Boland, started his own political party, which flopped. Boland dropped out of politics in 1976. Blaney remained into the 1990s. He was a Haughey supporter until 1987, when Haughey switched his position on the Anglo-Irish Agreement. Haughey was actually much closer to Lynch on the nationalism scale than he was to either of the other two. A highly publicized arms trial acquitted all three ministers from criminal prosecution in October 1970.[37]

Lynch followed a policy of cooperating with the British to contain the IRA while urging successive British prime ministers to enact social, economic, and political reforms in the province in order to undercut the organization's appeal. There was a rather absurd situation where neither the British nor the Irish foreign minister could openly discuss Northern Ireland because both claimed it — thus making it an internal matter — yet both were responsible for handling Anglo-Irish relations. British ambassador to Dublin John Peck, who later retired in Ireland, wrote that the divide on Northern Ireland policy did not run between parties in the Republic but within Fianna Fail itself.[38]

The Provisional IRA began an armed struggle in February 1971 followed by the Official IRA. The Official IRA ended its armed struggle in May 1972 with a unilateral ceasefire. A splinter organization, the Irish National Liberation Army, then split off in late 1974 and began its armed struggle in 1979 with the assassination of Airey Neave, Conservative spokesman on Northern policy. A third organization, Saor Eire (Free Ireland), carried out a series of bank robberies in the Republic in the spring of 1970 in order to finance operations, but it was only the equivalent of a single active service unit (ASU) of the Provisionals and soon faded from sight.[39]

Lynch also continued the party's rhetorical policy of referring to the province as an ahistorical, failed and illegitimate political entity. This was heartfelt — nearly all Irish nationalists of a certain age rejected partition. In February 2, 1972, after the British paratroop regiment killed thirteen demonstrators during an illegal protest march in Derry, a republican mob of about 30,000 organized by Provisional Sinn Fein marched on the British embassy in Dublin and burned it to the ground, despite the attempts of some 2,000 *garda* to protect it.[40]

Fine Gael and the Irish Labour Party returned to power in 1973 to form a coalition government. Under the Irish constitution, the Taoiseach handles Northern Ireland policy or Irish reunification, while the foreign minister often executes this policy through negotiations with the British government in London. Academic economist Garret FitzGerald, whose father was the Irish government's first foreign minister, became foreign minister under Taoiseach Liam Cosgrave, who was himself the son of a former taoiseach, William Cosgrave. Britain brought Ireland into co-sponsoring a peace initiative in Northern Ireland in December 1973.

In December 1973 three Northern Ireland political parties (the Alliance Party of Northern Ireland; the Social Democratic and Labour Party, or SDLP; and the Ulster Unionist Party, or (UUP) met at a teacher's training college in Sunningdale, England, to negotiate a power-sharing government for the province. Alliance had been instrumental in convincing London to make a requirement that any future devolved government be acceptable to both communities. The SDLP, founded in August 1970, about four months after Alliance, was the majority nationalist party in the province and would remain so until 2001. The three parties came up with a formula that allowed the Unionists to have a majority in the government, but to allow the other two parties to have a combined parity. As part of the negotiation, Dublin issued a statement saying that unity would only come about with the consent of the population of Northern Ireland. This obviously contradicted the constitution. Kevin Boland took the government to court for violating the constitution. The government was forced to defend itself by arguing that this was only a statement of government policy and not a refutation of the constitutional claim to Northern Ireland — which took away much of the political value of the joint statement for convincing the unionists. The deal also included a North-South dimension in the form of a Council of Ireland consisting of representatives from the Assembly and the Dail and with ill-defined powers. This became the boogeyman of unionist propaganda against the deal. Paisley coined the slogan, "Dublin is only a Sunningdale away." Labour minister Conor Cruise O'Brien warned both FitzGerald and Cosgrave about the dangers of the Council of Ireland but they were committed to it because the SDLP was.[41]

The power-sharing government began functioning on January 1, 1974. Prime minister Brian Faulkner lost a crucial vote of support in the UUP and was forced to resign with his supporters and form a new party, the Unionist Party of Northern Ireland. Faulkner had been the last prime minister when the Stormont parliament was prorogued in March 1972.

On March 13, 1974, Taoiseach Liam Cosgrave announced in the Dail that "The factual position of Northern Ireland is that it is within the United Kingdom and my government accepts this as a fact." He added that the province's constitutional position would not change without the consent of the majority. FitzGerald had arranged for him to make this statement. In May 1974 a general strike by loyalist workers who controlled the power plants for the province, along with the backing of the two main loyalist paramilitaries, led to the collapse of the power-sharing experiment. It would be another quarter century before the people of Northern Ireland would get another opportunity to share power.[42]

Lynch privately supported the Sunningdale agreement but felt constrained to oppose it in public because of his party's traditional policy. Lynch returned to power in 1977 and retired as Fianna Fail leader and taoiseach in December 1979. He was followed by Charles Haughey, who was the son-in-law of Sean Lemass. Haughey defeated George Colley in the leadership by six votes. Colley then became leader of the internal opposition. But when he died early in 1983, at age 57, while undergoing heart treatment. Desmond O'Malley then became leader of the internal opposition.[43] Haughey, in his more than a dozen years as party leader, had at least four different Northern policies.

First, from December 1979 to June 1981, he was in line with Lemass's and Lynch's policies of critical engagement with Britain. He held a famous "teapot" summit with British Prime Minister Margaret Thatcher in December 1980. But he oversold a rather innocuous phrase in the communiqué issued afterwards about addressing "the totality of their relations in these islands." He spun this as getting Thatcher to put British sovereignty in Northern Ireland on the table for discussion. The unionists in Northern Ireland were upset — especially Ian Paisley — which in turn upset Thatcher. She was very cold and aloof towards him for the rest of their relationship.[44]

Second, during the Falklands War Haughey went from initially supporting the European policy of supporting Britain against Argentina with trade sanctions to taking Argentina's side after a British nuclear submarine sunk an Argentine cruiser. The war ended in a British victory six weeks later, but Haughey continued his policy of verbally attacking Northern Ireland.[45] Haughey was opposition leader from November 1982 to February 1987.

In 1977 former Foreign Minister Garret FitzGerald became leader of Fine Gael. He began modernizing the party by bringing in new blood from academia and business, implementing new rules about leadership selection, and debating new policies. FitzGerald's great passion in life was peace in Northern Ireland. He sincerely believed in Irish unity, but believed that this would best come about by the Republic changing its constitution and culture to make it accommodating for unionists, who in any case were not eager to find a new home no matter how much change the Republic underwent. In the 1980s Fine Gael was briefly transformed from a Christian Democratic party to a Social Democratic party by a change in its economic and social policies. This did not make him popular with much of the party's old guard but did make coalition relations with Labour easier from 1982 to 1987.[46]

During this time Taoiseach Garret FitzGerald instituted a New Ireland Forum as an investigative forum to hold hearings on a future relationship with Northern Ireland. The Forum was originally the idea of John Hume, but FitzGerald modified it to invite the unionists and Alliance, all of whom turned down the invitation. The Forum consisted of the four nationalist parties on the island: the SDLP in Northern Ireland, and Fianna Fail, Fine Gael and the Irish Labour Party in the Republic. Both public and closed hearings were held in late 1983 and early 1984 and the report was issued on May 2, 1984.

The report called for three different possible future scenarios: a unitary united Ireland, a confederation of the two states or a federal state in which Northern Ireland was a province, and joint authority in Northern Ireland by Britain and Ireland. The latter was the preferred option of the SDLP, and the other two were put in to appease the nationalists within both Fianna Fail and Fine Gael. Before the report was issued, Haughey said that Fianna Fail would only support a unitary state and not a confederation/federation or joint rule. This reaction received as much publicity as the report itself. During the summer of 1984 Irish diplomats went on a publicity drive in Europe, London, and America to publicize the report. But after the report was officially released, a reporter asked Thatcher for her reaction to it at a European summit in November 1984. She gave her famous "out, out, out" reply. She publicly rejected all three approaches in a row. She well knew what unionists would accept — or at least she thought she did — and what they would reject.

On November 15, 1985, after nearly a year of consultations, Thatcher and FitzGerald publicly signed the Anglo-Irish Agreement, which allowed for Irish consultation on Northern Ireland policy.[47] Dublin opened up an office in a suburb of Belfast, Maryfield, in County Down, which served as a secretariat of the Anglo-Irish Division of the Department of Foreign Affairs. Periodically, various members of the DFA's Irish section would travel up to Ireland for a week's stay at the office escorted by Garda (Irish police) and the Royal Ulster Constabulary. They would liaise with the SDLP and with the Northern Ireland Office (NIO) and throw lavish parties while being ignored by the unionists. The diplomats would study internal policy in Northern Ireland and make suggestions about policing or other matters to the NIO. Haughey sent Brian Lenihan to Washington to lobby against the Anglo-Irish Agreement among Irish-American politicians in the Congress. Several politicians listened to Lenihan but ignored him — they all supported the Agreement.[48]

FitzGerald's motive for both the Forum and the AIA was to visibly reward the SDLP for its moderation by giving it tangible, visible gains. He hoped that by doing this he could marginalize or at least stop the growth of support for Sinn Fein, which had launched into electoral politics from its role in the hunger strikes in 1982. FitzGerald believed in strengthening the center against the extremes — he wanted another deal among those represented at Sunningdale. The SDLP was then divided between John Hume, who supported joint sovereignty or joint rule, and deputy leader Seamus Mallon, who was close to Fianna Fail and supported a unitary state. FitzGerald attempted to convince Thatcher about the importance of ending nationalist alienation in Northern Ireland, but the use of this quasi–Marxist language alienated Thatcher. She was mostly interested in whatever security cooperation she could get from the Republic. In her memoir she pronounced herself disappointed with the results of the AIA.[49]

Haughey returned to power about sixteen months after the AIA was signed. FitzGerald had hoped to remain in office long enough to have the AIA become accepted policy so that Haughey could quietly accept it when he returned to power. FitzGerald figured that one year should be sufficient to allow this to happen. When Haughey was first nominated as taoiseach in the Dail after being elected party leader, FitzGerald gave a very critical speech in which he referred to Haughey's "flawed pedigree." As a result Haughey felt great enmity, or even hatred, towards FitzGerald whom, ironically, he had attempted to recruit into Fianna Fail when both were students in Dublin during World War II. Haughey considered himself to be a self-made man, even if he married into power, where FitzGerald came from an elite family. So there is an element of Haughey automatically rejecting any initiative simply because FitzGerald proposed it. Although Haughey rejected the AIA for political and personal reasons, his advisor, Martin Mansergh, rejected it for principled ideological reasons.[50]

After he returned to power, Haughey began to quietly work the agreement. He was also persuaded by his Northern advisor, historian Martin Mansergh, to begin quiet contacts with Sinn Fein to see if a peace process could be started. This was the final period of Haughey's Northern Ireland policy. Mansergh, through two Clonard priests, Fr. Alex Reid and another less prominent priest, Raymond Murray, began a policy of talking with the Republicans in Northern Ireland and bringing them in from the cold. The two had written to Haughey in 1986 and suggested that he begin secret talks with Sinn Fein to bring them into a peace process. Haughey introduced Reid to Mansergh, who then conducted the talks in parallel with the Hume-Adams talks. Both Haughey and Hume had concluded in 1988 that the Republican Movement was not yet ready for peace based on the Hume-Adams talks.[51]

Mansergh is the son of a prominent Anglo-Irish historian, Nicholas Mansergh, who specialized in British Commonwealth history and the history of Anglo-Irish relations as well as early Free State history. After graduating from Oxford University with a doctorate in history for a dissertation on the French Revolution, Mansergh joined the Irish Department of Foreign Affairs. From there Haughey recruited him to become the chief policy researcher for the party. Mansergh was an Irish history buff who specialized in the history of the republican movement. He became both the party's token Protestant and its token intellectual — but a very influential one, who from 1981 to 2002 had more influence than most cabinet ministers by providing advice on economic policy, coalition negotiations, and Northern Ireland.[52]

Irish journalist and political historian Kevin Rafter has attributed Haughey's evolving Northern policy to two main factors. First, in the election in June 1981 that temporarily put FitzGerald into office for the first time, Sinn Fein ran several independent candidates in support of the republican hunger strike in Northern Ireland. They won two seats and took enough of the vote to keep Fianna Fail out of power. Some have interpreted Haughey's participation in the arms crisis of 1969–70 as an attempt to prevent himself from being outflanked by Irish nationalists, led by Neil Blaney and Kevin Boland, in his quest for the premiership. After Northern Ireland impinged on his drive for power a second time, he was determined to again neutralize it as an issue.[53]

Second, Mansergh then used his persuasion to convince Haughey to try to bring peace to Northern Ireland. In light of Haughey's corruption, which he was, of course, fully aware of, it seems reasonable to assume that he was trying to protect his historical legacy by trying to connect himself with peace in Northern Ireland and possibly reward Mansergh for his loyalty to him personally and to the party. In December 1991 during a European summit, Haughey proposed to Major that they draft a joint declaration as a means of starting a peace process in Northern Ireland. They had barely begun when Haughey lost power.[54]

Haughey fought five elections as party leader and never managed to win a majority because of poor vote management. His policy of not tolerating any deviation from the party line on various issues led to a split in the party in late 1985. After two leading members, Des O'Malley and Mary Harney, were forced out, they combined with a defector from Fine Gael, Michael McDowell — a "radical conservative" — to form the Progressive Democrats (PDs). The PDs based their appeal on a combination of integrity, a market-based economic approach, and liberal social policies. In 1989 Haughey was forced to form a coalition with the PDs so that he could remain in power.[55]

This alienated Albert Reynolds, a self-made businessman who had been among Haughey's early supporters in the 1970s. After losing an internal leadership challenge to Haughey in November 1991, Reynolds became the leader of Haughey's internal party opposition. Reynolds had won 22 votes in the challenge — the same number as Colley in 1982 — but this new "club of 22" was made up mostly of former Haughey supporters rather than of Colley supporters. Haughey was forced to resign the party leadership in February 1992, after he was caught out lying about the tapping of telephones of journalists a decade before.[56]

The likely contenders for the leadership were Reynolds and Finance Minister Bertie Ahern, who had taken over Reynolds's ministry after the latter's failed leadership challenge. The two quickly came to an arrangement that Ahern would support Reynolds for party leader now in exchange for Reynolds supporting him when he retired in a few years. After being elected Reynolds made a speech in which he announced that his two goals as taoiseach were to bring peace to Northern Ireland and to bring stability to Ireland's economy. The first goal surprised many as he had never expressed any interest in the province or in Irish unity in the past. Reynolds wrote in his memoir that his motive was all the relationships he had built with people from both communities in Northern Ireland as a businessman. For Reynolds the population of Northern Ireland was a reality rather than an abstraction, as it was for most Southern Irish politicians. FitzGerald also had a connection because he was a child of a mixed marriage and his mother came from a Northern unionist family.[57]

After leaving school, Reynolds secured a job in the Department of Finance. After a few years he risked his future by leaving to become an independent businessman promoting dance bands, which were a craze in Ireland in the 1950s and 1960s. Reynolds traveled all over the island and was successful at finding talent and promoting it. Then he left and became the owner of a pet food factory. He was also successful at this because there was a market for pet food in Ireland at the time and Reynolds knew how to take risks and had drive.[58]

In 1992 there were several indicators that the North was ripe for peace.

SDLP leader John Hume had renewed a dialogue with Sinn Fein leader Gerry Adams that had been broken off in 1988. British Northern Ireland secretary Peter Brooke had carried out a series of constitutional talks among the various Northern Ireland parties except for Sinn Fein. The talks had broken down after a few months. Mansergh had reported that Sinn Fein was interested in a peace process that included it. And on November 28, 1990, John Major, whom Reynolds knew when he was finance minister and Major was chancellor of the exchequer (finance minister), became prime minister. Reynolds got along well with Major and convinced him that peace in Northern Ireland was worth pursuing.[59]

But before he could pursue peace or repair the economy, he had to deal with party politics. There was a series of public hearings about corruption in the beef industry, known as the Beef Tribunal. Reynolds publicly characterized O'Malley's testimony before the Tribunal as "reckless, irresponsible, and dishonest." Because O'Malley fashioned himself as the standard of integrity, he was unwilling to back down and the coalition soon collapsed, leading to new elections.[60]

Elections were held on November 25, 1992, and Labour, running independently, doubled its seats from 16 to 33 after a campaign that was very critical of Fianna Fail on ethical issues. Fianna Fail lost nine seats and Fine Gael ten, so neither could easily form a coalition. Fine Gael leader John Bruton spoke of forming a "rainbow coalition" with Labour and the Progressive Democrats without having previously consulted with Spring. Spring was holding out for an Israeli-style prime ministerial rotation between himself and Bruton as Fine Gael had only a dozen more seats than Labour. But Martin Mansergh came up with the idea of Fianna Fail forming a coalition with Labour rather than with its traditional PD and independent partners. He came up with a proposed program that was very social-democratic sounding (Mansergh fancied himself a social democrat as well as a nationalist) and carrying the imprint of Labour. Spring abandoned any talk of a rotating premiership but insisted on becoming tanaiste (deputy premier) and foreign minister.[61]

Reynolds had baited the hook as well by telling Spring that the North was ready for peace. Spring was, like Lynch, a former sports star — soccer and hurling. He rose to the leadership of the party after only a year and a half after being elected to the Dail because of the sudden retirement of the party leader. He was not interested in economic issues. Although he grew up working class, Spring was culturally middle class. Other than John Rogers and Fergus Finlay, a couple of friends that he brought in as political advisors, he had no real friends in the party. He brought Finlay into the DFA with him to help him draft proposals.[62]

Once the coalition was up and running, Reynolds devoted himself to his twin goals. For peace he decided to go for a ceasefire and peace talks before decommissioning. Hume and Adams went through several drafts of a formula that they thought could become the basis of an Anglo-Irish peace initiative. Mansergh was the key draftsman of the language, along with a few from the DFA. The draft was then sent up North for Sinn Fein to review. Sinn Fein kept most of the language but made a few changes. Hume and Adams ended their dialogue in September 1993 and Hume presented the result to Dublin. The DFA then began redrafting the language in sessions with British civil servants. Finally, Reynolds and Spring were forced to hold a summit meeting to thrash out the language themselves. Reynolds was very upset when Major told him that they would have to start from scratch because his draft was "too green," meaning that the language was too republican and thus could not be sold to unionists.[63]

After a private session in which the two heads of government cleared the air, the process got back on track. Reynolds publicly abandoned Hume-Adams in order to save it. And on December 15, 1993, the two leaders held a joint press conference at 10 Downing Street at which they released the text of the Downing Street Declaration (DSD). The DSD called for self-determination for Ireland and the principle of consent. The two rival, and mutually exclusive concepts, were reconciled by self-determination being exercised separately in both polities on the island so that the unionists still retained a veto. It was "an Orange document written in Green language." Hume could argue that the Irish were determining their own fate rather than letting Britain determine it for them.[64]

During this time the DFA began drafting speeches for politicians at the rate of two or three per week. In the speeches, "Hume-speak" was converted into "peace-speak" so that the Republicans could be seduced into calling a ceasefire. Reynolds saw the Republicans, rather than the unionists, as his primary constituency in Northern Ireland, leaving the latter for Spring and Finlay. Mansergh continued to meet with Adams in an effort to draw the Republicans out of the ambiguous "armalite and ballot box" politics into democratic politics.[65]

The Clinton administration in Washington was drafted into this conversion process by granting visas to Republicans like Joe Cahill and Gerry Adams so that they could come to the United States and reassure their American supporters. This would prevent a situation where any dissident group would win major American support. In the administration it was the White House and the National Security Council against the State Department and Pentagon. There was a chain process of persuasion: Adams would convince Hume, who would then convince ambassador Jean Kennedy Smith in Dublin. She would then convince her brother, Senator Ted Kennedy, who would then persuade Clinton. If necessary, Reynolds would cut in to call Kennedy or Clinton directly. Cahill got his visa and the IRA called a ceasefire on August 31, 1994. Some six weeks later, the loyalists followed through with an umbrella organization that comprised their three main paramilitary organizations. Unlike the Republicans, the loyalists issued an apology for their past actions. David Andrews, who was foreign minister as this time, claimed that only Fianna Fail could have delivered the IRA, as the Republicans did not trust any other Southern Irish party.[66]

In the fall of 1994, two years after his fight with Des O'Malley, Reynolds got into another fight with his newest coalition partner. He nominated his attorney general, Harry Whelehan, to serve on the High Court. Whelehan was a conservative whom Labour naturally disliked because of his socially conservative views. After he was nominated it turned out that his office had overlooked several extradition requests from the Royal Ulster Constabulary for a pedophile Irish priest, Father Brendan Smyth, who had fled to Ireland. After Labour's campaign against Fianna Fail and ethical corruption in 1992, it was necessary for the party to take the high road. Spring had probably already decided to walk by the time the appointment was made. But Reynolds, possibly because of concessions already granted to Labour, was determined not to give in. And he was suffering from lack of sleep during the crisis. At one point Ruairi Quinn of Labour bluntly told him, "Albert, we've come for a head, either Harry's or yours — it doesn't look like we are getting Harry's."[67]

So, in December 1994, Reynolds finally resigned in the hope of saving the coalition. Later that day Whelehan also resigned from the High Court after only six days in office, too late to save the man who appointed him. Bertie Ahern was elected as the new party leader without opposition. Then it was revealed in the press that Ahern had known everything that Reynolds had known about Whelehan. In June, Fine Gael and the Democratic Left, which had been formed out of the Workers' Party by defecting deputies in 1992, each won a single by-election in Cork. This changed the coalition arithmetic and made a "rainbow coalition" of Fine Gael, Labour, and the Democratic Left possible. Ahern went from being the next taoiseach to being leader of the opposition overnight. Spring phoned Ahern at 2:00 A.M. on the morning of December 6, 1994, to inform him that Labour would not be going into coalition with him. Spring and Finlay were allowed to keep their positions and Fine Gael leader John Bruton promised to pursue the same policy on Northern Ireland as Reynolds had. Bruton even offered Mansergh the position of advisor on Northern Ireland, but Mansergh turned him down out of loyalty to Fianna Fail.[68]

At the final Dail session with Reynolds as taoiseach his colleagues and political rivals spoke of him as if they were giving eulogies at his funeral.[69] In his memoir Reynolds writes that Spring seemed determined to break up the coalition no matter what he did.[70] And this is probably true. Reynolds was careless in paying attention to the coalition arithmetic and too stubborn to be a great party leader in the age of coalitions. He was made for that earlier era when Fianna Fail ruled by itself, and he had never made the mental adjustments necessary for a new era. The same personality that led him to take great risks in business and for peace, also led him to get into fights with his coalition partners.

Spring and Finlay then went to work drafting the next major milestone of the peace process, the Frameworks Document of February 1995, which was his greatest achievement as foreign minister. This was a document that was a bit greener in order to try to appease the Republicans. This annoyed the unionists and David Trimble criticized it. But most other Unionists took a more relaxed approach. Spring had gone overnight from being the orangest member of the Reynolds government to the greenest of the Bruton government.[71]

The following month, Northern Ireland secretary Patrick Mayhew traveled to Washington to brief the Clinton administration on the peace process. He said publicly that Sinn Fein would have to do three things before they were admitted to talks: agree to decommissioning of weapons in principle, agree to the actual modalities of decommissioning, and actually begin some token decommissioning. These three conditions became known as the "Washington 3" and had the effect of freezing the peace process for the next two and a half years.[72]

Mansergh had broached the subject of decommissioning with Sinn Fein shortly before the ceasefire and had received an emphatic "no" as an answer. Finlay came up with the idea of setting up an international commission to deal with the subject. Spring presented the idea to Bruton as his own and then Bruton sold it to Major. The Mitchell Commission (or International Independent Commission on Decommissioning) was chosen in late November 1995 and presented its report in January 1996. The Mitchell Commission consisted of: former Senate Majority Leader George Mitchell of the United States, former Chief of Staff John de Chastelain of Canada, and former Prime Minister Harri Holkeri or Finland. The report called for no prior decommissioning and suggested holding elections to choose the parties to be represented in the peace talks.[73]

In February 1996 the IRA set off a major bomb in the Canary Wharf financial district of London, causing major damage and killing two people. Adams phoned in a last-minute warning to President Clinton before the bombing. Sinn Fein was determined to get rid of both the Conservatives in London and the rainbow coalition in Dublin — or at least John Bruton — before they rejoined the peace process by returning to a ceasefire. The Forum election was held in Northern Ireland in June 1996 and resulted in good showings by the Ulster Unionists, the Democratic Unionists, the SDLP and Sinn Fein. The loyalists were only elected by a top-up device that allowed for parties that were not elected but were in the top ten to be represented.[74]

In May 1997 an election in Britain resulted in Tony Blair and Labour coming to power with a large majority. The following month Ireland held an election with Labour, Fine Gael, and the Democratic Left all campaigning as part of one coalition. For the first time since 1981, Northern Ireland was a significant election issue with those for whom it was important, favoring Fianna Fail over the rainbow coalition. But David Andrews admits that there were no real policy differences between the two main parties in 1997, as there had been in the 1980s. Adams made clear his preference for Fianna Fail. Ahern ran a very personalized election emphasizing his youth. The election resulted in Fianna Fail returning to power in a coalition with the Progressive Democrats led by Mary Harney. Vote management techniques initiated by Ahern resulted in an extra nine seats in 1997 compared to 1992, with the same share of the vote.[75]

As soon as Fianna Fail was back in power, Mansergh began traveling North to meet with Adams and Martin McGuinness on a weekly basis. His job was to get them to persuade the IRA to call another ceasefire — one that would stick. After it was reported that the loyalists were conducting surveillance on him, Mansergh had to be warned by McGuinness not to take the train from Dublin to Belfast.[76]

Negotiations, which had been going on since the summer of 1996 without Sinn Fein, recommenced in September 1997 with Sinn Fein newly admitted after a second IRA ceasefire in August. The Democratic Unionists and the United Kingdom Unionist Party, which Conor Cruise O'Brien had joined as a member in the mid–1990s, walked out as soon as Sinn Fein entered the talks at Stormont. This allowed constructive discussions to begin. The serious bargaining took place in the last six weeks of negotiations — most of it in the final week. On January 12, 1998, the two governments issued the "Heads of Agreement" document summing up the progress that had been made so far. It outlined the subjects to be agreed upon and the basic range of solutions. It was much more favorable to the unionists than had been the previous Frameworks Document.[77]

Ahern spent much of his first nine months in office working on the peace process. During the final week of negotiations his mother, with whom he had been very close, died, and he went directly from the funeral in Dublin to the talks at Stormont without giving himself time to grieve. Ahern had presented a long list of functions to be handled by the North-South body — much longer than the Unionists were prepared to accept. John Taylor said he wouldn't touch it with a "ten foot pole." Ahern then whittled the list down to a much shorter version, which led many to suspect that the long list had been presented as a bargaining ploy. It gave the Unionists a visible victory after they had made so many concessions on decommissioning, prisoners, and power sharing.[78]

As part of the peace process Ahern agreed to amending the constitution so that there would be no more claim to the territory of Northern Ireland by the Republic. Reynolds had originally envisaged using this as a bargaining chip once he learned how important it was to unionists. He asked Mansergh what the British equivalent of Articles 2 and 3 was, and Mansergh told him that it was the Government of Ireland Act, which divided Ireland into two separate entities. Ahern agreed to give up the Articles in exchange for power sharing, a North-South body with real powers, and

Britain giving up the Government of Ireland Act. Britain passed enabling legislation so that in the future a simple majority in a referendum would determine the status of the province. The unionist veto remained but without a legal presumption of a union. Initially foreign minister David Andrews had begun by declaring the Articles sacrosanct in order to improve the Republic's bargaining position. This resulted in unionists and the Alliance walking out of the talks to show their displeasure with Andrews's statements.[79]

The Belfast Agreement was signed on Good Friday April 9, 1998, giving it the name by which it is commonly known — the Good Friday Agreement. It consists of three strands: Strand One, covering internal arrangements within Northern Ireland; Strand Two, covering the relations between Northern Ireland and the Republic (North-South); and Strand Three, covering relations between Ireland and the United Kingdom (East-West). This basic framework of strands had been in place since the constitutional talks of the early 1990s.

Two simultaneous referendums took place in the Republic and Northern Ireland on the Agreement. In Northern Ireland the yes vote was 71 percent, and in the Republic it was 94.5 percent. Importantly, there was a slight unionist majority for the Agreement. The turnout was much higher in the North than in the South. Because the IRA refused to decommission because it claimed that it was not a party to the Agreement, the UUP refused to begin power sharing with the nationalists. An Executive was not set up until early December 1999. It was at this point that the new text of Articles Two and Three of the Irish constitution went into effect. The language converted a claim into an aspiration and changed the focus from land to people. There was no longer a claim to Ireland being a thirty-two-county state; it was now a thirty-two-county nation within a twenty-six county state. Mansergh drafted the new language in time for the referendum.[80]

Many in the Fianna Fail parliamentary party did not want to amend Articles Two and Three. The party grassroots was also suspicious of the change. Ahern had Andrews lobby among them for support to convince them of the importance of the change in terms of peace and development.[81]

Two other major processes were also taking place simultaneously in Ireland alongside the peace process. The first was the Celtic Tiger economy, which began to take off with major increases in employment starting in 1995. The peak period of the Celtic Tiger lasted from 1995 to 2002, but the start was in 1993 and the after-effects continued until 2008, when the bubble in the property development market burst. During this time, which coincided with the height of the peace process, Ireland was spared the curses of Irish history — poverty and emigration. The end resulted in a major depression and a European Union bailout that was characterized as a loss of economic sovereignty. This, in return, resulted in the end of Fianna Fail's electoral dominance in 2010, after nearly eighty years.[82]

The second was the end of Catholic Ireland, a process which had begun in the 1970s but was much accelerated by three major scandals in the early 1990s. The first was the revelation in 1992 that Bishop Eamonn Casey, a popular senior clergyman, had a secret family. And then in 1994 it was revealed that Father Michael Cleary, an important church educator, had a family also, and the public also learned of the crimes of pedophile priest Brendan Smyth. In 1996 a documentary about the case in Northern Ireland revealed that the Church had a policy of simply moving pedophile priests on to new parishes, a policy also in effect in America. There was also a scandal about the abuse of unmarried pregnant women and their children in Church workhouses. These scandals, combined with European and American influences filtered through television and Irish novelists, combined to secularize a large portion of the population. By the turn of the millennium Ireland had mass attendance rates and other indications of religiosity comparable to other Western European countries rather than much higher as in the recent past — 91 percent in 1974 compared to only 55 percent in 2005. Irish sexual mores changed radically during the 1990s, possibly due to the wider availability of contraceptives, and possibly due to the lesser influence of religion.[83]

I contend that the peace process was independent of these two other phenomena, but that they helped to make it more acceptable to the country by weakening the national influence of the nationalist wing of Fianna Fail, which was full of pious traditionalists. Journalist Dick Walsh wrote, "When the going gets tough, Fianna Fail goes for the clerical vote."[84] And they gave those who looked to nationalism as compensation for poverty and unemployment a much better compensation.

It might also be true that with emigration to America and the British Empire in the nineteenth and early twentieth centuries largely replaced by emigration across the Irish Sea to the British mainland in the mid-twentieth century, from where naturalized British could regularly visit with their Irish relatives in the old sod that the enmity was reduced. After Ireland joined the European Economic Community with Britain in 1973, many Irish began seeking employment in Europe and were exposed to a post-nationalist point of view. Slowly and gradually, over several decades, Ireland became modernized and integrated into Western Europe.[85]

And Irish in the South had simply gotten used to the borders on maps and on the ground. They knew that if they wanted to go shopping in Northern Ireland they needed to convert their money into British pounds. Northern Ireland and Ireland had different political parties and different political systems and rules. Jack Lynch had concluded in the early 1970s that the Northern nationalists had more in common with the unionists than they had with Southern nationalists.[86] Historians reached the same conclusion in the mid–1990s.

The Republic had experienced terrorism that had spilled over from Northern Ireland from 1970 to the mid–1980s, but it had lessened over time. In the early 1970s there were a number of prominent robberies committed by republicans raising funds. In December 1972 there were a couple of bombs that went off while the Dail was debating new anti-terrorism legislation.[87] And in May 1974 the UVF set off three bombs in Dublin and Monaghan that killed 33 and wounded almost 300. Many to this day are convinced that they were the work of British intelligence, as the loyalists were not sophisticated enough to carry out simultaneous detonations.[88] There has been no solid evidence of this theory. The Republic had nearly a quarter century since the bombings to the surrender of the claim to get over the bitterness caused by the deaths. In the meantime, in 1985, the INLA kidnapped a prominent dentist in the Republic and engaged in a major shootout with the Garda.[89] In 1994 an IRA gang killed a Garda before the ceasefire.[90] So this might have driven home to many that the North was a place apart and the country was better off without it.

CHAPTER SIX

Palestinian Politics

Palestinian nationalism has grown up in conjunction with, and in reaction to, its rival, Zionism. Palestinian nationalism can be divided into four distinct periods with different organizing principles and national issues. The first period, the mandatory period, lasted from the early 1920s until *an nakba* in 1948. It was the period of the *hamulas* or clans (extended families), in which the leading Arab families in Palestine provided the leaders for the national cause and competition was more based on loyalty to a particular family than to an ideology. This is the period when the Palestinians were a proto-nation rather than a real nation, with allegiance and identity still being based more on a village or town than on the nation. The main tactics of this period are sectarian riots (or *pogroms*, to use the Russian term) and guerrilla warfare.

The next period was the period of exile from 1948 to 1964, when the Palestinians were absent from Arab politics. During this period many of the leaders from 1948 were overthrown in military coups d'état and replaced by military regimes — this occurred in Egypt, Syria, and Iraq (and in Jordan, King Abdullah I was assassinated by a Palestinian and King Hussein ibn Talal became monarch). Fatah was founded by a small group of Palestinian professionals living in Kuwait in 1958 but did not became a major actor at this time. Pan-Arabism, a sort of Arab fascism, became the leading Arab ideology.

The third period was the period of the *fedayeen*, which began at the start of 1965 and lasted until December 1987. In this period the Palestinians returned to Arab politics and after June 1967 became a leading actor and source of legitimacy for Arab regimes. A number of competing paramilitary organizations were formed around political entrepreneurs, who mainly derived their financial and military support from competing radical Arab regimes such as Egypt, Syria, Iraq, and Libya, with ideologies ranging from pan–Arabism to Marxism. But the real ideology of these organizations was return and revenge through armed struggle based mostly on terrorism. The main tactics of this period are guerrilla warfare, bombings, and hijackings of airliners.

The fourth period, which we are still in, is the period of internal Palestinian nationalism, in which Palestinians in Palestine — the occupied territories of Gaza and the West Bank — are the main actors and the competition is primarily between Fatah and two Islamist organizations, Palestinian Islamic Jihad and Hamas. This is the period in which Fatah embraces the two-state solution while the Islamists reject it. It is the era of both terrorism and negotiation. Its main tactics are bombings, both by planted bombs and suicide bombers, and drive-by shootings. It is the first era in which Palestinians are offered a clear ideological choice between two competing ideologies: secular nationalism and Islamism.

The mandatory period really began with the issuing of the Palestinian mandate to Britain by the League of Nations, based in Geneva, with the Balfour Declaration of 1917 calling for the creation of a Jewish national home in Palestine as part of the mandate in September 1922. The terms of the mandate had been decided at the San Remo Conference in 1920 and then modified by the exclusion of Transjordan from the terms of the mandate in 1922. Legally the mandate went into effect a year later with the signing of the Treaty of Lausanne, which formally ended the Ottoman Empire legally.

The main issue from the Arab point of view during the mandate was how to end the mandate as soon as possible without making concessions to Zionism. The Zionists were constantly pushing for higher immigration quotas and the right to purchase land from Arab landowners — usually absentee landlords — while the Arabs were pushing for restrictions on these rights to the greatest degree possible. The British were trying to fulfill their commitment to Zionism under the Balfour Declaration and the mandate while not causing a backlash that would endanger their political position in Muslim colonies or possessions such as India, Jordan, and Egypt. In this regard the British task was similar to the American one since 1970. Initially the Arab means of pressuring the British was through sectarian riots, as occurred in 1921 in Jaffa and again in August 1929 throughout Palestine. The Zionists could use counter-pressure at the League of Nations and in London.

Why were the Palestinians opposed to Zionism? There are several reasons, all of which are important. First, from the viewpoint of the Palestinians, Zionism amounted to a foreign colonial invasion from Europe. Such invasions are always resisted by native nationalist movements.[1] It should be remembered that it was the British Colonial Office that administered the mandate in Palestine. The only things that really differed in the Palestine mandate were that the Jewish settlers came not from a single country or pair of countries, as in Canada and South Africa, but from many European countries — but this did not make them any less foreign to the Palestinians — and that the mandate was internationally supervised. But the Palestinians were dealing with British colonial administrators as in any other British colony.[2]

Second, was that Zionism involved land dispossession, leaving peasants destitute. Zionism was unprecedented among settler colonialist movements in that it legally purchased the land at market prices, but it was the landlords who benefited from this rather than the peasants who farmed the land. These peasants then flocked to the towns and became recruits for the guerrillas during the Arab Revolt in the 1930s. During the second decade of British rule in Palestine from 1927–37, more than a quarter-million Jews settled in Palestine, which was twice as many as during the previous decade. Two-thirds of these immigrants lived outside of Tel Aviv, which meant major displacement in the settlements of the Jezreel Valley and coastal plain.[3]

Third, Islam has always regarded Judaism as solely a religion and not an ethnic identity as well. Judaism regards Jews as both a religion and a people.[4] But Islam, as a proselytizing religion like Christianity, involves easy conversion and retention of existing ethnic identities. Islam does not recognize that a religion has the right to a homeland — at least not one that supersedes Muslim claims on the land.

Fourth, Islam has always regarded Christians and Jews as "peoples of the Book" — adherents of Abrahamic religions that are to be tolerated but hold an inferior status to Muslims. They are known as *dhimmis* and the status as *dhimmitude* or toleration. Unlike pagans, they were not forced to convert to Islam at sword point, but they are treated as inferior subjects, who are not to be treated as equals of Muslims. Thus, in a dispute between Muslims and Jews, the Jews are expected to give way.[5]

When Palestinians and other Arabs write nationalist apologias for the Palestinian cause intended for Western audiences, they emphasize the first two factors. We now live in a postcolonial and secular era in the West, and so anti-colonial arguments have much more force. But these last two arguments, particularly the last, when reinforced with imported European anti–Semitism, have particular resonance in the fourth period, when Islam has once again returned as a major force within Palestinian nationalism.

The two main political families or *hamulas* during the mandate were the al–Husaynis (also spelled al–Husseinis) and the Nashishibis, both of Jerusalem. In March 1921 British high commissioner Sir Herbert Samuel, a Jew and a Zionist, appointed Haj Amin al–Husayni as the Mufti of Jerusalem responsible for representing Muslims and overseeing the Muslim holy sites on the Noble Sanctuary (*haram al-Sharif*), known in the West as the Temple Mount. Al-Husseini was only 25 years old at the time. This was after he had been sentenced in absentia to ten years in prison for his role in the Jaffa sectarian riots of April 1920.[6] He remained the Mufti of Jerusalem or Grand Mufti until 1937, when he was stripped of the title for backing the Arab Revolt against the British. At the same time Raghib Bey Nashishibi was the mayor of Jerusalem. The Nashishibis urged cooperation with the British as a more effective means of combating Zionism than confrontation.

In the mid–1930s a number of these clans established formal political parties. The Nashishibis founded the National Defense Party in late 1934. In mid–1935 the Khalidi and Budeiri clans established the Reform Party and in March 1935 the al-Husaynis established the Palestinian Arab Party. Of these three, the National Defense Party was the most moderate and its leaders met with some Zionist leaders and took into account short term Zionist goals when formulating their demands, but even this party rejected partition as a solution to the conflict.[7]

In April 1936 the Grand Mufti proclaimed a general strike against the British. He ran the Palestinian nationalist movement through the Arab Higher Committee, which consisted of religious and political leaders and was dominated by his supporters. His agents used coercion as a means of ensuring compliance by merchants with the strike. At the same time Jews were attacked — starting on April 15, 1936 when a truck carrying two Jews was stopped in Samaria and the occupants murdered — forcing Jews to restrict their travel in Arab areas and remain on Jewish settlements or in the Jewish portions of cities. The roads were the Achilles heel of the Zionist Yishuv (colony) in Palestine, as they were controlled by Arab villages. A five-man directorate of guerrilla chiefs ran the revolt under the guidance of the al-Husaynis. The Arab Revolt was preceded by a severe drought from 1931 to 1934 and widespread unemployment in 1935–36 after Zionist firms began laying off their Arab employees in response to League of Nations sanctions against Italy that caused an economic downturn.[8]

When the Peel Commission, appointed in response to the strike to come up with a solution, recommended partition and the establishment of separate Jewish and Arab states in Palestine in 1937, the Arabs rejected the findings. At this point a revolt was declared against the British mandate and Arab guerrilla groups began attacking British police and soldiers. From this point until the end of the mandate in May 1948 Palestine was effectively a land under military occupation. The Arab Revolt continued until September 1939 when the outbreak of World War II effectively ended it, but it had lost its momentum by January 1939. The high point was from September 1937, when the District Commissioner of the Galilee, Lewis Andrews, was murdered in Nazareth until January 1939 when Hassan Salame, one of the main guerrilla leaders, fled into Syria. It was effectively over by the spring of 1939. During the Revolt the main Arab tactics were arson, sniping against road traffic and civilians in cities, and crop burning and tree destruction in the countryside. The resolution of the Munich crisis at the end of September 1938 freed up the transfer of British troops from Britain and Egypt to Palestine. By 1939 more Arabs were being killed by other Arabs than by the British or the Jews. Some 30,000 middle-class Arabs fled Palestine to escape the violence.[9]

Amin al-Husayni snuck out of Palestine in disguise and traveled by boat from Jaffa to Beirut in October 1937. He remained in Lebanon for two years until pressure from the French mandatory authorities caused him to leave for Iraq. In May 1941 he supported the nationalist Arab revolt against the British led by Rashid Ali al-Kaylani. When it was crushed he fled to Tehran and hid in the Japanese embassy. He was supplied with an Italian passport under a false identity and made his way to Ankara, from where he flew on an Italian plane to Italy. He met with Il Duce Benito Mussolini on October 27, 1941. Mussolini, who had given pro–Zionist interviews in the early 1930s, proclaimed himself to be against Zionism and in favor of an independent Arab Palestine. The former Mufti then wrote to Hitler who sent a German aircraft to fly him to Berlin. He spent the war in exile in Berlin, although he carried out recruiting missions for the German armed forces in Bosnia and other Muslim areas under German control in Europe. He met with Hitler on November 28, 1941, in a personal audience and Hitler also proclaimed himself in favor of an independent Palestine. Al-Husayni then had Hassan Salame and other guerrilla leaders from the revolt flown to Germany for military training.[10]

At the end of the war he was arrested by the French on the Swiss border after Switzerland refused him political refuge and transferred to Paris. The Yugoslav government had a warrant for his arrest for war crimes and American Jews were pushing for his arrest and trial. On May 29, 1946, with the help of conservative politicians in Paris he was allowed to fly to Cairo. A few days later he was in Lebanon. He spent the remainder of his life until his death in 1974 in Cairo and Beirut. He spent the 1948 war in Cairo urging Egyptian participation in the war, while the Palestinian nationalist effort was run from Palestine by his cousin Jamal al-Husayni and a third member of the clan, Abd-al Qadir al-Husayni (a.k.a. Abdul Kadir Husseini), who was the commander of the Arab Army of Palestine.[11]

Hassan Salame had undergone a tank commander's course in Iraq and then was trained as a paratrooper by the Germans. On November 6, 1944, Salame parachuted into Palestine in a plot by Amin al-Husayni to poison the wells of Tel Aviv. The mission failed after his accomplices were captured, but Salame escaped and disappeared. He reemerged in 1947 as the number two man in al-Qadir al-Husayni's guerrilla army in charge of Jaffa, the coastal plain, Ramla, and Lod. On November 30, 1947, he started the Israeli War of Independence by opening fire on a Jewish bus near Jerusalem.[12]

Abd al-Qadir al-Husayni was killed during the Battle of Kastel in April 1948 when he accidentally walked into the line of fire of Hagana machine-gun after the Arabs had occupied Kastel and then abandoned it. By mid–May 1948, the civil war portion of the 1948 war between Israelis and Palestinians was over and replaced by an international war between Israel and the surrounding Arab countries. Two weeks later Salame was killed in battle with the Etzel at Ras al-Ain. This was after two previous attacks on his headquarters in February and April had failed to kill him. In late September 1948 an All-Palestine Government was set up in Gaza in the Egyptian-controlled territory. On October 1, 1948, Palestine was declared independent with Haj Amin al-Husayni as its president. But the "state" was really a creature of the Egyptian military occupation and was dissolved in 1959. At this point the former Mufti returned to Beirut where he lived in exile in a villa until his death in 1974. Before his death he gave his blessing to Yasir Arafat, a distant relative, as his successor.[13]

Some 3,000 to 6,000 Arabs were killed during the Arab Revolt of 1936–39, with the British and the Hagana and Etzel only responsible for about a quarter of that total.[14] The rest were victims of Arab in-fighting between rival guerrilla bands, using the revolt to settle personal scores, and crimes that occurred during the revolt. The revolt was defeated by the British applying counterinsurgency principles that they had learned as a result of their defeat in Ireland fifteen years before the revolt: the building of a fence to seal off the northern border, construction of police fortresses and concrete pillboxes to control the roads and Arab villages, and the use of torture during interrogation. Because many educated Arabs left during the revolt, the Palestinians found themselves lacking a real officer class in 1948.[15]

In 1948 the Jews beat the Arabs because the former had developed a real national consciousness and leadership and the latter had not. The Jewish Agency and Hagana spent the next decade preparing for war and having its fighters gain experience either in the British-sponsored Palmakh, or in the British army during World War II. Few Palestinians actually did any fighting during World War II with either side and so were at a disadvantage. The Yishuv used funds raised in the diaspora to purchase weapons and munitions on the surplus arms market following World War II and some nations like France provided them free of charge. By comparison the Arab states only invested in their own armies, which also were inexperienced. This left the various Arab guerrilla forces without adequate ammunition for their rifles. And most of their plans were revealed to Hagana intelligence by informers. The various Arab states were fighting at cross-purposes in order to win limited territorial gains at the expense of both the Palestinians and the Jews. Jordan was fighting to win control of the West Bank, while Egypt wanted to control Gaza. The various Arab armies did not coordinate their actions with each other or with the two irregular forces — Abd al-Qadir al-Husayni's Palestinian army and the foreign volunteers led by Fawzi al-Kawakji. The Israel Defense Forces knocked the various Arab armies out of action one by one and after July 1948 fielded more men than the Arabs did. The Palestinians lost an estimated 12,000 killed and between half and three-quarters of a million people were left homeless — most within Palestine itself.[16]

A prosperous engineer from an obscure branch of the al-Husayni hamula who had taken the adopted name of Yasir (also spelled Yasser) Arafat founded an organization named Fatah in Kuwait in October 1959. Fatah is a reverse acronym for Palestinian liberation movement (*harakat tahrir filastin*) and means *conquest* in Arabic. It was founded by Arafat and a number of Palestinian acquaintances that he had made in Egypt when he headed the Palestinian students association in Cairo. Arafat deliberately kept Fatah's ideology as vague and broad as possible so as to not rule out any potential sources of funding in the Arab world. Thus he was not a Nasserist, nor a Ba'athist, nor a Marxist, nor an Islamist because he wanted to be able to attract support from people identified with all of these groups and not preclude support from the Gulf states. His only ideology was Palestinian nationalism.[17]

Arafat was born in Cairo in 1929 to a merchant who had moved there from Palestine, but for political reasons he always claimed that he was born in either Gaza or Jerusalem. As a teenager he served in the 1948 war with the Muslim Brotherhood's volunteers. He spent much of his time going into the battlefields in western Egypt from 1941–42 to recover abandoned weapons with which to equip the fighters. In the spring of 1948 he traveled from Cairo to Jerusalem to fight the Zionists, but probably did not see any action before the Palestinian war effort collapsed. Under the Muslim Brotherhood he participated in guerrilla raids against British soldiers in the Canal Zone in the early 1950s and gained some military experience. During the 1956 war he served as a lieutenant in the Egyptian army in command of an ammunition dump. He did not see action.[18]

In the mid–1960s there were a number of competing movements for the banner of Palestinian nationalism. First was the Palestine Liberation Organization created at an Arab summit meeting in East Jerusalem and presided over by a Palestinian named Ahmed Shukeiry, who was a former Saudi diplomat and aide to Amin al-Husayni. The PLO was created by Egypt in order to take the Palestinian issue away from Iraq and Syria so as to avoid Egypt getting dragged into another war with Israel. Palestinian units were created within the Egyptian, Jordanian and Syrian armies that were to serve as an army for the PLO.[19]

Second was Arafat's Fatah which had organized itself in a number of Palestinian refugee camps. Arafat had acquired a few weapons from Syria and had his recruits trained in guerrilla warfare and sabotage by the Syrian army. On the night of December 31, 1964, a Fatah team carried out the first raid by Fatah in an unsuccessful attempt to sabotage the Israeli national water project that carried water from Lake Kinneret (the Sea of Galilee) to the Negev Desert. Fatah would carry out a number of other missions over the next two-and-one-half years until the Six Day War, which frightened the Israelis more than causing any real damage to the economy.[20]

Third was George Habash's Arab Nationalist Movement (ANM). The ANM was a Nasserist pan–Arabist movement organized among Palestinians in Lebanon, Syria, and Jordan. Habash was a young doctor who worked in the refugee camps in Lebanon where he founded the movement in 1948. He soon founded the Progressive Front for the Liberation of Palestine (PFLP) in 1967 as a Marxist alternative to Fatah. A number of his lieutenants would, over the next decade, split off and found their own Front organizations with similar ideologies such as the Democratic Progressive Front for the Liberation of Palestine (DFLP — the Progressive label was soon dropped), founded by Nawaf Hawatme. Both the PFLP and the DFLP advocated overthrowing the conservative Arab governments such as Jordan and Lebanon, whom they thought were too pro–Western. They would then use their territories and resources to launch the liberation of Palestine. It was the DFLP that was responsible for sparking the Black September Jordanian civil war through a mass hijacking of Western airliners that were then flown to Jordan and blown up.[21]

During the Six Day War, Shukeiry made a number of blustering statements that discredited him and led to his replacement by an interim chairman of the PLO in 1968. The following year Arafat took over as chairman of the PLO by bringing in all of the major fedayeen movements: Fatah, the PFLP, the DFLP, the PFLP-General Command, and so on. Arafat accomplished this by giving the smaller organizations disproportionate representation in the Palestinian National Congress (the Palestinian legislature in exile that ran the PLO) and because he had the backing of Egypt's Nasser, who had been the force behind the creation of the PLO in 1964. Thus, by 1969 Arafat had united the various competing movements of Palestinian nationalism.[22]

The official strategy of the PLO for two decades was a guerrilla war that would weaken the Israeli economy through attrition, cause new immigrants to return to their countries or origin, and dissuade Jews from coming to Israel. Before June 1967 he spoke of Fatah serving as the catalyst for a general war, in which the Arab armies would defeat Israel. For under-standable reasons he ceased speaking of this after June 1967.[23] In reality this strategy allowed poor Palestinian youths to gain some status as resist-ance fighters while serving as justification for subsidies for the cause from the Gulf states that allowed the leadership to live well. Those Palestinians who had the necessary professional training emigrated from the Middle East to the West and Latin America.[24]

By the early 1970s some Palestinian intellectuals in the territories and in the West were speaking of a two-state solution in which the Palestinians would settle for an independent state alongside Israel in the West Bank and Gaza. Professor Walid al-Khalidi published an article, "Thinking the Unthinkable," in which he argued for such a solution.[25] In October 1974 at the Rabat summit, the Arab League recognized the PLO as the only organization entitled to speak for the Palestinians about the future of the territories.[26] At the same time the PLO adopted the "phases strategy," by which any territory liberated from Israel would be used to liberate all of Palestine. Western apologists for the Palestinians claimed that this was recognition of a two-state solution in disguise. But Israel saw it as a con-tinuation of the non-sectarian, democratic state that would result in the expulsion of many Jews from Palestine — all those who came after the start of "the Zionist invasion" (the PLO was silent as to whether this invasion dated from 1882 or from 1917). The secular, democratic state was never official Fatah or PLO policy but was rather a DFLP policy suggestion that was rejected but then used as propaganda in the West.[27]

Initially the PLO strategy was based on guerrilla warfare conducted from both Jordan and southern Lebanon (Fatahland), which Beirut had recognized in two separate agreements as being a base for operations against Israel. But after July 1971, when the last fedayeen were expelled from Jordan by the Jordanian army — many crossing the Jordan River to end up in Israeli prisons — the PLO could count only on southern Lebanon as a base for operations. After the First Lebanon War in 1982 and the Fatah revolt the following year, the PLO was forced to go into exile. Its new headquar-ters were located in a suburb of Tunis over a thousand miles from the homeland. Its fighters were scattered around the Arab world. Suddenly the PLO was left without even the pretense of an armed struggle strategy.

For three years Arafat equivocated about whether or not to pursue a joint negotiating strategy with King Hussein of Jordan that would allow the king to negotiate on behalf of the Palestinians. Arafat was afraid of causing a major split in the organization and the fedayeen did not trust King Hussein after Black September. It was a dilemma that Gerry Adams would confront a decade later in deciding whether or not to pursue negotiations on an internal settlement in Northern Ireland. In the winter of 1985 Arafat and King Hussein signed an agreement for a joint negotiation strategy. Finally, in 1986 after the PLO had equivocated for too long, King Hussein called the whole thing off. The PLO would have to find its own way back.[28]

There was in Palestinian nationalism a fundamental conflict of interests after June 1967 between the insiders under Israeli occupation and those living in exile abroad. The primary interest of the former was in ending the occupation and gaining independence. The primary interest of the latter was to return to their homes — or the site of their ancestors' homes — in Palestine. But relatively few of the original Palestinian homes were still standing, as Israel had systematically bulldozed abandoned villages into the earth after 1948. Homes in cities such as Jerusalem, Jaffa, Haifa, Safed, and Tiberius were declared forfeit and given out to Jewish immigrants arriving from Europe or the Middle East.

Because Arafat was an outsider whose constituency was the Palestinians in the refugee camps and the West, it seemed unlikely that he would suddenly switch constituencies by abandoning them for the Palestinians living in the territories. But as the years passed Arafat must have realized that the only way for him to return to Palestine and salvage something from his life of nationalist activism was through Israel. This was not a sudden epiphany but a gradual and growing realization.

In December 1987 a traffic accident between an Israeli truck driver with bad brakes and several cars sparked off the Intifada.[29] This soon spread from Gaza to the West Bank as Israel tried to end attacks on isolated patrols by using deadly force. Arafat and the PLO leadership were caught off guard by the outbreak of violence. Televised scenes of Palestinian stone throwers confronting Israeli soldiers firing on them and defense minister Yitzhak Rabin's infamous order to break bones returned the Palestinian issue to the forefront of Western consciousness. West Bank insiders were anxious that this opportunity not be wasted through the presentation of outdated unrealistic demands. Feisal al-Husayni, the son of slain commander Abd al-Qadir al-Husayni, and Sari Nusseibeh, the son of former

Jordanian Defense Minister Anwar Nusseibeh, urged Arafat to adopt the two-state solution.[30]

A year after the outbreak of the Intifada, Yasir Arafat made a speech in which he surrendered to American demands and recognized 242 as the guiding basis for negotiations and renounced terrorism. Outgoing secretary of state George Shultz responded by opening a dialogue with the PLO. Unfortunately not everyone in the PLO got the message or agreed with it. Within 18 months after its opening the dialogue was suspended after a minor organization within the PLO, the Palestine Liberation Front of Mahmoud Abu al-Abbas (not to be confused with Arafat's successor)carried out a raid on a Tel Aviv beach from the sea. Several people were killed and Arafat refused to condemn the raid or expel the PLF from the PLO. Washington, under George H.W. Bush and Jim Baker, got out of the peacemaking business for two years.[31]

After the Iraqi invasion of Kuwait in August 1990 the Palestinian Intifada began to wane as Israeli arrests of activists and the effects of curfews took their psychological toll on ordinary Palestinians. International media focus also shifted from Palestine to the Persian Gulf and Iraq. After the war Baker made an effort to convert the political capital that the Bush administration had accumulated into a settlement of the Israeli-Palestinian problem. Baker twisted arms to get Prime Minister Yitzhak Shamir to attend the Madrid Conference in October 1991. Shamir and the Syrian foreign minister traded insults, while the Palestinians appeared statesmanlike in contrast. The two-day ceremonial conference in Madrid led to a process of bilateral negotiations in Washington between Israel and a Jordanian-Palestinian delegation and with the Syrians. Arafat then used his influence over the Palestinian negotiators from the territories to prevent any progress in the negotiations in Washington.

Meanwhile Yossi Beilin and Shimon Peres had launched an unofficial track negotiation with PLO representatives in Norway outside Oslo, known as the Oslo process more because of official Norwegian sponsorship than its actual location. After a few months Rabin upgraded this negotiation to official status by including an Israeli attorney practicing in the United States, who was a reserve colonel in the IDF, in the negotiations. Peres and Arafat wrapped up the remaining issues in a marathon telephone call from Stockholm to Tunis in August. The following month the agreement was signed in a dramatic ceremony on the White House lawn.[32]

As Arafat was slowly opening the door to negotiations in the late 1980s, his first real ideological opposition was being formed in Gaza. The Muslim Brotherhood was founded in Ismailia in March 1928 by Hassan al-Bannas. It was founded as a religious, social, and political movement, as Islam does not recognize the split between the spiritual and secular realms that exists in Christianity. By the 1930s it had spread to Gaza. Under the Israeli occupation it was tolerated by the authorities as long as it did not engage openly in politics. Israel was happy to promote religion as an alternative to secular Palestinian nationalism. From this tolerance some have inferred or suggested that Hamas was somehow an Israeli creation. This is far from the truth.[33]

Hamas, which means "zeal" or "enthusiasm" in Arabic, is an acronym for Islamic Resistance Movement (*harakat al-Muqāwamah al-'Islāmiyyah*). Initially it was considered in the West to have been founded in the winter of 1988 a few months after the outbreak of the Intifada. Mosab Hassan Yousef, a son of one of the founding members of Hamas, claims in his memoir that it was secretly founded in Hebron in 1986 before the Intifada. Wikipedia claims that it was founded in December 1987, and Mideast Web claims that it was founded in February 1988, after the outbreak of the Intifada.[34]

Initially Hamas engaged in guerrilla warfare against the IDF in Gaza and the West Bank by engaging in kidnappings of hitchhiking Israeli soldiers, drive-by shootings and bombings of groups of Israeli soldiers, and other forms of attacks through its military wing, the Qassem Brigades, named after a Muslim cleric who was killed by the British in 1935.[35] But by the mid–1990s, when the Oslo agreements were being implemented, the organization graduated to terrorism by bombing Israeli buses and other targets in an effort to torpedo the Oslo process. Originally Hamas's political headquarters were in Amman. But the attempted assassination of Khalid Mishal in Amman in 1997 by the Mossad led the organization to transfer its external headquarters to Damascus. There it joined the various Palestinian Front organizations and Hezbollah. Initially the organization was funded primarily from Palestinians in the diaspora and other Arabs and Muslims and by various scams. Iran supported the much smaller Palestinian Islamic Jihad. But after the Al-Aksa Intifada broke out at the end of the Oslo process, Iran gradually began funding Hamas. Hamas had close relations with Hezbollah dating from the mass expulsion of Hamas leaders

143

and activists from the territories by Rabin in December 1992. Hezbollah, which was founded by the Iranian Islamic Revolutionary Guard Corps a decade earlier, began making contacts with the refugees and did some training and networking until they were readmitted into the territories.[36]

With Hamas's political bureau in Damascus, the connection with Tehran tightened. This was despite the fact that Palestinians are Sunnis and Iranians are Shi'ites. The two sides had more than enough in common through Islamism and anti–Zionism to bridge the sectarian divide. The outbreak of the Green Revolution in Iran in June 2009 following a controversial presidential election led Hamas to gradually reassess its relationship with Tehran. The outbreak of the Sunni revolt in Syria in the spring of 2011 led Hamas to reorient itself away from Tehran and Damascus and towards Cairo, which was then in the process of being taken over by the Muslim Brotherhood.[37]

From its origin, Hamas was an ideological and practical threat to Fatah hegemony. Fatah could tolerate the emergence of rival secular movements as long as they supported Fatah's leadership of the PLO. All these rival organizations faded into obscurity over the decades as their rejection by the West and their intrigues in Arab politics led to further splits and splinters. But Hamas, which was as independent of foreign influence as was Fatah, was an ideological threat. As pan–Arabism faded in the Arab world following the death of Nasser in September 1970 and the defeat of Saddam Hussein by America in 1991, Islamism emerged as the new ideological answer and hegemon. During the seven years of the Oslo process the Palestinian Authority gained a well-deserved reputation for corruption as the PLO's exile leadership used Western funding to buy loyalty and build big houses in the territories. In contrast Hamas used its own sources of funding to run charities that provided much-needed social services to the Palestinians in the territories, particularly Gaza. This strengthened the loyalty of the population to Hamas and gave it an opening to preach their brand of religious nationalism.[38] The Arab Spring movement of 2010–11 has only strengthened the appeal of Islamism in the region.

During the Oslo process Arafat had a strategy of playing Israel and Hamas off against one another by alternately giving in to Israeli pressure and arresting Hamas and Islamic Jihad terrorists, and then releasing them from prison. Over time, especially after the Likud returned to power in mid–1996, Arafat tended to make fewer efforts to appease Israel as his own political standing among the population faded and Israel seemed to cooperate less with him.[39] Finally, starting in October 2000 with the outbreak of the Al-Aksa Intifada, Fatah and Hamas ceased temporarily to be deadly enemies and became rivals pursuing a joint strategy of terrorism. This then changed again in November 2004 with the death of Arafat and the election of Mahmoud Abbas/Abu Mazen as his successor as president of the Palestinian Authority and leader of Fatah in January 2005. Abbas abandoned the strategy of armed struggle for one of negotiation. Unfortunately for him, Ariel Sharon was prime minister and had no intention of giving up the West Bank for a Palestinian state that any real Palestinian leader could accept. Abbas had to outwait Sharon before he could implement his strategy of liberation through negotiation.

But in order to implement this new strategy he had to retain the confidence of the Palestinian population of the territories. Abbas shared many if not most of Arafat's defects and little of his charismatic image. Abbas lacked Arafat's guerrillas' background — he had not escaped from West Bank homes minutes ahead of the Israelis — nor fought at Karameh and other legendary battles that gained in stature in the retelling.[40] And he was not connected to the mandatory era through his family pedigree. Only six years younger than Arafat, Abbas was a political scientist by training who served as a diplomat for the PLO before Oslo. Arafat liked to play Abbas off against Ahmed Qurei, a.k.a. Abu Ala'a, promoting one as his primary political advisor and then demoting him in favor of the other. Both had major roles in the negotiation process at Oslo, supervising the talks from Tunis. This pattern continued during the post–Oslo period when President Bush forced Arafat to create the office of prime minister and fill it with Abbas. After Abbas resigned in frustration after a few months Arafat appointed Qurei to take his place. Arafat and Abbas were not on speaking terms when Arafat died and some conspiracy theorists speculate that Arafat was poisoned by Abbas.[41] This seems unlikely for someone who eschewed violence.

Since 2002 Israel under Sharon had been engaged in a policy of "targeted killings" of Hamas, Islamic Jihad, and Fatah leaders.[42] This culminated in the assassination of Hamas leader Sheikh Ahmed Yassin on March 23, 2004, by the Israeli Air Force (IAF) after a previous IAF attempt had failed in September 2003. His successor, Abdel Aziz al-Rantisi, was killed on April 17, 2004, after having been seriously wounded in a previous attempt in June 2003. In late September 2004 Izz al-Din al-Sheikh al-Khalili, a Hamas liaison between Gaza and the West Bank was assassinated by a bomb in Damascus in reprisal for two Hamas bus bombings in August, which Hamas claimed were reprisals for the killings of Yassin and Rantisi.[43]

These killings helped to push Hamas to make a major change in strategy away from terrorism, which had been its strategy from 1994 to 2005, to elections. In municipal elections on December 23, 2004, Hamas won control of nine councils compared to Fatah's 17, or 75 seats compared to Fatah's 135. On January 23, 2005, Hamas and Palestinian Islamic Jihad declared a unilateral ceasefire in order to allow newly elected PLO president Mahmoud Abbas to negotiate with Israel. In the Cairo Declaration of March 17, 2005 a *hudna,* or truce, for all of 2005 was declared and Hamas called for a reform of the PLO to include the Islamists. Hamas wanted to share power with Fatah at the national level, but the latter was not prepared to grant this. In 1992–93 Hamas suggested to Arafat that it should get 40 percent of the seats in the Palestinian National Council, the PLO's parliament, but Arafat was unwilling to grant this. In the January 2005 Gaza local elections, Hamas took control of seven out of ten local councils with 75 councilors out of 118. There was an over 80 percent voting rate, similar to that in the previous election.[44]

George W. Bush wanted to promote democracy in the Arab world so he pressured Israel to allow legislative elections in the Palestinian territories. The elections were held, despite Israeli misgivings and fears that Hamas might win, in January 2006. Fatah released two separate lists of candidates because the Young Guard (insiders from the territories) and the Old Guard (those who returned from Tunis) were not able to agree on a single list. The elections were considered by international monitors to be the most free in the history of the Arab world. The elections were won by Hamas with 74 seats to Hamas with 45 and other lists with 13 just two months before Israeli elections, which replaced Sharon with Ehud Olmert, his deputy. Ismael Haniyeh became prime minister. Once again there was a centrist Israeli government in power, but the Palestinians were in no position to negotiate seriously.[45]

Hamas was surprised by and unprepared for the scope of its victory — it wanted to share power with Fatah rather than assume power by itself. In the West much of the commentary was that this was mainly a protest vote against PA corruption rather than a vote in favor of Hamas's positions on Israel. Israeli historian Benny Morris claimed that it occurred because of the Islamist religious trend in Palestine. Journalist Paola Caridi claims that it was a case of a victory by civil society over the establishment.[46]

Any final settlement between Israel and the Palestinians will involve major concessions and compromises on both sides. Each side can only make those compromises if it feels a need to do so — willingness — and feels strong enough to be able to withstand a nationalist backlash for having made those compromises — ability. Arafat may have lacked the willingness to make important concessions on the right of return and Jerusalem at Camp David in July 2000, but he certainly felt that he lacked the ability.

In June 2007 Hamas carried out a coup in Gaza, capturing Fatah leaders and overrunning Fatah military camps in skirmishes that lasted for five days after Fatah security chiefs provoked a reaction. A few Fatah men were thrown to their deaths off of high buildings by their Hamas captors. In the fighting between the two factions, 160 Palestinians were killed and over 700 wounded. Suddenly there were three states instead of two involved in any future settlement scenario: Israel, the West Bank and Gaza (Hamastan). This meant that Jerusalem suddenly had a viable excuse not to negotiate with the Palestinians.[47]

In late November 2007, George W. Bush, under pressure from secretary of state Condilezza Rice, opened up a peace conference at Annapolis, Maryland. This peace process, the second of the Bush presidency, resulted in a number of meetings between Olmert and Abbas. But Olmert, whose personal popularity among the Israeli public had dipped to as low as three percent following the feeble showing by the IDF in the Second Lebanon War in the summer of 2006, was in no position to make major concessions to the Palestinians beyond those made by Barak at Camp David. Bush soon lost interest in the peace process and put no pressure on Israel to compromise. Abbas, who knew that Olmert was essentially a weak lame duck prime minister, made no official response to Olmert's last offer, and the peace process ended.[48]

Despite the ideological differences between Hamas and Fatah, the election victory of the former in January 2006 essentially returned the conflict back to the situation before December 1988 — some seventeen years. What happened after this was a situation where figures aligned with Hamas would make moderate-sounding statements in lectures in the West or in interviews with the press while Hamas spokesmen denied them. This

147

was the same game that the PLO played throughout the 1970s and 1980s in an attempt to test the waters and improve the organization's image. The game works much better in Europe than in America. The Palestinian strategy was the stages strategy, of taking over territory without making peace. The Hamas strategy is similar. Hamas figures have spoken of long-term *hudnas*, or truces, in which Hamas would coexist with Israel for a set period of time in exchange for Israel withdrawing from all the territories. But the terms that Hamas demands are terms that Israel would only agree to in exchange for a full peace treaty that is final. Hamas well knows this and, like the PLO before it, is engaged more in an exercise in weakening Israel's image and improving its own by feigning moderation by offering what it knows Israel could never accept.[49] It was the same game played by the PLO in the 1980s. Some excuse this by allowing that Hamas as an Islamist organization could never openly accept the legitimacy of Israel — but that is the whole point. This is dhimmitude all over again. If Israel is ever weak enough to accept the terms that Hamas has on offer, Hamas will probably demand different terms.

Between 2000 and December 2008 the Palestinians, mainly Hamas and Islamic Jihad, lobbed thousands of Qassam rockets and mortar rounds on Israeli settlements near Gaza, such as the town of Sderot. In November and December 2008 more than a hundred rockets and a hundred mortar shells were fired on Israeli Negev settlements before Israel responded on December 27, 2008, with Operation Cast Lead. Cast Lead lasted until January 18, 2009 — two days before President Obama's inauguration. During this whole time Israel was unable to completely suppress the firing of rockets by superior firepower. Hamas had maintained a unilateral ceasefire for over a year in 2005. Jerusalem and Washington, after the January 2006 election, had decided on a strategy of regime change through boycott. Israel in March 2006 began a siege of Gaza. Operation Cast Lead was intended to provoke a popular revolt against Hamas in Gaza, which it failed to do. But while raising Hamas's regional profile and reputation, it did hurt its image among many Palestinians.[50] After Cast Lead, Israel really lacked a political policy on how to deal with Hamas rule in Gaza.[51]

The pattern of Zionist-Palestinian relations in Palestine since 1936 has been one of incompetent use of violence by the Palestinians, leading to a competent and more powerful use of counterviolence by their opponents, which has left the former in a worse-off position. The use of assassination and random terrorism by the al-Husayni-led Palestinian movement in the revolt led the British to bring in reinforcements from the Empire and then crush the rebellion with the help of the Zionist leadership. This resulted in the leadership going into exile.

In the next round in 1948 the Palestinian forces backed up by the Arab armies lost to the Hagana, Palmakh, and IDF, supported by foreign volunteers and the Revisionist undergrounds. This led to the exile or expulsion of most of the Arab population within the armistice lines except in the Galilee.

In the next major round from 1967–73, the fedayeen of Fatah contributed to a crisis that resulted in the defeat of the Arab armies and the loss of the rest of mandatory Palestine to Israeli control. After 1967 the Palestinians gained their one real military victory with the help of the Jordanians at the Battle of Karameh in March 1968. So what did they do then? They turned on those same Jordanians, resulting in their expulsion from Jordan. They then attempted to liberate Palestine by rocket attacks on border settlements from southern Lebanon and by terrorist attacks against Israeli targets in Europe. This resulted in much of the terrorist leadership being killed in Europe by Mossad assassination teams.[52] The Black September leader, Ali Hassan Salame, got away but was later assassinated in Beirut in January 1979.[53]

The Palestinian Intifada of 1987–93 led to the only real Palestinian political gain through the use of violence. This is because the West Bank leadership, led by Feisal al-Husayni and Sari Nusseibeh, led to the Oslo process. But then, Arafat, who was suffering from corruption and a poorly-negotiated agreement, was losing popularity to the Islamists. So he rejected the best deal he was likely to get — without offering counter-proposals. He then returned to violence — whether he initiated it, as the Israeli Right alleges, or merely followed the popular lead, as the Israeli Left argues is irrelevant. The Israeli Center-Left was decimated. Arafat had his hero's death under siege in Ramallah until nearly the end and a mass funeral.

Since the mid–1990s Hamas and Palestinian Islamic Jihad have been using greater levels of terrorism: bus bombings, suicide bombers, and drive-by shootings of civilians. Israel under Sharon finally countered with a series of assassinations of the Hamas and PIJ leaderships.

Accompanying Palestinian rejectionism has been the empowering of a successively more ruthless set of opponents. The Arab Revolt helped to lead to the rise of David Ben-Gurion, at the expense of Chaim Weizmann, as head of the Zionist movement.[54] The 1967 victory and Palestinian terrorism led to the rise of New Zionism and the replacement of Labor with the Likud. Then Islamist violence in 1996 led to Shimon Peres's defeat at the hands of Benjamin Netanyahu. Arafat's rejection at Camp David led to the election of Ariel Sharon in 2001 and 2003. In 1949 Arafat's Zionist equivalent, Yitzhak Shamir, was a marginal political figure, running for the Knesset on the Fighters' List and being defeated. After 35 years of Arab rejectionism, he was prime minister.

Palestinians should contemplate the tragedy of their own history and that of the ancient Jews. Successive failed revolts by the Jews led to harsher Roman reprisals and the eventual exile of much of the Jewish population from Palestine/Eretz Israel.[55] Another escalation in the round of violence could lead to another mass expulsion.

They should also learn from modern Irish history. A quarter century of Irish republican terrorism did not result in the British leaving or the unionists embracing a united Ireland. Finally, Sinn Fein cut its losses and retrieved what it could from the stalemate of the struggle. They did this by finally saying yes to what was on offer at the time instead of rejecting it. The Good Friday Agreement of 1998 was a worse settlement from the republican perspective than what was to be offered from Sunningdale in 1973–74, which the IRA rejected. Palestinian one-staters and their leftist allies are now full of praise for the bi-nationalism of the Ihud, which both mainstream Zionists and Palestinians rejected in 1946–48. When the Zionist leadership was offering bi-nationalism in the 1920s, the Palestinians were not interested.[56]

There is today a Palestinian national consensus accepted by both Hamas and Fatah in favor of an agreement with Israel based on the 1949 armistice lines and the right of return.[57] Mahmoud Abbas in November 2012 went beyond this consensus by accepting that he could only return to Safed as a tourist. A Fatah Central Committee member explained that Abbas was only expressing his personal opinion and not conceding the right of return.[58] Whether or not he would stick to this in negotiations is an open question.

The best way to test whether Israeli *mizrakhanim* (Orientalists) and historians like Barry Rubin and Benny Morris are correct about Hamas or Western journalists like Paola Caridi and Paul McGeough are would be for Washington and Brussels to pressure Ramallah into allowing Hamas into a reformed PLO. As far back as 1991–92 Hamas had discussed with Arafat being included in the PLO with 40 percent of the seats in the PNC, but this was more than Arafat was willing to concede. In 2005 his successor was also unwilling to share power with Hamas at the national level.[59] The PLO could then negotiate a peace deal with Israel and the situation could be put to the test. But so soon after the failure of the Oslo process, this is very unlikely to take place, especially because Hamas offers only a long-term truce and not a peace treaty in exchange for the territorial concessions and refugee return demanded of Israel.

Italian journalist Paola Caridi compares Hamas to the Christian Democrats (of Germany and Italy, El Salvador and Venezuela).[60] But the Christian Democrats did not support suicide bombers and other forms of terrorism even though Germany was under Western occupation following World War II and continued to remain under de facto partial Soviet occupation until 1990. Henry Siegman, a former president of the American Jewish Committee for sixteen years, compared Hamas to the Zionist movement — presumably to Etzel and Lehi — as a political movement that used terrorism in the mistaken belief that it was the only way to rid their country of foreign occupation.[61] This is a more accurate comparison.

In the first decade of the twenty-first century, Palestinians and their Western supporters began advocating a one-state solution. Israeli new historian Benny Morris saw three precursors to this: Arafat's rejectionism in 2000, the rise of Hamas in 2006–7, and Tony Judt's article in the *New York Review of Books* rejecting Zionism in 2003.[62] Morris notes that back in the 1940s the Arabs rejected bi-nationalism completely and among the Jews it was proposed only by a small intellectual organization of German-speaking Jews with less than a hundred members, *Agudat Ihud,* and the HaShomer HaTzair Marxist-Zionist youth movement, which then abandoned it in 1948 when it merged with an irredentist Marxist Party, Ahdut ha'Avoda, to form Mapam.[63] Today mizrakhim (Oriental Jews), and ultra–Orthodox and Russian Jews are all poor candidates for bi-nationalism and Arab rejection is greater than or equal to Jewish rejection. Thus, the one-state solution in terms of a state that is not dominated by one of the parties is a non-starter.[64]

CHAPTER SEVEN

American Politics and the America-Israel Alliance

Political Zionism has always believed in having the support of great powers. Shortly after writing his seminal pamphlet *Der Judenstaat (The Jewish State)* and holding the First Zionist Congress, Zionist movement founder Theodor Herzl started his quest for a national charter for Palestine from one of the great powers. He first appealed to the Ottoman sultan, who had no interest in granting one as he knew how unpopular it would be with Muslims throughout the Ottoman Empire. So Herzl followed Kaiser Wilhelm II to Palestine — the only time he bothered to visit the object of his desire — for an audience with him to convince him to use his influence with the sultan to win a charter for the Zionists. He then turned to the French, the Pope, anyone at all who might be able to influence the sultan.

Finally he had his first break in 1902 when he secured a friendly audience with British foreign secretary Joseph Chamberlain. Chamberlain agreed to look into establishing a Jewish settlement in El Arish, in the northern Sinai Peninsula, next to Palestine. But the British representative in Egypt, Lord Curzon, vetoed the idea because it would be too difficult to supply it with fresh water and because he did not want to cause problems with the native Egyptians. Nonetheless, Chamberlain promised to see what he could do for the Zionists.

The following year after the Kishniev pogrom in Romania showed the need for a place where Jews could go free from religious prejudice, Chamberlain offered to see about settling the Jews in part of British East Africa, what is today Kenya but has gone down in Zionist historiography as the Uganda Affair. Herzl agreed as a temporary measure but found very strong opposition from the Russian Zionists at that year's Congress. Herzl promised that it would only be a temporary measure — a "night shelter —

until the Jews could settle in Palestine. But he nearly split the Zionist movement, and he died from a heart attack in 1904.[1]

Chaim Weizmann, a young Russian Zionist activist living in Germany who taught chemistry, decided that the British connection was the thing of the future. He moved to Britain and became a chemistry professor at the University of Manchester. He spent the rest of his life lobbying the British government on behalf of the Zionist movement and winning the elusive national charter — the Balfour Declaration — from British foreign secretary Arthur Balfour in November 1917. After the war this translated into a League of Nations mandate for Palestine from Britain, with the language of the Balfour Declaration written into the language of the mandate.[2] Only the coming to power of Adolf Hitler in Germany ensured a sufficiently large level of European immigration to Palestine to make the Zionist dream appear viable. But this same immigration was perceived by the local Arabs as a severe threat.[3] The grand mufti Haj Amin al-Husseini led a general strike in Palestine in April 1936 that soon turned into an insurrection. As mentioned earlier, this turned into a partition plan that was soon canceled.

The final decade of the mandate led to severe friction between the British colonial authorities administering the mandate, on one hand, and the Arab and Jewish subjects, on the other. After a three-year Arab Revolt from April 1936 to September 1939, a Hebrew Revolt by the Revisionist undergrounds broke out in February 1944 and lasted until November 1947.[4]

The leader of the Jewish Agency and first prime minister of Israel, David Ben-Gurion, had as one of his basic political maxims that Israel should never act without the support of at least one great power. Before declaring independence on May 14, 1948, he ensured that he had the support of both the United States and the Soviet Union. Washington provided diplomatic support at the United Nations and Moscow supplied badly needed arms through Czechoslovakia.

By the early 1950s Israel had lost the support of Moscow, as Stalin was an anti–Semite who saw the Arabs as a better partner than the Jews in the Middle East.[5] Israel managed for a few years without any powerful supporter until the insurrection against French rule by Algerian nationalists on November 1, 1954, gave Israel and the French a mutual enemy. That enemy was Egyptian president Gamal abd al-Nasser, who supported both the Algerian nationalists and the Palestinian Fedayeen organizations. Two years later, in November 1956, Israel colluded with both Britain and France in an attack on Egypt. The connection with London was only temporary and ad hoc, but the alliance with France endured for another decade, until the Six Day War of June 1967.[6]

From Truman to the present there have been elements in both American political parties that have supported both the Zionists and the Arabs in the Middle East. Among the Democrats the Zionists were supported mostly by rank-and-file Jews from non–Orthodox denominations and by the American labor movement. At the same time Arab-Americans, academics and members of mainstream Protestant and Catholic denominations with missionary activities in the Middle East supported the Arabs. Among the Republicans it was mostly business interests and those anti–Communists with a global perspective who supported the Arabs. After 1980, when Evangelical Protestants became a largely Republican constituency, they, along with more conservative Jews, supported Israel.[7] Because the traditionally Arabist State Department and business interests were able to lobby the president directly, Zionist and pro–Israel groups have concentrated on lobbying the Congress as a counterweight to the executive branch.

President Harry Truman ignored the advice of Secretary of State George C. Marshal to recognize de facto Israel's independence only minutes after Ben-Gurion had declared it.[8] His successor, general Dwight D. Eisenhower, took a less risky approach. Eisenhower started the tradition of American presidents sending diplomatic envoys to the region to attempt to negotiate either an informal or formal peace between Israel and its Arab neighbors by sending Texas oilman and future treasury secretary Robert Anderson in 1955.[9] Eisenhower threatened Israel with a cutoff of donations from American Jews if Israel did not promptly withdraw from the Sinai, which, it had just conquered in 1956. Ben-Gurion withdrew in March 1957 and correct relations with Washington were soon restored. This was the low point in America-Israel relations.[10]

Eisenhower's successor, president John F. Kennedy, was also cool towards Israel in an attempt to build better relations with its Arab neighbors. Kennedy also hassled Jerusalem about the nuclear reactor that it was building near Dimona.[11] But in 1962 Kennedy did agree to sell Hawk surface-to-air missiles to Israel. Israel did not need the missiles badly, as its air force was, and still is, the best in the region, but it wanted the sale as a precedent for future sales.[12]

Kennedy's vice president, Lyndon B. Johnson, had been a good friend of the Jewish state as Senate majority leader in the 1950s. When he became president following Kennedy's assassination in November 1963, relations between the two countries gradually improved. In 1965 he agreed to sell A-4 Skyhawk attack aircraft to Israel, although these did not begin arriving until after the June 1967 war. After the war the United States also agreed to sell F-4 Phantom fighter bombers to Israel as well. Gradually the Israeli Air Force transitioned over from French aircraft to American aircraft during the late 1960s and early 1970s.[13]

Lyndon Johnson was too preoccupied with the Vietnam War to attempt to make peace between Israel and its neighbors. But he did give Foreign Minister Abba Eban the green light for Israel to act to end the blockade imposed on it by Egypt, and he dispatched Robert Anderson, Eisenhower's envoy, to Cairo to ascertain Nasser's intentions in late May 1967. Prime Minister Levi Eshkol, who had served as a deputy defense minister under Ben-Gurion, kept in mind Ben-Gurion's maxim even though the two men had become bitter political enemies by this time. Ben-Gurion cautioned against acting as he was afraid that Israel lacked great power support. His protégés, Defense Minister Moshe Dayan, Foreign Minister Eban, and Rafi leader Shimon Peres, ignored him.[14]

Richard Nixon was the first Republican president since Eisenhower and had been Eisenhower's vice president. Growing up in southern California he had developed mildly anti–Semitic attitudes, but he did not let them interfere with his political views or foreign policy.[15] He chose the foreign policy advisor of his rival, Nelson Rockefeller, as his national security advisor. Henry A. Kissinger was rather unusual for a senior American government official. Born Heinz Kissinger in a small town in Bavaria, Germany, he had been forced to flee from Germany with his family after the Nazis came to power. At Harvard University Kissinger studied philosophy, history and political science, eventually earning his doctorate in the latter field and becoming a Harvard professor. He also, for several years, ran a special seminar for foreign government officials, and through it became acquainted with future Foreign Minister Yigal Allon of Israel and future Prime Minister al-Masri of Jordan. Kissinger, like Nixon, was a realist — meaning that he focused on the balance of power, security, and national interest rather than on morality in determining and analyzing foreign policy. Nixon and Kissinger were a close team during the former's almost six years in office as president.[16]

During the Nixon administration Israel became an American client state, as Nixon and Kissinger were determined to resist the spread of Soviet influence in the Middle East. During Nixon's first term, Kissinger had responsibilities everywhere except the Middle East, which was generally left to Secretary of State William P. Rogers. Rogers attempted to negotiate a peace settlement in the region, but soon settled for negotiating an end to the War of Attrition along the Suez Canal between Egypt and Israel. Kissinger had developed a close relationship with Israeli Ambassador Yitzhak Rabin, relying on him for military advice in dealing with the Vietnam War. Kissinger secretly encouraged Jerusalem to resist pressure from Rogers for concessions.[17]

Kissinger's initiation into the politics of the region came in September 1970 when he managed the Black September crisis, when Palestinian fedayeen challenged the authority of the Jordanian government by hijacking aircraft in Europe and landing them in Jordan. King Hussein of Jordan decided to put an end to the state-within-a-state of the fedayeen organizations. Syria intervened by sending tanks into northern Jordan, which the Jordanian army was able to destroy. IAF aircraft made passes over the battlefield in northern Jordan in coordination with Washington to make clear to Damascus that Israel would intervene militarily rather than see the king overthrown. By saving another American client (which America had inherited from the British), Israel had demonstrated its useful to Washington.[18]

Over the decades of the Cold War, Israel had an opportunity to acquire several state of the art Soviet weapons systems, such as an Iraqi MiG-21 fighter jet, T-55 and T-62 tanks, BMP-1 infantry fighting vehicles, and Russian radar systems, which, were captured either in wars between 1967 and 1982 or in special operations by Israeli intelligence. Israel was quick to share the intelligence from these systems with friendly Western powers, foremost among them the United States. It also shared its experience in combating Soviet air defense systems along the Suez Canal in 1969–70 with the United States Air Force, which was then engaged in fighting those same systems in Vietnam.[19] Israel also developed a number of agents within important Arab countries such as Egypt, Syria and

Lebanon, either by subverting Arabs or by inserting Arabic-speaking Jews. It was this intelligence about Soviet activities in the Middle East, as well as analysis of Arab politics in its neighbors, that made Israel of some value to America as an ally during the Cold War. But unlike what one-state supporter academic Virginia Tilley claims, Israel probably was not able to provide a great deal of political intelligence about the Gulf states, which supplied the West with much of its oil.[20]

The other major service that Israel provided was in supplying arms and training to the militaries of Third World regimes that Washington wished to support but could not afford to be seen supporting openly either for diplomatic reasons or because of congressional restrictions due to human rights violations. Israel, along with Brazil and South Africa, is a major non–European exporter of arms to the Third World. Israel was able to provides arms or military services to many countries in both sub–Saharan Africa and Latin America and could be counted on to supply captured Soviet small arms to rebel movements like the Contras in Nicaragua. This became especially important during the Reagan administration in the 1980s.[21]

For twenty years from 1968 to 1988 superpower rivalry was a major factor in the politics of the Middle East. During this time support for Israel became an issue in American presidential elections starting in 1968.[22] Initially candidates competed for the Jewish vote, which peaked as a percentage of the total electorate in the 1950s and 1960s. During this time Jews made up about three percent of the total population with this figure dropping off to about 2.5 percent by the 1990s and to between 2.1 and 1.7 percent in 2010. But because the rate of voting was so much higher than among other ethnic groups for reasons of class, Israel, and the Holocaust, Jews actually made up between five and eight percent of the actual voting public. And because Jews are concentrated in a few states with large electoral vote totals, like New York, Florida, Illinois, Pennsylvania, New Jersey, Massachusetts and California, their votes could be critical in a tight election.[23]

Eventually a candidate's position on Israel became important to other voting publics besides Jews, such as Evangelical Protestants and those who voted on the basis of foreign policy. Evangelical Protestants became an important Republican constituency starting in 1980 and became even more important in 2000 for George W. Bush. This gave the America Israel Public

Affairs Committee (AIPAC) a major constituency in both political parties.

Over the decades AIPAC, which was founded in 1953, was quick to point out these services provided by Israel. AIPAC soon developed strong influence on Capitol Hill with the Congress by providing members of Congress from both parties with background information and with good references to a number of allied political action committees that provided funding to political candidates. Initially relying mainly on American Jews to pressure members of Congress through letter-writing campaigns or phone calls, AIPAC has expanded in recent decades to develop solid ties with Evangelical Protestant Christians and other non–Jews.[24]

AIPAC developed a number of themes in its pro–Israel message to Congress that were based upon a selective filtering of the truth. That is to say, its basic message was true but not the whole truth. AIPAC has had four main themes.

First, it asserts that Israel is the only democracy in the Middle East. This is mostly true. Lebanon was a very dysfunctional and corrupt consociational democracy from 1943 until 1976 when Syria occupied it. Lebanon regained a measure of freedom when Syria withdrew its army from Lebanon in 2005, but Hezbollah, which is allied to both Syria and Iran, has remained as a political party with its own private army, and this has prevented democracy from being restored in Lebanon. Turkey has recently emerged as a democracy, but with significant restrictions on freedom of speech and the press.

Israel, as outlined previously, is a dysfunctional democracy when it comes to resolving the Arab question, and it is an ethnic democracy in that the Arab minority is kept out of government by a general agreement of parties. But most Americans conceive democracy as majority rule and certain basic freedoms (those enumerated in the First Amendment of the Constitution) that do exist in Israel, so it is a democracy. And certainly in comparison to its neighbors it is democratic.

Second is the theme that Israel is an outpost of Western civilization and is under threat from its Arab neighbors. This was much truer in Israel's first decades than it is today. Since June 1982 when the IDF destroyed the Syrian air force in a single day over Lebanon and fought the Syrian army for about a week, Israel has not fought the conventional forces of any of its Arab neighbors. It has fought Hezbollah guerrillas for two decades in

158

a guerrilla campaign in southern Lebanon from 1982 to 2000 and then in a semi-conventional war in the summer of 2006. It has fought Hamas guerrillas in the summer of 2006 and in December 2008 and January 2009 before Obama was inaugurated president. Israel does face a military challenge from farther powers such as Iraq under Saddam Hussein in the 1990s and Iran today. But its biggest threat comes from Arab terrorism, which annually kills fewer people than car accidents.

Third is the theme that Israel has been a loyal ally serving American interests. The Jewish Yishuv in Palestine fought on the Allied side in both world wars. Jewish volunteers helped to conquer Palestine for the British in 1918. In North Africa Jewish volunteers fought in the British army against the Germans and Italians from 1940–43 and in the final year of the war the Jewish Brigade fought as an independent unit in the British army in Italy. In 1950 Israel was too young a state and too politically divided to send troops to Korea. But Israel identified itself as part of the Western camp throughout the Cold War.

In many ways Israel's record of alliance with the West is comparable to white South Africa's record. In both world wars the Union Defence Force served as part of the British war effort in both Africa and Europe and South Africa considered itself as part of the West during the Cold War. But in September 1914 many Afrikaner nationalists revolted and fled into German South West Africa rather than fight against their former foreign supporters in Germany. During World War II John Vorster was interned as a threat to national security. He served as prime minister from 1966 to 1978.[25] Likewise the Likud leaders of the late 1970s and 1980s fought against the British during World War II. Yitzhak Shamir, prime minister from September 1983 to June 1984 and from October 1986 to June 1992, was part of an underground organization that attempted to form an alliance with Nazi Germany in 1941. Shamir fought against Britain during the Hebrew Revolt, as did Menachem Begin.[26] Pro-Israeli Americans and apologists for apartheid South Africa rarely have mentioned this background.

Critics of Zionism also cite the attack on the American intelligence ship *U.S.S. Liberty* in June 1967 by the Israeli Air Force and Israeli Navy as a deliberate assault. Israel argues that it was a tragic error and paid $6.9 million compensation to the U.S. government and the victims.[27] This has not had much effect on American public opinion. Much more lasting is the impression that Israel also puts its own interests above American interests and causes problems for the United States in the region through its settlement activities on the West Bank.

But by contrast the Palestinians do not have a mixed record: they were always either neutral or on the other side during the twentieth century. During World War II Haj Amin al-Husseini and Hassan Salame fought against the British in Iraq in 1941 and then were in Germany for the remainder of the war.[28] Yasir Arafat aligned the PLO with the Soviet Union from when he took over in 1969 until the demise of the Soviet Union. In 2000 Arafat bought a shipload of arms from Iran.[29]

And fourth is the legacy of the Holocaust, from which Jews can only be protected by a strong Jewish state. Critics claim that Israel is exploiting the memory of the victims of the Holocaust for its own political needs. But political Zionism claimed since its foundation that anti–Semitism was growing in Europe and that if a Jewish homeland were not established in Palestine and the Jews resettled there, the results would be very tragic. The Holocaust seemed to far exceed the predictions of Zionist leaders. Asking Israel to stop talking about the Holocaust is like asking academics not to mention the predictions that they made that were proven true. And when one considers that Zionist leaders are also politicians, this does seem to be asking quite a bit.[30]

A legitimate critique of Zionism is that it has only succeeded in transforming anti–Semitism into anti–Zionism and transferring it from Europe to the Middle East. It has also concentrated many Jews into one place, thus making them vulnerable. But because of Zionism, Jews are political actors and thus have their own fate at least partially in their own hands.

Combined, these four themes are very powerful and strike a deep chord among ordinary Americans. Combine these rational political arguments with non-rational religious arguments that have widespread support and Israel has an unbeatable position in relation to its foes in America.

As Washington's interactions with its client, Israel, expanded during the mid–1970s to encompass the early peace process between Israel and its neighbors, so too did AIPAC. AIPAC was involved in a number of high-profile political battles with the Ford, Carter, and Reagan administrations between 1975 and 1982.

The first of these occurred in March 1975 when Israel failed to make what Secretary of State Henry Kissinger considered to be generous enough concessions in the negotiations on a further Israeli pullback in the Sinai. Kissinger returned to Washington and convinced President Ford to announce a "reassessment" of the American-Israeli relationship as a means of pressuring Jerusalem to make concessions. AIPAC went to work drafting a letter of support for Israel and urged senators to sign it. Seventy-six senators signed the letter effectively giving it the strength of a "sense of the Senate" resolution and neutering the administration's attempts to pressure Israel to make concessions. The Sinai II agreement was signed on September 1, 1975, after a further Kissinger shuttle in August. Kissinger essentially bribed Israel to make the required concessions with military aid and a new Memorandum of Understanding. President Sadat of Egypt came up with the idea of manning warning stations within the Giddi and Mitla Passes with American monitors. The agreement was completed but Kissinger's shuttle diplomacy had reached its limit. It would take Sadat flying to Jerusalem and speaking in the Knesset to get Israel to agree to withdraw from all of Egyptian territory seized in 1967.[31]

Carter also went to battle against AIPAC in the summer of 1978 over the sale of F-15 Eagle air-superiority fighters to Saudi Arabia. Carter won and AIPAC lost. After Kissinger's shuttle diplomacy petered out after September 1975, Washington turned increasingly to arms sales as a method of maintaining influence and rewarding clients. Carter arranged to have the arms sales of modern fighter aircraft to Egypt (F-5s), Israel (F-16s, F-15s) and Saudi Arabia (F-15s) presented to the Senate as a single package that would either be approved or rejected. Egypt and Israel were getting about half as many aircraft as they originally requested, while Saudi Arabia was getting all that it had asked for. Israel and AIPAC's real objection was not to the aircraft sale to Egypt, its actual enemy, but to Saudi Arabia, its potential enemy. There was worry that if there were a revolution in Saudi Arabia the aircraft could end up being used by Israel's enemies. The fight took place over several months in 1978 and slowed down the peace negotiations between Egypt and Israel. In the end the Senate approved the sales by a vote of 54–44.[32]

The next real crisis came after the Egyptian-Israeli peace treaty was signed in Washington in March 1979. There was a dispute over a settlement freeze that prime minister Menachem Begin had agreed to. Begin claimed that he had agreed to a ninety-day freeze in order to allow the autonomy talks to get started. President Jimmy Carter claimed that Begin had agreed

161

to a settlement freeze until the autonomy talks were completed and an agreement reached. Because of the vehemence that both leaders used in stressing their positions it is likely that there was a genuine misunderstanding over what was agreed to. AIPAC naturally took Begin's side and argued that it was a minor disagreement between friends. Carter was forced to eventually drop the matter.[33] Begin knew that Egypt and Israel had diametrically opposed positions on autonomy and so an agreement was unlikely. He was determined to settle the West Bank with Jewish settlements and so would never have agreed to such an indefinite freeze.

When President Ronald Reagan came into office in January 1981 he was the most pro–Israel president to date. This is due to several factors. First, he had spent his career in Hollywood and so knew many Jews and had many Jewish friends. Second, he was an avowed anti–Communist and so it was natural that he sided with a country that was an enemy of the Soviet Union and whose enemies were supported by the Soviets. Third, as a genuine Presbyterian Christian, he believed that the Holy Land was the homeland of the Jews. Fourth, he was very aware of what happened in Europe during the Holocaust.[34] Yet he managed to have two major disputes with Israel.

The Reagan administration had a mixed range of views towards Israel and the Middle East. Reagan's first secretary of state, Al Haig, was very pro–Israel, as was UN ambassador Jeane Kirkpatrick. But secretary of defense Casper "Cap" Weinberger, who had a long-term relationship with Reagan that Haig lacked, was from an anti–Zionist Jewish family and had served in a senior position at Bechtel Corporation, which had major construction projects throughout the Arab world, before coming to the administration. He was accompanied by Haig's replacement, George Shultz, who was also a senior person at Bechtel — the president — and had previously served as labor secretary and secretary of the treasury in the Nixon administration. Shultz ended up getting along very well with Israel once Shimon Peres replaced Yitzhak Shamir as prime minister. Several others, such as National Security Advisor Robert McFarlane, were sympathetic to Israel but wanted to balance America's ties with Israel with those in the Arab world.[35]

Reagan was determined to sell AWACS military aircraft to Saudi Arabia for both foreign policy and economic reasons. He wanted to assure Saudi Arabia's support for American policy in the region. He also wanted to recycle petrodollars by selling American weapons to Arab countries. The five AWACs aircraft and additional air-to-air missiles for the F-15s sold in 1978 cost $8.5 billion but were essential to Saudi Arabia having a robust defensive capability over the Persian Gulf. Reagan personalized the deal and claimed that he was single-handedly fighting numerous lobbyists from AIPAC. Administration aides told senators that it was "Reagan or Begin." The sale went ahead on a narrow 52 to 48 vote in the Senate in October 1981.[36]

Reagan was not afraid to unilaterally sanction Israel for actions that he deemed were in opposition to American interests such as the June 1981 bombing of the Osirak nuclear reactor in Iraq or the December 1981 application of Israeli law to the Golan Heights, namely, de facto annexation. Usually he would merely delay supply of previously agreed to military equipment to Israel until the dispute was resolved or until Reagan thought that Israel had got the point. Such measures would enrage the prickly Begin, who would call in U.S. ambassador Sam Lewis for an official protest.[37] But Reagan could get away with things that Ford or Carter could not have gotten away with because Israel's American supporters knew that Reagan was a friend of Israel and because Reagan had the first loyalty of those supporters who were Republicans.

There was a major row between Reagan and Begin after the IDF invaded Lebanon in June 1982 and put Beirut under siege. After being shown pictures of a Lebanese child who had been injured in an Israeli barrage, Reagan had a gut reaction against what Israel was doing. American pressure was instrumental in dissuading Israeli forces from entering Muslim West Beirut in August. As a result of the war Reagan issued an American peace plan, drafted by the State Department's Bureau of Near East Affairs in consultation with Arab governments but not Israel, calling for a final settlement of the Israeli-Palestinian conflict based on an Israeli withdrawal from the West Bank and Gaza with Jordan assuming sovereignty over an autonomous West Bank and Gaza. While this would have been acceptable or at least negotiable with a Labor Party government, to the Likud it was anathema.[38]

The main job of AIPAC was to lobby Congress to serve as a counterweight to the administration in power and keep up the levels of economic and military aid to Israel. Since 1975 these had held steady at a combined total of about $2–3 billion per year plus a further $1.5 to $2 billion in economic aid to Egypt annually after the signing of the peace treaty with Israel. This amounted to about 45 percent of the annual foreign aid allocation of the United States. AIPAC justified this high level by arguing that the defense budget amounted to a much higher level of de facto military aid to Western Europe by helping to pay for their annual defense costs. And AIPAC argued that the intelligence and other benefits that Israel provided to the United States were worth the expense. Much of the military aid is spent in the United States and it can be argued that it is a subsidy to the defense industry.[39]

During the 1980s AIPAC began to change by hiring Christian staffers who could serve as an outreach to the Christian Zionists. The lobby also began to attract more Republicans who were Likud supporters. This caused problems when Labor returned to power in June 1992. This was because Rabin prioritized the peace process whereas many AIPAC staffers and board members were interested in causes that appealed more to the Likud. An example was the drive to get the United States government to move the embassy from Tel Aviv to Jerusalem. Because the original 1947 UN partition plan had called for Jerusalem to remain an international city, most countries refused to locate their embassies there even though it had been Israel's capital since early 1949. Israel had learned to live with having two de facto capitals: Tel Aviv as the diplomatic capital and Jerusalem as the parliamentary and executive capital. But it was a sour point with the Israeli government and Israelis that foreign governments and the media would refer to Tel Aviv as Israel's capital. When he first came to Washington in 1992, Rabin had harsh words for AIPAC's leadership behind closed doors.[40]

In 1985 AIPAC's deputy director of Foreign Policy Research, Martin Indyk, a former Australian intelligence official, set up the Washington Institute for Near East Policy as a think tank designed to provide policy output that would influence the executive branch and the media. Indyk created WINEP with AIPAC's blessing and with funding from many AIPAC donors. It was designed to provide more academic-quality and independent research than AIPAC put out. WINEP concentrates on the internal affairs of Middle Eastern countries except Israel and on the foreign and defense policies of these countries. It also provides Israel-friendly prescriptions for the peace process. WINEP has become a serious player in Washington and a supplier of foreign policy officials for both parties. Indyk later served as an ambassador to Israel and as assistant secretary for Near

East affairs in the Clinton administration and is now at the Brookings Institution in a senior position.[41]

At least twice Washington has attempted to intervene in Israel's domestic politics — both times on behalf of Labor. The first time was in the fall of 1991 when Washington refused to supply Israel with loan guarantees for $10 billion in private loans used to resettle Soviet Jews in Israel. The right-wing coalition of Yitzhak Shamir wanted Washington to co-sign on the loans so that if Israel were forced to default, the American taxpayer would pay for them. Washington refused to do this causing many Russian immigrant voters in Israel to vote for Labor in the May 1992 election. Washington then quickly agreed to supply the Rabin government with the guarantees.[42]

The second time was in 1998 when President Clinton persuaded Ehud Barak to hire some of his top election aides such as pollster Stanley Greenberg and two others to work for the Labor Party. It was no secret that Clinton did not get on well with Benjamin Netanyahu and blamed him for the deterioration in the peace process. Clinton saw Barak as likely to restore the momentum to the peace process that had been lacking since Rabin's murder. Both of these instances involved perfectly legal and acceptable uses of leverage.[43]

Israel has also returned the favor by interfering in the American presidential election process on behalf of the Republicans. Bibi Netanyahu has gone out of his way to emphasis his disagreements with President Obama in the hope that American Jews might defect from the Democrats to the Republicans and thereby help to elect a Republican president.

The closest relationship between an American president and an Israeli prime minister has to be that between George W. Bush and Ariel Sharon. This relationship was even closer than that between Bill Clinton and Yitzhak Rabin, whom Rabin regarded as a surrogate father figure. This is because Bush and Sharon became acquainted when both were making their way up the political ladder and had few foreign friends.

Bush went on a governors' tour of Israel. One of AIPAC's more effective techniques was to arrange for tours of Israel for American government officials on which they would be shown Israel's pre–June 1967 borders, meet with senior IDF officers and government officials, and be made to feel special while being fed a line of government *hasbara,* or propaganda. The tour was in November 1998 when he was governor of Texas and Sharon was foreign minister but soon to be out of office. Sharon took Bush up on a helicopter tour over the center of Israel and showed the vulnerability of the country to a foreign attack as well as lecturing him about his battles from the 1948, 1967, and 1973 wars. Sharon had planned on just giving him a briefing on the ground with maps but his aide convinced him that it was worth his time in case one of the governors should run for higher office and be elected.[44]

During the presidential transition following the cliffhanger 2000 American election several Clinton administration officials including Clinton himself warned President-elect Bush and future Secretary of State Colin Powell not to trust Yasir Arafat. Clinton blamed Arafat for the failure of the Camp David summit in July 2000 and the outbreak of the Al-Aksa Intifada in October. Bush decided that there was little payoff in getting involved in Mideast peacemaking as long as Arafat was alive and in charge of the Palestinian Authority.[45]

The terrorist attacks on September 11, 2001, gave the new Bush administration a focus and a purpose that it previously lacked. It also led to a further bonding between Israel and Washington as Sharon was quick to describe Arafat as a local Osama Bin Laden. Bush, who was prone to think in terms of absolutes — good and evil, and so on — rather than in shades of gray, was quick to pick up on Sharon's characterization of Arafat.[46]

Sharon spent his first three years as prime minister combating the Al-Aksa Intifada. Bush, during this time, made a number of bold innovations to American Middle East policy. Bush was the first sitting president to call for the creation of a Palestinian state. Clinton refrained from calling for the creation of a Palestinian state so as not to prejudice the Israeli-Palestinian negotiations and because Rabin never officially recognized that this would be the result of the Oslo process. Bush also brought the European Union, Russia, and the United Nations in as partners in the peace process, termed the Quartet. And in June 2004 he both called on the Palestinians to choose another leader besides Arafat and recognized the legitimacy of Israeli settlement blocs by declaring them a reality that must be taken into account in any final settlement.[47]

The Road Map plan failed after Arafat outmaneuvered prime minister Mahmoud Abbas, whose position was created as a result of American pressure, and because Israel refused to carry out its obligations regarding settlements. The Bush administration did not involve itself again in Middle

East diplomacy until the final year of Bush's presidency. By then it was too late.[48]

There have been two serious attempts by the United States to negotiate a comprehensive solution to the Arab-Israeli conflict. The first was the Rogers Plan, introduced by Secretary of State William P. Rogers in December 1969. This effort was not important to the Nixon-Kissinger foreign policy team and Kissinger, in fact, undermined it by letting Rabin know that Israel would pay no price for standing firm. The national unity government of Golda Meir objected to it and Rogers after a few months settled for negotiating a ceasefire in the War of Attrition between Egypt and Israel. This went into effect in August 1970 with Egypt quickly violating it by moving their surface-to-air missiles forward as the ceasefire was being implemented.[49] The second was by Jimmy Carter in 1977. Once President Anwar Sadat went to Egypt, Carter like Rogers before him quickly settled for negotiating a bilateral Egyptian-Israeli deal, in this case a peace treaty.[50]

The Arabs after 1967 favored negotiating with Israel as a bloc so that they could maximize their negotiating leverage and compel Israel to retreat to the 1949 armistice lines. Israel insisted on dealing with the Arabs on a bilateral basis for two reasons. First, this would counter the Arab strategy and increase Israel's bargaining leverage. And second and more importantly, with no trust between Israel and the Arabs and Israel exchanging tangible assets — territory — for intangible assets — aspects of peace, Israel wanted to have each Arab leader prove himself to Israel as a reliable partner before Israel gave up territory. Israel was able to convince Washington of the validity of this concept. Israel has never been able to negotiate on multiple tracks simultaneously. In 1974 there was a choice between negotiating a separation-of-forces agreement with Jordan or a second agreement with Egypt. Since 1979 the choice has been between the Palestinian track and the Syrian track. Washington has gone along with Jerusalem's preference for the Syrian track, thrilled that Israel appears ready to seriously negotiate with someone. Only once the Syrian track has failed, has Jerusalem then come under pressure from Washington to make a deal with the Palestinians.

The failure of the Bush administration to become engaged led to the creation of a grassroots counter–AIPAC known by the Hebrew name of Brit Tzedek v'Shalom (Alliance for Justice and Peace). The organization was created from a meeting of former Jewish liberal activists from the 1960s and 1970s in April 2002.[51] Its first president was Marcia Freedman, a former one-term Knesset member from Shulamit Aloni's Citizens' Rights Movement (Ratz), one of the forerunners of Meretz.[52] The idea was to create an organization that could involve Progressive Jews, especially those from Reform and Conservative backgrounds, to lobby for a two-state solution. Brit Tzedek began actively recruiting members in the fall of 2002 and soon had chapters in most American cities with major Jewish populations.[53] Because the organization could have no real impact on a Republican administration, it spent the period up through 2008 in a growth mode initiating discussions about Israeli policy in non–Orthodox synagogues.

Starting in 2006 there were rumors of a possible merger of Brit Tzedek with Americans for Peace Now, the American fundraising arm of the Israeli peace movement, and the Israel Policy Forum, a liberal Zionist think tank, to form a new lobbying organization to be bankrolled by Jewish financier George Soros.[54] In the end no major merger occurred. Jeremy Ben-Ami, a Democratic activist and scion of a very established Zionist family in Israel, formed J Street as a Progressive Israel lobby in Washington on April 15, 2008. The following year the Brit Tzedek chapters became J Street chapters but APN and the Israel Policy Forum remained separate.[55]

J Street, unlike AIPAC, does have its own political action committee to provide funding for candidates that it approves of. It also has a university division for liberal Zionist students. Unfortunately for J Street, it has very few Republican supporters. J PAC, its PAC, did support one Republican official, a Lebanese-American representative from Louisiana.[56] But due to peer pressure within the party he was forced to break off his association with J Street in 2010. J Street declined to endorse Obama for reelection in 2012 so as not to antagonize any Republican supporters but all of JPAC's endorsed candidates were Democrats.[57] Thus J Street is almost more a symptom of the problem of American polarization when it comes to the Middle East than part of the solution. J Street has also chosen not — at least for now — to imitate AIPAC and create its own think tank. It has grown very rapidly in its four years of existence — from 1,500 at its first conference in 2009 to 2,500 at its third conference in 2012 — but still attracts only a fraction of the crowd that AIPAC attracts to its annual conference.[58] J Street conferences concentrate more on educating their membership about Israeli politics and policy than on getting them into positions in Senate and House staffs on Capitol Hill or involved in political campaigns.[59]

Engaging in successful Middle East peacemaking has a political cost for American presidents. This is because peacemaking involves putting pressure on Israel to make concessions that it probably would not otherwise make. This pressure in turn antagonizes some American supporters of Israel, who then will vote against the president who applied it. Thus, it is no accident that no American president has been electorally rewarded for successful peacemaking. Kissinger failed to stop the impeachment process against Nixon in 1974. Ford failed to be elected president in 1976. Carter failed to win reelection in 1980. Reagan won reelection without any peace agreement, as did Clinton. George H.W. Bush failed to win reelection after pressuring Israel in 1991. George W. Bush did not engage in serious peacemaking and was reelected.

At best J Street can serve to counteract some of AIPAC's pressure on Congress, but only on Democrats. J Street can influence only Democratic presidents. And it cannot change the reality of Israeli or Palestinian politics. J Street cannot prevent pro–Likud Democrats from defecting to a Republican candidate in presidential elections. And it does not really recruit new voters for a Democratic president or nominee than he would otherwise have. Thus, J Street is really, whether this was Ben-Ami's intention or not, mainly a way of siphoning more dollars to liberal Democrats in Congress from Progressive Jews with guilty consciences.

So an American president with many foreign and domestic items on his agenda has to decide if he is going to spend limited political capital on Middle East peacemaking. Most presidents in the future will probably imitate Obama and at most make a rhetorical stab at the problem. The only time this is likely to change is if a war in the Middle East shakes up things sufficiently, as occurred in October 1973, to make a major effort appear both urgent and likely to succeed.

CHAPTER EIGHT

Lessons from the Cases

So what lessons can be drawn from the three Western democratic (two Israeli and one South African) cases of territorial withdrawal and the single case of a native renunciation of irredentism? First, we'll examine the Western cases (Sinai, Gaza, Namibia) and their lessons and then the lessons for the Palestinians from Fianna Fail.

The first lesson is that conservative nationalist regimes like to make peace with other governments or the international community rather than with revolutionary liberation movements or terrorist organizations. Begin made peace with the Egyptian military regime led by Anwar Sadat. This was after Sadat had proven his good intentions by honoring the separation agreements that he made with Labor governments in the mid–1970s. He then came to Jerusalem. Begin was basically continuing a policy already started by Rabin.

Begin considered Arafat to be another Hitler and the PLO to be an illegitimate terrorist organization. Netanyahu later conducted minimal negotiations with the PLO under Arafat. He did this only to honor already established commitments made on Israel's behalf by Labor under Rabin and Peres. The National Party negotiated with Western mediators starting with Henry Kissinger, extending through the Western Contact Group and finally with Chester Crocker. It also dealt directly with two foreign military regimes — Angola and Cuba. The South African leadership was wary of SWAPO — and with good cause. In April 1989 SWAPO violated the ceasefire transitional arrangements by having PLAN conduct a mass infiltration of guerrillas into Namibia. Pretoria then demanded the right to physically resist this violation and defeated the invasion.[1]

Ariel Sharon was so wary of the PLO that he refused to coordinate Israel's unilateral withdrawal from Gaza with Mahmoud Abbas and his lieutenants. Netanyahu resigned from the government rather than take part in the withdrawal. And the Likud Central Committee refused to support it. And both Rabin and Barak attempted to conclude agreements with Syria before they attempted to negotiate with the Palestinians. So this is a nonpartisan Israeli preference.

Secondly, the Likud has always refused to withdraw from the core of the historic homeland of *Eretz Israel,* the Land of Israel (Palestine in Hebrew). Sharon withdrew from Gaza, but that was the area that was historically under foreign rule — under the Philistines. Namibia was never considered part of the Afrikaner homeland but a defensive buffer state like the Sinai.[2] The National Party only six years later did give up control of South Africa but that was because whites had always been a minority in South Africa and F.W. de Klerk saw a conflict lasting decades and resulting in both black rule and an economically-ruined country. He wanted to avoid that and negotiate from a position of strength.[3] Obviously the leaders of the Likud and the other parties of the Right do not see a similar conflict and end for Israel. They face a liberation movement that has lacked the moral restraint of the African National Congress in South Africa and has embraced terrorism. And they receive economic and military aid from the United States rather than facing trade sanctions. Today the BDS (boycott, divestment, sanctions) movement is about the same stage that the divestment movement was against South Africa in the late 1970s.

Netanyahu has been cleverer than Yitzhak Shamir about his rejectionism, but Shamir's famous adage that "The Arabs are the same Arabs and the sea is the same sea" was a favorite of his.[4] Like Sharon and unlike Olmert, Netanyahu has only spontaneously made concessions that he knows are unacceptable to the Palestinians. He has supported a two-state solution on the condition that the Palestinians accept Israel as a Jewish state. This is unacceptable on two counts. First, it is seen as surrendering the return of refugees demand before negotiations. Second, it would mean making a concession about the nature of Israel that Palestinian Israelis refuse to accept.[5] And of course, Netanyahu demands an undivided Jerusalem — as did all Israeli governments up until July 2000.

Regarding the Namibian case there are a number of important differences. First, the last time Israel fought with an Arab army over the West Bank was in March 1968, when Arafat was still in the process of gaining control of the PLO and an interim leader was in place, at the Battle of Karameh. Israeli tanks, infantry and paratroopers invaded the East Bank to attack the town of Karameh, which housed a concentration of Fatah, in reprisal for a number of terrorist attacks. Jordan came to the aid of their Palestinian brethren, who then two years later in September 1970 tried to overthrow the monarchy. The Jordanians inflicted punishment on the Israelis, although Israel claimed a victory in the battle, and the PLO claimed the credit for their recruiting efforts.[6] Fourteen years later another Arab army, the Syrians, came to the aid of the PLO in southern Lebanon. The Syrians fought for about a week, in which time they lost most of their air force to the Israeli Air Force's fighter pilots, and then agreed to a ceasefire. Israel went on to drive the PLO out of Beirut. When Fatah attempted to come back to Lebanon Syria instigated a rebellion against Arafat. So, Arab regime relations with the PLO have been much more volatile than those between SWAPO and Angola.[7]

Second, the Palestinians never were as proficient at guerrilla operations as was PLAN. Hezbollah managed, like PLAN in Namibia with the South Africans, to make the Israeli occupation very costly. So that in the summer of 2000 Barak ordered the IDF out of Lebanon. But there were never Israeli settlers in southern Lebanon even if the Zionists had originally envisioned the area south of the Litani River as part of the future Jewish state.[8] The Israeli settlement of the West Bank is more like American settlement of the United States or the Boer expansion across South Africa, except under twentieth and twenty-first century conditions. It is like the period before the War of 1812 when the Indians still had powerful foreign allies. So Israel continues to settle the West Bank without annexing it formally.[9]

Third, because Namibia was never annexed by South Africa and was populated by different native peoples than in South Africa, it developed its own liberation movements. South Africa could credibly exit Namibia knowing that it would not be used as a launching pad for raids into South African territory. The same is not the case for the West Bank. Fatah has attempted to differentiate between the territories by declaring that Israeli settlers in the West Bank along with Israeli soldiers are legitimate targets during intifadas, but the Israeli public is not buying the distinction — largely because Arafat never had the discipline to follow through. After the stages strategy of 1974 and the Al-Aksa Intifada, Israelis are reluctant to trust the Palestinians. The Right also tries to blur the organizational boundaries and have the public treat Fatah like Hamas. The only hope for the Palestinians would be if a new organization came along that was dedicated to waging an armed struggle solely to liberate the territories and not Israel. But Palestinian history argues against that option. Splinter groups are usually more extreme rather than more moderate than the organization that they split from. To have credibility in Palestinian eyes they need a heroic past as guerrilla or terrorist operatives, but such a past destroys their credibility in the eyes of much of the Israeli public.[10]

Now as regards the Palestinians and the Irish, the differences are important. While there are many similarities between Ireland and Palestine and between Fianna Fail and Fatah,[11] the differences are important. The first major difference is that Fatah is the more moderate of the two main Palestinian liberation movements. To its nationalist and religious Right is Hamas. Hamas is where Fatah and the PLO were before December 1988 when the PLO conceded Israel's right to exist. In Ireland Fianna Fail was the party on the nationalist and religious Right and the parties that were its opponents and/or coalition partners — the PDs, the Irish Labour Party, the Democratic Left and Fine Gael — were all more open and less nationalist. Fine Gael and Labour paved the way for changing the Articles by their discussion of the issue and their joint statements with the British at Sunningdale in December 1973 and at the signing of the Anglo-Irish Agreement in November 1985. Rather than facing resistance from these rivals, the Fianna Fail leaders knew that they would receive support. After all, Haughey had expelled future PD leader Mary Harney from the party over her support for the AIA in a Dail vote.[12]

The second major difference is that Palestine is situated in a region that has been often times hostile to compromise and concessions from the Arab side in the name of peace. Unelected Arab regimes have traditionally used rhetorical, military and economic support for the confrontation with Israel over Palestine as a legitimizing device. In contrast to this, Western Europe, the United States, and Canada were all supportive of the Northern Ireland peace process. There was a diaspora of republicans in the United States (primarily in New York, Philadelphia and Boston) that was initially opposed to giving up the dream of a united Ireland but the influential Irish-Americans in government and business supported the peace process and supported the non-violent SDLP.[13] The European Union provided crucial funding for programs to employ former loyalist and republican prisoners.

The Arab Peace Plan of 2002 seems to have changed this record. It promises peace for Israel with all the Arab states if it gives up the occupation and returns to the 1949 armistice lines ("1967 borders"). But the plan also embraces the right of return for Palestinian refugees and has been seemingly offered in a non-negotiable form. Unfortunately, Jerusalem has been unwilling to take the Arab League up on its initiative and seek clarification on points in dispute such as refugees and Jerusalem. This is partly because the plan was offered at the same time as a major terrorist bombing in March 2002 that sparked an Israeli reoccupation of the West Bank.

Whenever it negotiates or reacts to an Israeli or American offer, the PLO must take into account how its response will affect its popularity vis a vis Hamas. In 1976 Henry Kissinger journeyed to Africa in two major rounds of shuttle diplomacy in an attempt to solve the Namibian and Rhodesian conflicts. In the Rhodesian case he failed because the situation was not yet ripe. As Africanist and negotiations theorist I. William Zartman has written in numerous texts, ripeness consists of three components: valid negotiators, a hurting stalemate, and a formula that offered a way out. Rhodesia was lacking valid negotiators on the African side and a hurting stalemate. There were three competing liberation movements and four liberation leaders all competing to represent the African side. Only one of the African leaders, Joshua Nkomo even was willing to meet with Kissinger and then only for about ten minutes while Kissinger explained the procedure of his shuttle. The other leaders refused to meet with him and the most radical, Robert Mugabe, kept the others from offering major concessions when the negotiations met in Geneva in October 1976. After a week the talks had made little progress. The talks ended up breaking up for Christmas and never reconvening. Kissinger did not even chair these talks as he knew a hopeless situation.[14]

Hamas in many ways has the same chilling effect on negotiations that Robert Mugabe and ZANU had in 1976 in Rhodesia. In 2008 Mahmoud Abbas never even gave a formal reply to Ehud Olmert's last negotiation offer.[15] When Al Jazeera leaked what were claimed to be the positions from the talks, the PLO denied that it had made the concessions attributed to it. Until the Hamas-Fatah conflict is resolved or until Fatah is much stronger than at present there can be no successful Israeli-Palestinian negotiation.

It has been suggested that an interim solution based on negotiating an agreement on the basis only of the "security" and "borders" bundles of issues and leaving out Jerusalem and refugees be the basis for Palestinian independence. Then over time Israel and Palestine could negotiate solutions to those problematic issues, which caused the collapse of negotiations in 2000 and 2008 respectively, as legal equals. The theory behind this is that over time the existence of borders would tend to erode Palestinian (and Israeli) irredentism. A good case might be made that this is what occurred in the Republic of Ireland regarding Northern Ireland in the decades following partition. But *if* the public's approval was contingent on the lessening of religiosity that occurred during the 1990s and the Celtic Tiger economy than this phenomenon is likely not transferable to Palestine because of the strengthening of religion as a force in the region in general and in Palestine over the last three decades as well as the continued poor economy. If, however, Palestinian entrepreneurism could be unleashed and the state would stop actively instigating against Israel, then it might be possible that over time irredentism could be eroded. But Palestine would be much more vulnerable to regional influences — especially negative ones — than Ireland was. But the issue is of sufficient importance that the factors affecting the Irish referendum vote of May 1998 are worth further investigation.

So this means that a negotiated resolution of the Israeli-Palestinian conflict is very problematic from both ends at present. But the cases point towards another possibility for progress in another track of the peace process. Israel and Syria conducted peace negotiations on and off since 1992. The problem was that Syrian President Hafiz al-Assad was unwilling to give the external confidence-building measure equivalent to Sadat's trip to Jerusalem that any Israeli government needs to reassure the electorate before making major territorial concessions. In 2000 they came close but Barak got cold feet at the last minute and Assad, who was dying, was focused on managing his succession.[16] It may well be that the Assad regime has always needed a peace process much more than peace. When the Cold War ended Assad needed a new relationship with Washington in order to replace that with Moscow, which was no longer a real superpower and could no longer afford to pretend to sell him expensive weapons. Later his son also needed an improved relationship after his regime was implicated in the Hariri assassination in Beirut in 2005.[17]

But the Syrian civil war/rebellion has effectively closed the track since it began in 2010. It will take a new majority Sunni regime to make peace with Israel. A majority regime with political legitimacy will not need the conflict with Israel as a source of legitimacy as the minority Alawite regime has needed it. The fascist Ba'ath Party has needed the conflict with colonialism and Zionism as a source of legitimacy as have all radical military regimes in the Arab world. The peace between Jerusalem and Cairo remained a Cold Peace because the military regime needed to keep its distance from Israel so as not to aggravate too much the Egyptian street and so as not to return to the state of isolation that it fell into in 1978–79. This is not to advocate that Washington actively assist in the overthrow of the Syrian regime. We have little idea who would replace it. Peace with Israel after regime change is only a possibility — not a certainty or even a probability. Regime change is also not without risk or cost. And there is a good chance that the Assad regime, as in 1982, will survive with the help of the various sectarian minorities (Christians, Kurds, Druze) that are wary of Sunni rule. If it survives there would be little chance of a successful peace deal on the Golan at least not until the regime had regained regional and international legitimacy.

The Syrian front of the peace process is not only hostage to events in Syria itself (and potentially in the neighboring countries that affect those) but also to events in Egypt. So far the Egyptian military has managed to remain in charge by sacrificing Mubarak, its head for thirty years. It has also stripped the parliament and the presidency of most real powers. It remains to be seen whether President Muhammad al-Morsi and the Muslim Brotherhood tolerate the military's leading role in the future. The Egyptian-Israeli peace treaty is likely to be one of the main issues or key terrain features over which the future battles are fought. The Brothers could move to either completely cancel the peace treaty or to permanently end diplomatic relations with Israel, thus turning the cold peace into a frozen one. This would be very popular with intellectuals, many of whom are Marxists or former Marxists, and thus a means of winning their support for the Brotherhood in a confrontation with the military. The intellectuals in both Egypt and Jordan have always been hostile to the peace treaties with Israel because their main function was to spread pan–Arabism and anti–Zionism (often identical with anti–Semitism) in Arab societies. This would return them to their former prestigious role in Egypt under Gamal abd al-Nasser and under Sadat before the separation of forces agreements.[18]

If the peace treaty with Egypt is either cancelled or significantly watered down, this will make it much easier for future Likud governments to avoid entering into new agreements or serious negotiations with other Arab states. If Egypt cancels its peace treaty with Israel, it will make it harder for King Abdullah or his successor to maintain his country's peace with Israel. Jordan would likely then return to the pre–1994 situation of de facto peace with Israel without the formality because it is in the interest of the Hashemite regime to do so.

Four things are necessary for a two-state solution to be enacted: a Palestinian government that is able and willing to offer positions that a likely Israel government will accept; an Israeli government that is able and willing to offer positions that a likely Palestinian government will accept; an outside mediator or mediators that are able to help bridge the gaps and maintain the momentum in the peace process; and, most difficult of all, that these three things should occur simultaneously. I have already discussed the difficulties with the first two parts. The third part is also problematic because Israel's main mediation partner in the peace partner from 1969 to present has been thoroughly penetrated by Israel and Israel and the peace process have become partisan issues.

While significant achievements were registered in the first ten years of the peace process from 1969 to 1979, little progress was made over the next thirteen years. If progress also seems nonexistent in the peace process since Bill Clinton issued the Clinton Parameters in late December 2000 this is easily explained. Simply subtract all the time when there was either a Likud or national unity government in power in Israel,[19] or when Arafat was in power or both. Then of the remaining time, look at whether Washington was committed to mediating Middle East peace. At best, the situation was ripe only in 2006 to 2008. And I would argue that the poor performance of the IDF and the Israeli government in the Second Lebanon War in the summer of 2006 fatally compromised Kadima as a peace partner for the remainder of its term. And in 2006 President Bush and Secretary of State Rice had their hands full with Iraq and midterm elections.

On January 22, 2013, elections were held for the nineteenth Knesset (parliament) in Israel. The Likud, which had merged with Avigdor Lieberman's *Israel Beitenu* party in November to form a joint list known as Likud Beitenu, came in first with 31 seats; this was a substantial drop of eleven seats for the combined totals of the two parties. Next came *Yesh Atid* (There Is a Future) with 19 seats. Yesh Atid was a Center party headed by Israeli broadcast journalist Yair Lapid, the son of former Shinui leader Yosef

"Tommy" Lapid. Yesh Atid had a similar message to that of Shinui of fighting the ultra–Orthodox parties and ending their exemption from military service. Kadima was reduced from 28 seats to only two under Shaul Mofaz, just barely passing the entry barrier to the Knesset. But former Kadima leader Tzipi Livni formed her own list, haTnua (the Movement), which won six seats. Most of Kadima's former voters from 2009 appear to have gone to Yesh Atid. Adding up Kadima's two seats, Livni's six seats and Yesh Atid's 19 seats leaves us with a total of 27 seats, one less that Kadima had in the previous election. Labor emerged with 15 seats — a gain of two over its 2009 total and a modest improvement. But much more significant were the totals in the religious camp: Jewish Home 12 seats, Shas 11, and United Torah Judaism seven seats for a total of 30 seats. It appears that large numbers of Likud and possibly Israel Beitenu voters from 2009 voted for Naftali Bennett's Jewish Home party. Meretz doubled its representation to six seats. The three Arab parties had a grand total of 11 seats.

What this amounts to is a continuation of the trends noted in the first chapter with the Likud still holding a veto. In the coalition bargaining phase Yesh Atid teamed up with Jewish Home to oppose concessions to the ultra–Orthodox parties, which for the first time in decades ended up in the opposition. This is probably good for civil rights and democracy in Israel but bad for the prospects of an Israeli-Palestinian peace deal. Netanyahu swallowed up his biggest external competitor, Lieberman, but a new one emerged in the form of Naftali Bennett.

In the Northern Ireland peace process success was achieved because for both the British and Irish governments the peace process was a bipartisan issue. Tony Blair in opposition supported John Major in his mediation in Northern Ireland and the same was true of Major's successors in regard to Blair's mediation. In Ireland the opposition parties supported Albert Reynolds's active pursuit of ceasefires in Northern Ireland and when they came to power they continued the policy and Prime Minister John Bruton even offered to put Martin Mansergh in charge of contacts with the Republicans. While the peace process was an issue in the 1997 election, it was a case of Fianna Fail claiming that it could do a better job rather than being opposed to the peace process. Thus continuity was maintained over 13.5 years until peace was stabilized in 2007.[20]

In the 1970s and 1980s the Republicans were better stewards of the peace process because the Democrats were partially compromised by the role of American Jews in their fundraising and elections. But by the 1990s the situation had begun to reverse itself as the largely Reform and Conservative Jewish communities became alienated from Likud governments over the Lebanon War and its definition of who is a Jew.[21] At the same time Evangelical Protestant voters were playing an increasingly important role in the Republican Party because of their rejection of Democratic social policies on issues such as abortion, gay rights, etc. These Evangelical voters were supportive of Israel's Likud governments because they saw them fulfilling Biblical prophecy and leading to End Times scenarios as revealed in the Book of Revelations.[22] This can be seen in the difference between George H. W. Bush's Israel policy with its use of loan guarantees for absorption of Soviet Jewry in 1992 that helped to elect Rabin prime minister, and his son George W. Bush's relationship with Ariel Sharon. Bush *pere* had a East Coast view of foreign policy from the Cold War, where Bush *fils* had a Texas view of foreign policy based on loyalty to allies and Evangelical beliefs. Bush sr. was from the Wall St. wing of the party; Bush jr. was allied with the social conservative wing.[23]

While George W. Bush could be excused for not pursuing the peace process vigorously during his first term both because of the 2000 failure at Camp David and the Al-Aksa Intifada and the invasion of Iraq, he did attempt to make up for it late in his second term. But like Bill Clinton he waited until his final year in office before pursuing it vigorously. While John McCain might have pursued the peace process had he been elected in 2008, by the time of the 2012 primaries the dynamics of the Republican Party had changed.[24] Mitt Romney secured his nomination only by avoiding any talk of foreign policy that would offend the Republican Right and generally sticking only to immigration as a foreign policy issue. In the general election this did not change either as Romney concentrated solely on economic policy as an election issue.[25]

Obama will face problems in his second term as well. The Republicans since 2010 have pursued a strict policy of non-cooperation with Obama in the belief that keeping him from making political achievements would prevent his reelection. This is made easier by the fact that they genuinely disagree ideologically with his policies. If the Republicans retain control of the House or gain control of the Senate or both in 2014 it will be even more difficult for Obama to mediate in the Middle East. His mediation efforts in his first term were more pro forma than real, a payback to Progressive Jews who supported him in 2008.[26] It will probably take at least the first half of his second term for Syria to sort itself out — an end to the civil war and a new government to consolidate and establish itself. That will leave him with at most two years for a peace process. And the election of his successor and his lame duck status will cripple him in his final year leaving him with effectively a single year.

Obama visited Israel in March 2013 and made a speech comparable to his 2009 Cairo speech, but which was meant to assure an Israeli audience by noting Israel's long historical roots in the Middle East going back millennia while calling for Israelis to support a two-state solution. None of what he said seemed to signal a new peace initiative in the Middle East, although newly confirmed Secretary of State John Kerry, the unsuccessful 2004 Democratic presidential nominee, is said to be interested in reviving the Israeli-Palestinian peace process. If he does attempt this he will encounter the same problems that Obama and Clinton encountered in 2009 and 2010.

The alternative would be for Obama or a future Democrat president to attempt to limit Israel's settlement enterprise. This could be done by using existing pressure points and signaling American displeasure with Israeli policy. In such an attempt symbolic actions are probably more effective than serious cuts to aid. But because the Republicans have chosen to politicize Middle East policy, this attempt might well fail because the Israeli Right knows that a future Republican administration would reverse it. Without bipartisan support, such a policy is likely to be ineffective and without pressure on both sides on the Palestinian track mediation is also likely to fail.

J Street, Americans for Peace Now, and Israeli and Palestinian peace activists have preached the belief that the window on the two-state solution is closing. Many in Israel and the West Bank/Gaza argue that the window has already closed. They argue that with more and more settlements on the West Bank there will be less land to bargain over and that the large percentage of religious Zionists and settlers in the IDF's officer corps will make a repeat of the settlement evacuations of 1982 and 2005 impossible. They may be right.

But I believe that given the difficulties inherent in any of the varieties of the one-state solution (apartheid, bi-national state, Arab dominance) that like power sharing in Northern Ireland the two-state solution retains a compelling logic as the only possible solution. Neither will the Arabs soon reconcile themselves to the occupation nor will Israeli Jews be content to return to the insecurities of a time without a state. In Northern Ireland power sharing failed twice (1974, 2002) before finally succeeding on the third try with the support of the Democratic Unionists. What pushing it into the future means is that both sides will pay a higher price in terms of deaths, economic misery, and loss of legitimacy until the situation is ripe in the future for a two-state solution. Over half of the casualties in The Troubles occurred after the failure of Sunningdale in May 1974.

So what does this all mean in terms of broader American foreign policy? During the Cold War we were taught that America had four main interests in the Middle East: first, protecting the flow of oil to itself and its allies at a reasonable price; second, preventing the continued penetration of the Soviet Union into the Muslim Middle East; third, the security of Israel; and fourth, the peace process between Israel and its Arab neighbors. The fourth was really a way of reconciling the third interest with the first two, because of their obvious clash. American support for Israel hurt it politically with the anti–Zionist and anti–Semitic Arabs and Iranians and thus helped to pave the way for further Soviet penetration and threaten the safety of oil access. Since the end of the Cold War in 1990 there has been little sign of a systematic reexamination of American interests in the region as a result of changed circumstances.[27] The sole accommodation with reality seems to be substituting Al-Qaeda and terrorism for the Soviet Union. Since the end of the Cold War the United States has invaded Iraq twice (1991, 2003), and become engaged in expensive counterinsurgency campaigns in both Iraq and Afghanistan.

I would argue that these wars with all their cost in blood and treasure have not made the United States more secure and have cost it influence and political capital around the world. They made the United States economy weaker and detracted from the ability of the Obama administration to pursue its goals not just in the region but elsewhere — Afghanistan and Pakistan. The Arabs and Iranians have an inherent interest in selling their oil at market prices around the globe. To attempt to artificially raise the price by cutting production will simply encourage the West to invest in research for substitute sources of energy and conservation. And future administrations should pursue policies that encourage conservation of fossil fuels through taxation and, if necessary rationing.

Al-Qaeda deliberately targeted the United States in New York and Washington in an attempt to drag the United States into intervening militarily in Arab and Muslim countries. They knew that such intervention would expose more Muslims to the infidel with his foreign and idolatrous customs and would result in more support for terrorism against the regimes that supported the Americans. They were too weak to directly defeat their more moderate opponents in Saudi Arabia, Egypt and elsewhere in the Arab World and the repressive regimes ruling these countries so they employed the indirect approach as good students of military history. They nearly succeeded. The United States should now militarily disengage from Afghanistan and the Arab Middle East and restrict its presence to the embassies, consulates, and universities of the pre–Cold War era. Washington can continue to support Israel's security by selling it or supplying it with essential weapons systems as it now does with Taiwan, while continuing to condemn its continued colonization of the West Bank. When Israel and the Arabs are finally ready for peace and the situation is ripe Washington can reengage in the peace process, hopefully with the aid of the European Union, which has more influence on the Palestinians than Washington does.[28]

The State Department can better prepare for the few fleeting windows of opportunity for successful mediation when the situation is ripe by ensuring that all senior diplomats in the region are given theoretical training in international mediation either by the Department or at the U.S. Institute of Peace or in leading American or Israeli universities. The Arabists who have spent their time serving in embassies in the Arab World should also be trained in Israeli politics by either taking a course or by acquiring a textbook on the subject and acquainting themselves with the mechanics of the Israeli party system, coalition building, and the history of the main parties and blocs. If this advice is heeded future political appointees who serve as secretaries of state will be ensured of knowledgeable advice even if they have no background in the region. This was the case with most American secretaries of state over the last forty years. Cyrus Vance, Alexander Haig, George Shultz, Madeleine Albright, Colin Powell, and Condi Rice all lacked wide background in the Middle East. Henry Kissinger handled the Jordan crisis of September 1970 and monitored Soviet escalation in Egypt in 1969–70 as national security advisor; Warren Christopher, Clinton's secretary in his first term, had handled the Iran hostage negotiations. And Hillary Clinton was First Lady during her husband's mediation at Camp David. Not all future secretaries will be the quick studies that Kissinger turned out to be.[29]

Chapter Notes

Introduction

1. On the alliance see Sasha Polakow-Suransky, *The Unspoken Alliance: Israel's Secret Relationship with Apartheid South Africa* (New York: Pantheon, 2010).
2. On South Africa's regional foreign and defense policies see Robert S. Jaster et al., *Changing Fortunes: War, Diplomacy and Economics in Southern Africa* (New York: Ford Foundation, 1992); Brian Pottinger, *The Imperial Presidency* (Johannesburg: Southern Book Publishers, 1988); and Gavin Cawthra, *Brutal Force: The Apartheid War Machine* (London: IDAF, 1986).
3. Oren Yiftachel, *Ethnocracy: Land and Identity Politics in Israel/Palestine* (Philadelphia: University of Pennsylvania Press, 2006).
4. Thomas G. Mitchell, *Native vs. Settler: Ethnic Conflict in Israel/Palestine, Northern Ireland and South Africa* (Westport, CT: Greenwood, 2000), pp. 15–20.
5. See Chapter Four, "South Africa Leaves Namibia," for more background.
6. Ian S. Lustick, *Unsettled States, Disputed Lands: Britain and Ireland, France and Algeria, Israel and the West Bank-Gaza* (Ithaca, NY: Cornell University Press, 1993).
7. Both the British and Irish governments gave up their constitutional claims to the territory. Belfast Agreement is the formal title preferred by unionists and Good Friday Agreement is the popular title used by nationalists and journalists.

Chapter One

1. Husseini was involved in talks along with Sari Nusseibeh with Meir Amirav from the Likud in the late 1980s. When word of the talks leaked out, Amirav was disowned and forced to resign from the party. Sari Nusseibeh, *Once upon a Country* (New York: Farrar, Straus and Giroux, 2007), pp. 252–59.

2. Most analysts use May 1977 as the start date because this is when power actually changed hands, but I prefer the previous election, as this is when the Likud first demonstrated that it was close enough to prove a threat to the Alignment. Likewise, analysts differ over when this period of two-party dominance came to an end, with most placing it in 2003, when the Left was decisively defeated in the Knesset election; however, one could also argue for 1999 or even 1996.
3. See the discussion of this in Neill Lochery, *Israeli Labour Party: In the Shadow of the Likud* (Ithaca, NY: Cornell University Press, 1997); Asher Arian, *The Second Republic: Politics in Israel* (Chatham, NJ: Chatham House, 1998), pp. 142–45.
4. Colin Shindler, *A History of Modern Israel* (Cambridge: Cambridge University Press, 2008), pp. 123–46; Ofira Seliktar, *The New Zionism* (Washington, DC: The Carnegie Endowment for International Peace, 1983).
5. Don Peretz and Gideon Doron, *The Government and Politics of Israel* (Boulder, CO: Westview, 1997), pp. 264–68.
6. Gideon Doron and Michael Harris, *Public Policy and Electoral Reform* (New York: Lexington Books, 2000), pp. 79–87; Arian, *Second Republic*, pp. 224–25.
7. Arian, *Second Republic*, p. 107, Table 5.1.
8. Ibid.
9. The two terms, *Sephardim* and *mizrakhim*, are usually used interchangeably but there are slight differences in that many Sephardim emigrated from Iberia to the rest of Europe. I use lower case for *mizrakhim* because *Mizrakhi* was the acronym for *Merkaz Rukhani* (spiritual center), the party that preceded the National Religious Party.
10. Glenn Frankel, *Beyond the Promised Land* (New York: Touchstone, 1994), pp. 142–44, 315–16; Peretz and Doron, *Government and Politics of Israel*, pp. 50–55; Arian, *Second Republic*, pp. 212–13; Yonathan Shapiro, *The Road*

to *Power* (Albany, NY: SUNY Press, 1991), p. 166; Eric Silver, *Begin: The Haunted Prophet* (New York: Random House, 1984), p. 158.

11. The three were: Marshal Henri Petain (1934–45), General Charles de Gaulle (1944–46, 1958–69), and General Marie-Pierre Koenig (1951–55). Weimar Germany also had several former generals as politicians, most notably President Hindenburg and General Erich Ludendorff. But Weimar Germany was too unstable to compare well to Israel.

12. These were the so-called Know Nothings, who founded the American Party in mid–1855.

13. For further details see Thomas G. Mitchell, *Indian Fighters Turned American Politicians* (Westwood, CT: Praeger, 2003).

14. Basil Williams, *Botha, Smuts and South Africa* (New York: Hodder and Stoughton, 1948).

15. Examples include the national flag, the national anthem, and the official status of the white languages.

16. Ned Temko, *To Win or to Die* (New York: W.W. Morrow, 1987), pp. 180–83.

17. Robert Slater, *Rabin of Israel* (New York: St. Martin's Press, 1993), pp. 353–59.

18. Roni Sofer, "Ehud Barak splits from Labor Party," ynetnews.com, Jan. 17, 2011.

19. Smuts's expected successor had died in 1948.

20. Baram, Burg, Sarid and Beilin were the most important of these defections.

21. Susan Hattis Rolef, *Political Dictionary of the State of Israel* (New York: Macmillan, 1987), pp. 18, 172; Robert Slater, *Warrior, Statesman: The Life of Moshe Dayan* (New York: St. Martin's Press, 1991), pp. 328–29.

22. There was no party to replace the United Party that was acceptable to English-speaking whites until the mid–1970s.

23. It is the thesis of Michael F. Holt, a historian who specialized in the politics of the antebellum period, that the Whigs largely died out because the old issues became less relevant when the expansion of slavery became a major issue, starting in 1848. See Michael F. Holt, *The Rise and Fall of the American Whig Party* (New York: Oxford University Press, 2003).

24. Thomas G. Mitchell, *When Peace Fails: Lessons from Belfast for the Middle East* (Jefferson, NC: McFarland, 2010), and Michael Kerr, *Transforming Unionism: David Trimble and the 2005 General Election* (Portland, OR: Irish Academic Press, 2006).

25. The Whigs nominated the American Party presidential nominee Millard Fillmore as their own nominee after he had already been nominated. The year 1852 marked the last presidential election in which the Whigs ran an independent nominee.

26. Peres was running the defense ministry at age 29 under David Ben-Gurion and was responsible for Israel's arms purchases from Europe in the 1950s and the creation of Israel's military nuclear effort in the late 1950s. Arens was a professional aeronautical engineer who played a major role in Israel's fledgling aircraft industry.

27. Labor had the same number of seats after the 2003 and 2006 elections, but in general the formula is correct.

28. Mark Rosenblum, "After Rabin: The malaise of the Israeli Zionist Left," in Robert O. Freedman, ed., *Contemporary Israel* (Boulder, CO: Westview Press, 2009), p. 52.

29. Ofir Abu, Fany Yuval and Guy Ben-Porat, "'All that is Left': The demise of the Zionist Left parties, 1992–2009," in Asher Arian and Michal Shamir, eds., *The Elections in Israel 2009* (New Brunswick, NJ: Transaction, 2011), pp. 41–68.

30. These were Shinu,i led by Amnon Rubinstein, which began as a protest movement after the Yom Kippur War of 1973, and the group of former generals and technocrats organized around Yigael Yadin. Yadin retired from politics in 1981 a broken man. Arian, *Second Republic*, pp. 133–37.

31. "Centre Party," *Wikipedia,* accessed June 25, 2012.

32. Gregory S. Mahler, *Politics and Government in Israel* (New York: Rowman and Littlefield, 2004), p. 181; "Shinui," *Jewish Virtual Library,* accessed June 25, 2012; "Shinui leader resigns in Israel," *BBC News Online,* Jan. 25, 2006.

33. Giora Goldberg, "Kadima goes back: The limited power of vagueness," in Shmuel Sandler, Manfred Gerstenfeld, and Hillel Frisch, eds., *Israel at the Polls, 2009* (New York: Routledge, 2011), pp. 31–50.

34. Journalist Robert Slater coined the term and applied it to Dayan and Rabin; it was later applied to Sharon as well.

35. Itamar Rabinovich, *The Lingering Conflict* (Washington, DC: The Brookings Institution, 2011), pp. 177–80.

36. Goldberg, "Kadima goes back," pp. 35–36.

37. Ibid., p. 41.

38. Einat Gedalya, Hanna Hertzog and Michal Shamir, "Tzip(p)ing through the elections: Gender in the 2009 elections," in Arian and Shamir, *The Elections in Israel,* pp. 165–89.

39. Akiva Eldar, "Israel's new politics and the fate of Palestine," *National Journal,* Jul.–Aug. 2012; Shmuel Sandler and Hillel Frisch, "The 2009 Knesset elections: A foreign policy perspective," in Sandler, Gerstenfeld, and Frisch, *Israel at the Polls,* pp. 142–64.

40. Amy Teibel, "Mofaz beats Livni to head of Israel's Kadima Party," *Yahoo News Online,* Mar. 27, 2012.

41. Ibid.

42. Judi Rudoren, "Leader of Israel's Centrist party Kadima agrees to join Netanyahu's coalition," *New York Times,* May 7, 2012.

43. Orly Halpern, "No future for Kadima, says Livni," *The Daily Beast: Open Zion,* June 14, 2012; Attila Somfalvi, "Haim Ramon to form new political party," *Ynetnews.com,* July 3, 2012; Moran Azulay, "Kadima MKs mull quitting the party," *Ynet,* Oct. 17, 2012. Azulay reported that discussions had been held between groups of Kadima MKs and Likud and Labor.

44. Abraham Diskin, "The Likud: The struggle for the centre," in Sandler, Gerstenfeld, and Frisch, *Israel at the Polls,* pp. 51–68.

45. These parties all resigned from the coalition just as Barak was departing for the U.S. to meet with Arafat and Clinton at Camp David in July 2000.

46. Ian Lustick, *Unsettled States, Disputed Lands: Britain and Ireland, France and Algeria, Israel and the West Bank-Gaza* (Ithaca, NY: Cornell University Press, 1993), pp. 257–58.

47. Ibid., pp. 242, 290–91.

48. Arian, *Second Republic,* pp. 118–27, 130; Colin Shindler, *The Land beyond Promise: Israel, Likud and the Zionist Dream* (New York: I.B. Tauris, 2002), pp. 107–8, 279; Aaron D. Rosenbaum, "Tehiya as a permanent nationalist phenomenon," in Gregory S. Mahler, *Israel after Begin* (Albany: State University of New York Press, 1990), pp. 71–90; Akiva Eldar and Idath Zerfal, *Lords of the Land* (New York: Nation Books, 2009).

49. Hendrik Spruyt, *Ending Empire: Contested Sovereignty and Territorial Partition* (Ithaca, NY: Cornell University Press, 2005).

50. Ibid., pp. 252–53, 266–68.

51. Mahler, *Politics and Government,* p. 56; Vladimir Ze'ev Khanin, "Israel's Russian Parties," in Freedman, *Contemporary Israel,* pp. 97–114.

52. Nadav G. Shelef, *Evolving Nationalism* (Ithaca, NY: Cornell University Press, 2010), pp. 181–88.

53. Glenn Frankel, *Beyond the Promised Land* (New York: Touchstone, 1996), pp. 152, 154–57.

54. Etta Bick, "The Shas phenomenon and religious parties in the 1999 election," in Daniel J. Elazar and Ben Mollov, eds., *Israel at the Polls, 1999* (New York: Routledge, 2001), pp. 55–100.

Chapter Two

1. Eran Kaplan, *The Jewish Radical Right* (Madison: University of Wisconsin Press, 2005), p. 5; Colin Shindler, *The Triumph of Military Zionism* (New York: I.B. Tauris, 2010) p. 11.

2. Kaplan, *The Jewish Radical Right,* pp. 5, 8; Joseph B. Schechtman, *Fighter and Prophet: The Vladimir Jabotinsky Story, The Last Years* (New York: Thomas Yoseloff, 1961), pp. 125–26.

3. Howard M. Sachar, *A History of Israel from the Rise of Zionism to Our Time* (New York: Alfred Knopf, 1996), p. 187; Susan Hattis Rolef, ed., *Political Dictionary of the State of Israel* (Jerusalem: Jerusalem Publishing House, 1987), p. 61; Sasson Sofer, *Begin: An Anatomy of Leadership* (New York: Basil Blackwell, 1988), p. 61.

4. Kaplan, *The Jewish Radical Right,* pp. 24, 33–35.

5. Ibid., pp. 14–20; Shindler, *The Triumph of Military Zionism,* pp. 143–61, on the Maximalists.

6. Schechtman, *Fighter and Prophet,* pp. 304, 331; Shindler, *The Triumph of Military Zionism,* p. 184.

7. Avi Shlaim, *The Iron Wall: Israel and the Arab World* (New York: W.W. Norton, 2001), pp. 12–16, 598–99.

8. Schechtman, *Fighter and Prophet,* p. 447.

9. Ibid., p. 307.

10. Ibid., pp. 304, 314, 321–22.

11. Ibid., pp. 452, 470–71; Shindler, *The Triumph of Military Zionism,* p. 203. The Education Ministry has its teachers teach about all the Zionists in pre-state Palestine who were hanged by the British.

12. Shindler, *The Triumph of Military Zionism,* pp. 206–10; Amos Perlmutter, *The Life and Times of Menachem Begin* (Garden City, NY: Doubleday, 1987), pp. 85–89; Ned Temko, *To Win or to Die* (New York: William Morrow, 1987), pp. 46–49; Schechtman, *Fighter and Prophet,* p. 381.

13. Shindler, *The Triumph of Military Zionism,* pp. 213, 218.

14. Perlmutter, *The Life and Times of Menachem Begin,* pp. 95–98.

15. Ibid., pp. 99–127.

16. Ibid., pp. 128–91, for a scholarly treatment of the Revolt. For first-person accounts from an Etzel perspective, see Menachem Begin, *The Revolt* (Tel Aviv: Steimatzky's, 1983) and Shmuel Katz, *Days of Fire* (Tel Aviv: Steimatzky's, 1968). On Begin's propaganda function, see Sasson Sofer, *Begin: An Anatomy of Leadership* (New York: Basil Blackwell, 1988), p. 70.

17. Perlmutter, *The Life and Times of Menachem Begin*, pp. 211–17; Temko, *To Win or to Die*, pp. 111–14.

18. Perlmutter, *The Life and Times of Menachem Begin*, pp. 218–34; Temko, *To Win or to Die*, pp. 117–23; Israel Eldad, *The First Tithe* (Tel Aviv: The Jabotinsky Institute, 2008), pp. 387–400.

19. Perlmutter, *The Life and Times of Menachem Begin*, pp. 240–48; Yonathan Shapiro, *The Road to Power: Herut Party in Israel* (Albany: SUNY Press, 1991), p. 73.

20. Shapiro, *The Road to Power*, pp. 106–9.

21. Perlmutter, *The Life and Times of Menachem Begin*, pp. 244–47; Temko, *To Win or to Die*, pp. 129–34.

22. Peter Y. Medding, *The Founding of Israeli Democracy, 1948–1967* (New York: Oxford University Press, 1990), pp. 63–70.

23. Colin Shindler, *The Land beyond Promise: Israel, Likud and the Zionist Dream* (New York: I.B. Tauris, 2002), pp. 55–61.

24. Temko, *To Win or to Die*, pp. 167–68; Perlmutter, *The Life and Times of Menachem Begin*, pp. 277–79; Medding, *The Founding of Israeli Democracy*, pp. 185–86, 193–96.

25. Temko, *To Win or to Die*, pp. 169–72; Perlmutter, *The Life and Times of Menachem Begin*, pp. 280–88; Medding, *The Founding of Israeli Democracy*, pp. 226–27. Asher Arian is an exception in dating the founding of the Second Republic to 1993 with the start of the Oslo process: Asher Arian, *The Second Republic: Politics in Israel* (Chatham, NJ: Chatham House, 1998), p. 1.

26. Perlmutter, *The Life and Times of Menachem Begin*, pp. 288–93.

27. Temko, *To Win or to Die*, pp. 179–83.

28. Ibid., pp. 184–87; Ariel Sharon, *Warrior* (New York: Simon & Schuster, 2001), pp. 274–86.

29. Sharon, *Warrior*, p. 341.

30. Rolef, *Political Dictionary of the State of Israel*, pp. 119, 187.

31. Temko, *To Win or to Die*, pp. 193–97; Perlmutter, *The Life and Times of Menachem Begin*, pp. 313–18; Sharon, *Warrior*, pp. 348–54; Shindler, *The Land*, pp. 78–82; Ilan Peleg,

Begin's Foreign Policy, 1977–1983: Israel Moves to the Right (Westport, CT: Greenwood, 1987), pp. 44–45.

32. Shindler, *The Land*, pp. 83–87; Perlmutter, *The Life and Times of Menachem Begin*, pp. 319–27.

33. Peleg, *Begin's Foreign Policy*, pp. 148–56, 192–95; Perlmutter, *The Life and Times of Menachem Begin*, pp. 372–76.

34. Sofer, *Begin*, pp. 81–82; 234–36; Temko, *To Win or to Die*, pp. 287–90.

35. Peleg, *Begin's Foreign Policy*, p. 53. Peleg is an Israeli who lives in the U.S. Shindler is a British Jew.

36. Ibid., p. 54.

37. For his background see his memoir, Yizhak Shamir, *Summing Up* (Boston: Little Brown, 1994); Shindler, *The Land*, pp. 174–86; and Glenn Frankel, *Beyond the Promised Land* (New York: Touchstone, 1996), pp. 26–39.

38. Arian, *Second Republic*, p. 126.

39. Frankel, *Beyond the Promised Land*, pp. 37–38; Michael Bar-Zohar, *Shimon Peres* (New York: Random House, 2007), pp. 401–13; Ziva Flamhaft, *Israel on the Road to Peace* (Boulder, CO: Westview Press, 1996), pp. 45–92.

40. Flamhaft, *Israel on the Road to Peace*, pp. 163–66.

41. Ibid., p. 170.

42. Shindler, *The Land*, p. 274; Perlmutter, *The Life and Times of Menachem Begin*, p. 355; Nir Hefez and Gadi Bloom, *Ariel Sharon: A Life* (New York: Random House, 2006), pp. 264–66.

43. Hefez and Bloom, *Ariel Sharon*, p. 265; Giora Goldberg, "The Likud: Moving toward the Center," in Daniel J. Elazar and Shmuel Sandler, *Who's the Boss in Israel* (Detroit, MI: Wayne State Univ. Press, 1992), pp. 49–51.

44. Hefez and Bloom, *Ariel Sharon*, p. 302.

45. Richard Stengel, "King Bibi," *Time*, May 28, 2012, pp. 35–36.

46. Roger Friedland and Richard Hecht, *To Rule Jerusalem* (Berkeley: University of California Press, 2000), p. 512.

47. Paul McGeough, *Kill Khalid* (New York: The New Press, 2009), pp. 132–50.

48. Dennis Ross, *The Missing Peace* (New York: Farrar, Straus and Giroux, 2005,) pp. 256–494.

49. Ibid., pp. 293–322.

50. Ibid., pp. 415–94; Hefez and Bloom, *Ariel Sharon*, pp. 326–28.

51. Hefez and Bloom, *Ariel Sharon*, p. 328.

52. Ibid., pp. 354–55.

53. Ibid., pp. 19–25; Sharon, *Warrior*, p. 25; Gilad Sharon, *Sharon: The Life of a Leader* (New

York: Harper, 2011), p. 28. Sharon claims that his father was a Mapainik, but his father sided with the Revisionists during the Arlozoroff murder trial in 1934 and was opposed to the *saison* conducted by the Palmakh/Hagana against the Jewish undergrounds in 1944. Plus the Sharon and Begin families had a close relationship from the coming of Zionism in their hometown of Brest, Belarus (then in the Russian Empire and then Poland). See Temko, *To Win or to Die,* p. 185. Sharon's grandmother had midwifed Begin's birth. Shindler, *The Land,* p. 282, on Sharon's Mapai membership.

54. Sharon, *Sharon,* pp. 345–46; Hefez and Bloom, *Ariel Sharon,* pp. 344–47.

55. His kitchen cabinet was known in English as the septet or in Hebrew as the *shevia* for the number of its members.

56. Hefez and Bloom, *Ariel Sharon,* pp. 465–66.

57. For Clinton that constituency was Irish-Americans, not American Jews.

58. On the speech, see James Mann, *The Obamians* (New York: Viking, 2012), pp. 142–48.

59. Steven Lee Myers, "Amid Impasse in Peace Negotiations, America's Chief Middle East Envoy Resigns," *New York Times* May 13, 2011; Josef Federman, "Benjamin Netanyahu: No Settlement Freeze," *Huffington Post,* Sept. 27, 2011; Mann, *The Obamians,* p. 324; Scott Wilson, "Where Obama Failed on Forging Peace in the Middle East," *Washington Post,* July 14, 2012 .

60. Stengel, "King Bibi."

61. Marcia Freedman, a former Israeli MK and the first president of Brit Tzedek veShalom, was fond of saying that Sharon was willing to give the Palestinians a state "with 42 percent of the West Bank, not 41 percent and not 43 percent."

62. Israel is today defined as a "Jewish democratic state." Liberal Zionists want to see it redefined as "a Jewish state and a state of all its citizens." Arabs want to see it redefined simply as a state of all its citizens.

Chapter Three

1. Sasson Sofer, *Begin: An Anatomy of Leadership* (New York: Basil Blackwell, 1988), pp. 98–99, 104, 107–08, 110.

2. Ibid., pp. 111–12, 115.

3. Ibid., p. 114.

4. Ibid., p. 125.

5. Ibid., pp. 124, 129.

6. Ibid., pp. 126–27, 128.

7. "Rabat Summit," *Wikipedia,* accessed August 7, 2010.

8. Ned Temko, *To Win or to Die* (New York: W.W. Morrow, 1987), pp. 199–200.

9. Sofer, *Begin,* p. 134.

10. Boutros Boutros-Ghali, *Egypt's Road to Jerusalem* (New York: Random House, 1997), pp. 133–34, 225–26.

11. *Plugot Makhatz,* or strike, companies were the full-time components of the mainstream Zionist militia, the Hagana, and provided the leading offensive component to the Israeli army in 1948. They were commanded by Yigal Allon and his deputy, Yitzhak Rabin. Dayan helped to found the Palmakh along with Yigal Allon, but shortly later was forced out when he lost his eye in the invasion of Vichy Syria in 1941.

12. Amos Perlmutter, *Israel: The Partitioned State* (New York: Charles Scribners' Sons, 1985), pp. 205, 207–8, 217.

13. On Weizman, see Ezer Weizman, *The Battle for Peace* (New York: Bantam, 1981).

14. Aaron David Miller, *The Much Too Promised Land* (New York: Bantam, 2008), p. 170.

15. William Quandt, *Peace Process, Revised Edition* (Berkeley: University of California Press, 2001), pp. 188–90.

16. Ibid., p. 191; Miller, *The Much Too Promised Land,* pp. 171–72; Silver, *Begin,* pp. 170–72.

17. Silver, *Begin,* pp. 175–76; Sofer, *Begin,* p. 182.

18. Sofer, *Begin,* pp. 132–35.

19. Amos Perlmutter, *The Life and Times of Menachem Begin* (New York: Doubleday, 1987), pp. 341–42; Temko, *To Win or to Die,* pp. 216, 218; Silver, *Begin,* p. 178; Weizman, *The Battle for Peace,* pp. 123–24.

20. David Reynolds, *Summits* (New York: Basic Books, 2007), pp. 289, 291.

21. Quandt, *Peace Process,* pp. 194–97.

22. Sofer, *Begin,* p. 188; Moshe Dayan, *Breakthrough* (New York: Alfred Knopf, 1981), p. 140; Weizman, *The Battle for Peace,* pp. 338–39.

23. Ibid., p. 189; Miller, *The Much Too Promised Land,* pp. 173–74; Quandt, *Peace Process,* p. 197.

24. Reynolds, *Summits,* pp. 305, 307, 309, 337.

25. Ibid., pp. 305, 316.

26. Boutros-Ghali, *Egypt's Road,* pp. 46, 136, 139–40, 143.

27. Reynolds, *Summits,* pp. 303, 304.

28. Ibid., pp. 314, 316, 339–40. Sadat had wanted to become an actor before becoming an officer. Begin graduated from law school in Warsaw.
29. Quandt, *Peace Process*, pp. 197–203; Miller, *The Much Too Promised Land*, pp. 174–79; Silver, *Begin*, p. 192; Temko, *To Win or to Die*, pp. 227–28; Reynolds, *Summits*, p. 318. Madeline Albright wrote in her memoirs that Senator Edmund Muskie's Polish was better than Brzezinski's Polish. She worked for both of them.
30. Silver, *Begin*, pp. 196–98; Reynolds, *Summits*, p. 329; Quandt, *Peace Process*, p. 201.
31. Boutro-Ghali, *Egypt's Road*, pp. 43, 144, 163.
32. Sofer, *Begin*, p. l96; Quandt, *Peace Process*, p. 203; Reynolds, *Summits*, pp. 330, 335.
33. Sofer, *Begin*, p. 195; Temko, *To Win or to Die*, pp. 233–34; Perlmutter, *The Life and Times of Menachem Begin*, pp. 355–56; Reynolds, *Summits*, p. 335. Arens voted against and Shamir abstained.
34. Quandt, *Peace Process*, pp. 209–237; Miller, *The Much Too Promised Land*, pp. 179–84, for a detailed assessment of the issues involved. Reynolds, *Summits*, p. 341; Dayan, *Breakthrough*, p. 303; Weizman, *The Battle for Peace*, p. 381.
35. Boutros-Ghali, *Egypt's Road*, pp. 160, 166–67, 176, 178, 180, 190; Dayan, *Breakthrough*, p. 173.
36. Boutros-Ghali, *Egypt's Road*, pp. 195–96, 199, 218.
37. Ibid., pp. 200, 230, 237, 239.
38. Shibley Telhami, *Power and Leadership in International Bargaining* (New York: Columbia University Press, 1990), pp. 164–65, 170–72, 176–80, 182. For confirmation of his points, see Boutros-Ghali, *Egypt's Road*, pp. 165, 190; Dayan, *Breakthrough*, p. 154.
39. "Moshe Feiglin," *Wikipedia*, accessed August 9, 2010; Reynolds, *Summits*, p. 321.
40. He was involved in the assassination of the Egyptian prime minister under the monarchy in the late 1940s.
41. The most authoritative Sharon biographies are his own autobiography, *Warrior* (New York: Simon and Schuster, 1989), and for his later political career after 1988, and by his son Gilad Sharon, *The Life of a Leader* (New York: HarperCollins, 2011). From what Gilad writes of his paternal grandparents, they were neither Revisionists nor socialists.
42. Ibid., p. 221.
43. Ibid., pp. 209–13; Nir Hefez and Gadi Bloom, *Ariel Sharon: A Life* (New York: Ran-

dom House, 2006), p. 430; Mark Matthews, *Lost Years: Bush, Sharon and Failure in the Middle East* (New York: Nation Books, 2007), pp. 341–43; Freddy Eytan, *Sharon: A Life in Times of Turmoil* (Paris: Studio 9, 2006), p. 143.
44. This author wrote his doctoral dissertation partially on the Indaba. See Thomas G. Mitchell, *Black Faces, White Heads: Internal Settlements in Southern Africa* (doctoral dissertation, Los Angeles: University of Southern California, 1990).
45. Hefez and Bloom, *Ariel Sharon*, pp. 435–36.
46. Eytan, *Sharon*, pp. 149–50.
47. Ibid., p. 151; Hefez and Bloom, *Ariel Sharon*, p. 441.
48. Eytan, *Sharon*, pp. 152–54.
49. Ibid., p. 156; Charles Enderlin, *The Lost Years: Radical Islam, Intifada, and Wars in the Middle East 2001–2006* (New York: Other Press, 2007), pp. 230–31, 237.
50. Enderlin, *The Lost Years*, p. 244; Uri Dan, *Ariel Sharon: An Intimate Portrait* (New York: Palgrave Macmillan, 2006), pp. 234, 240–41, 243, 246. The date of the interview is not given by Dan, but September 2004 is listed in the chapter title.
51. Dan, *Ariel Sharon*, p. 240.
52. The Hebrew for the United Nations is *uumot meuhadot*, or *uum* for short.
53. Hefez and Bloom, *Ariel Sharon*, pp. 400–12, 483, for a good summary of the scandals.
54. Sharon was famous for eating shellfish and other foods forbidden by Jewish dietary law.
55. Enderlin, *The Lost Years*, pp. 152–53.
56. Gilad Sharon, *Sharon*, pp. 5–45; he claimed authorship of the plan in a memo he wrote for his father.
57. Hefez and Bloom, *Ariel Sharon*, pp. 447–48.
58. Glenn Kessler, *Confidante: Condoleeza Rice and the Bush Legacy* (New York: St. Martin's Press, 2007), p. 126.
59. Ibid., p. 446.
60. Eytan, *Ariel Sharon*, p. 311, see pp. 310–12 for the text of the full letter; Enderlin, *The Lost Years*, p. 235.
61. Eytan, *Ariel Sharon*, p. 159; Hefez and Bloom, *Ariel Sharon*, pp. 449–50; Enderlin, *The Lost Years*, p. 238.
62. Hefez and Bloom, *Ariel Sharon*, p. 451; Enderlin, *The Lost Years*, p. 240; Eytan, *Ariel Sharon*, p. 160.
63. Enderlin, *The Lost Years*, pp. 241–42.
64. Hefez and Bloom, *Ariel Sharon*, pp.

454–55; Matthews, *Lost Years*, p. 371; Eytan, *Ariel Sharon*, pp. 160–61.

65. Hefez and Bloom, *Ariel Sharon*, pp. 455, 459–60; Eytan, *Ariel Sharon*, pp. 161–62; Enderlin, *The Lost Years*, pp. 246–50. In 2012 Arafat's widow produced clothes that she claimed were his at the time of his death and on which were found strong traces of polonium. The providence of the clothes were never established and the readings seemed quite strong for over seven years after the event, but her claims fit into the Palestinian narrative and so were readily believed.

66. Hefez and Bloom, *Ariel Sharon*, pp. 461–62; Eytan, *Ariel Sharon*, p. 163; Enderlin, *The Lost Years*, p. 251.

67. Hefez and Bloom, *Ariel Sharon*, p. 463; Enderlin, *The Lost Years*, p. 254.

68. Hefez and Bloom, *Ariel Sharon*, pp. 463–64.

69. Matthews, *Lost Years*, pp. 371–72.

70. Ibid., pp. 464–65; Eytan, *Ariel Sharon*, pp. 163, 166.

71. Enderlin, *The Lost Years*, pp. 256, 259–60.

72. Matthews, *Lost Years*, p. 381; Enderlin, *The Lost Years*, p. 264.

73. Matthews, *Lost Years*, pp. 381–84.

74. Enderlin, *The Lost Years*, pp. 262–63.

75. Ibid., pp. 264–65; Hefez and Bloom, *Ariel Sharon*, p. 467.

76. Matthews, *Lost Years*, p. 388; Enderlin, *The Lost Years*, pp. 266, 285; Eytan, *Ariel Sharon*, p. 280.

77. Matthews, *Lost Years*, pp. 386–87; Dan, *Ariel Sharon*, pp. 272–73, Hefez and Bloom, *Ariel Sharon*, p. 469.

78. See Hefez and Bloom, *Ariel Sharon*, pp. 471–85; Eytan, *Ariel Sharon*, pp. 200–247; and Dan, *Ariel Sharon*, pp. 274–81, on the creation of Kadima and Sharon's strokes and medical treatment. Kessler, op. cit., p. 134.

79. Matthews, *Lost Years*, p. 386.

80. Itamar Rabinovich, *The Lingering Conflict* (Washington, DC: The Brookings Institution, 2011), p. 162.

81. Kessler, op. cit., pp. 134–35.

82. Many of these settlers formed the Third Way party for the 1996 election and then joined the Likud as a faction.

Chapter Four

1. Peter Katjavivi, *A History of Resistance in Namibia* (London and Paris: James Currey/OAU/UNESCO, 1988), p. 10.

2. http://www.history.com/this-day-in-history/germans-surrender-southwest-africa-to-union-of-south-africa, accessed July 2, 2012.

3. Theresa Papenfus, *Pik Botha and His Times* (Pretoria: Litera, 2010), pp. 64, 69.

4. Ibid., p. 69.

5. Andre du Pisani, *SWA/Namibia: The Politics of Continuity and Change* (Johannesburg: Jonathan Ball, 1985), pp. 334–35, and an interview with the author in Johannesburg in December 1988.

6. Papenfus, , *Pik Botha and His Times*, pp. 83, 89, 114, 124.

7. Ibid., p. 509, claims 1974; http://www.sahistory.org.za/places/namibia gives the 1973 date.

8. For South African versions of the invasion, see Hilton Hamann, *Days of the Generals* (Cape Town: Zebra Press, 2006), pp. 21–45; Magnus Malan, *My Life with the South African Defence Force* (Pretoria: Protea, 2006), pp. 133, 139–40.

9. Brian Pottinger, *The Imperial Presidency: P.W. Botha, the first 10 years* (Johannesburg: Southern Book Publishers, 1988), pp. 14, 24–25.

10. Ibid., pp. 3–6, 49–77, 201–3; Robert M. Price, *The Apartheid State in Crisis: Political Transformation in South Africa, 1975–1990* (New York: Oxford University Press, 1991), pp. 101–46; Malan, *My Life with the South African Defence Force*, p. 231.

11. See Piet Nortje, *32 Battalion* (Cape Town: Zebra, 2004), for an overview of the Angolan ethnic groups and the process by which Chipenda's men became part of the SADF.

12. Papenfus, *Pik Botha and His Times*, p. 508; Piero Gleijeses, "From Cassinga to New York: The Struggle for the Independence of Namibia," pp. 201–25 in Sue Onslow, ed., *The Cold War in Southern Africa* (New York: Routledge, 2009,) pp. 207–8.

13. Papenfus, *Pik Botha and His Times*, pp. 511–12.

14. Herbert Weiland and Matthew Braham, eds., *The Namibian Peace Process: Implications and Lessons for the Future* (Freiburg, Germany: Arnold Bergstrasser Institute, 1994), pp. 13–14, 18, 45.

15. Ibid., pp. 13, 46, 183.

16. Du Pisani, *SWA/Namibia*, pp. 334–35; Weiland and Braham, *The Namibian Peace Process*, p. 42.

17. Weiland and Braham, *The Namibian Peace Process*, pp. 27, 30, 34–36.

18. Ibid., p. 24; Chester A. Crocker, *High Noon in Southern Africa: Making Peace in a*

Rough Neighborhood (New York: W.W. Norton, 1992), pp. 64–70.

19. Pottinger, *The Imperial Presidency*, pp. 133–44, 227–43; Price, *The Apartheid State in Crisis*, pp. 192–217; Papenfus lists Pik Botha as the head of the *verligte* camp in 1977 *Pik Botha and His Times*, p. 519.

20. On MK's offensive, see Stephen Davis, *Apartheid's Rebels* (New Haven: Yale University Press, 1987). For legal reasons the UDF never specifically and formally aligned itself to the ANC as such, but it made general pronouncements of support for the liberation movements, and it later announced its support of the 1956 Freedom Charter, which clearly aligned it with the ANC rather than the rival PAC. COSATU also swore fealty to the Freedom Charter. In 1988 academics and journalists began to refer to "the mass democratic movement," meaning the ANC/UDF/COSATU, in the way that Irish Republicans referred to the Republican Movement to mean Sinn Fein/IRA.

21. Geldenhuys, *At the Front*, p. 298. Former Rhodesians and mercenaries who had fought in both Rhodesia and Namibia compared PLAN guerrillas to ZIPRA rather than to ZANLA.

22. Gleijeses, "From Cassinga to New York," p. 201; Malan, *My Life with the South African Defence Force*, p. 256.

23. Pottinger, *The Imperial Presidency*, pp. 221–24.

24. David Welsh, *The Rise and Fall of Apartheid* (Johannesburg: Jonathan Ball, 2009), pp. 292–304.

25. George P. Schultz, *Turmoil and Triumph* (New York: Charles Scribner & Sons, 1993), p. 1122.

26. Malan, *My Life with the South African Defence Force*, pp. 261–63.

27. Ibid., pp. 265–66; Papenfus, *Pik Both and His Times*, p.556; Hamann, *Days of the Generals*, pp. 85–86.

28. Geldenhuys, *At the Front*, pp. 228–29; Piet Nortje, *32 Battalion* (Cape Town: Zebra, 2004), p. 236; Malan, *My Life with the South African Defence Force*, p. 267; Heitman, *War in Angola*, p. 266.

29. Malan, *My Life with the South African Defence Force*, pp. 270–72; Fred Bridgland, *The War for Africa: Twelve Months That Transformed a Continent* (Gibraltar: Ashanti, 1990), pp. 257, 311–12, 315; Clive Holt, *At Thy Call We Did Not Falter* (Cape Town: Zebra, 2005), p. 93.

30. Dick Lord, *From Fledging to Eagle* (Johannesburg: 30 Degrees South, 2008), pp. 373, 380, 394–404; 438–39; 441–42, 498–99. Lord

doesn't even have an entry for the Cheetah in the index of this book because they were never used over Angola. "Cheetah," *Wikipedia*, accessed April 3, 2012.

31. Bridgland, *The War for Africa*, p. 262; Geldenhuys, *At the Front*, p. 164; Heitman, *War in Angola*, p. 343.

32. Heitman, *War in Angola*, p. 281; Bridgland, *The War for Africa*, pp. 331, 368.

33. Nortje, *32 Battalion*, back flap. Nortje gives no source for his contention that the capture of Cuito Cuanavale was a South African war aim. The books consulted were: Geldenhuys, *At the Front*; Malan, *My Life with the South African Defence Force*; Bridgeland, *The War for Africa*; Heitman, *War in Angola*; Holt, *At Thy Call They Did not Falter*; Hamann, *Days of the Generals*; Onslow, *Cold War in Southern Africa*; Willem Steenkemp, *South Africa's Border War, 1966–1989* (Gibraltar: Ashanti, 1989); Tim Ransden, *Border-Line Insanity* (Victoria, BC, Canada: Trafford, 2007). Holt and Trafford were mildly critical of the South African war effort. Piero Gleijeses was very critical. The rest were supportive.

34. Bridgland, *The War for Africa*, p. 244; Holt, *At Thy Call They Did Not Falter*, p. 108; Hamann, *Days of the Generals*, p. 97.

35. Heitman, *War in Angola*, p. 281.

36. The Ratel was a family of Infantry Fighting Vehicles (IFVs) that came in several different versions. The basic version was equipped with a 20mm main gun. One version mounted a mortar. And one version carried a turret from the Eland (Panhard) armored car with its 90mm main gun. Another mounted antitank missiles.

37. The 1975–76 Angolan operation did not really involve the SAAF or the SAN. Geldenhuys, *At the Front*, pp. 183, 235–36; Malan, *My Life with the South African Defence Force*, p. 278, Bridgland, *The War for Africa*, p. 282; Heitman, *War in Angola*, p. 345.

38. Malan, *My Life with the South African Defence Force*, p. 283; Holt, *At Thy Call They Did Not Falter*, p. 109; Steenkemp, *South Africa's Border War*, p. 158; Geldenhuys, *At the Front*, p. 240.

39. Steenkemp, *South Africa's Border War*, p. 155.

40. Ramsden, *Border Line Insanity*, pp. 359, 362; Papenfus, *Pik Botha and His Times*, p. 578.

41. Papenfus, *Pik Botha and His Times*, p. 578; Geldenhuys, *At the Front*, pp. 272–73.

42. Gleijeses, "From Cassinga to New York," p. 216; Geldenhuys, *At the Front*, pp. 277–79.

43. Papenfus *Pik Botha and His Times,* pp. 579–80, 582; Shultz, *Turmoil and Triumph,* pp. 1128–29.
44. Robert S. Jaster et al., *Changing Fortunes: War, Diplomacy and Economics in Southern Africa* (New York: Ford Foundation, 1992), pp. 58–59.
45. Robert S. Jaster, *South Africa in Namibia: The Botha Strategy* (Lanham, MD: University Press of America, 1985), pp. 69–74, 110–13.
46. Weiland and Braham, *The Namibian Peace Process,* p. 56.
47. Price, *the Apartheid State in Crisis,* pp. 277–78; Jaster et al., *Changing Fortunes,* pp. 13, Pottinger, *The Imperial Presidency,* p. 201; R.W. Johnson, *South Africa: The First Man, The Last Nation* (London: Phoenix, 2004), pp. 194–95; Welsh, *The Rise and Fall of Apartheid,* pp. 348, 371; Ken Flower, *Serving Secretly* (Alberton, Republic of South Africa: Galago, 1987), pp. 155–59; Martin Meredith, *The Past Is Another Country: Rhodesia: UDI to Zimbabwe* (London: Pan, 1980), pp. 127, 145–46, 194–95. Hendrik Verwoerd, the South African prime minister at the time of Rhodesian UDI, had warned Ian Smith not to take the step; Smith had ignored the warning.

Chapter Five

1. Elaine A. Byrne, *Political Corruption in Ireland, 1922–2010* (New York: Manchester University Press, 2012); see the early chapters for corruption; see also before Charles Haughey, p. 221, on voters; Fintan O'Toole, *Ship of Fools* (New York: Public Affairs, 2010), pp. 35, 37.
2. Byrne, *Political Corruption in Ireland,* pp. 89–90; Stephen Collins, *The Power Game: Ireland under Fianna Fail* (Dublin: O'Brien Press, 2001), pp. 39–41.
3. Collins, *The Power Game,* pp. 130–33; Byrne, *Political Corruption in Ireland,* pp. 235–36.
4. Colm Keena, *Haughey's Millions* (Dublin: Gill and Macmillan, 2001), pp. 36–37, 43–44, 46–49, 72, 76; 274; O'Toole, *Ship of Fools,* pp. 29–30; Byrne, *Political Corruption in Ireland,* pp. 146.
5. Keena, *Haughey's Millions,* pp. 104, 144, 148–49, 151, 161,
6. Ibid., pp. 164, 167–68.
7. Ibid., pp. 178, 181, 183–84, 186, 190; O'Toole, *Ship of Fools,* p. 29.
8. Keena, *Haughey's Millions,* pp. 205, 211.
9. Ibid., pp. 216–17.

10. Ibid., pp. 245–48; 262, 282, 292; Byrne, *Political Corruption in Ireland,* p. 158.
11. Byrne, *Political Corruption in Ireland,* pp. 108–18, on the Beef Tribunal.
12. Collins, *The Power Game,* pp. 246–48, 269–72; Ruairi Quinn, *Straight Left: A Journey in Politics* (Dublin: HodderHeadline, 2005) pp. 288, 310; Albert Reynolds, *My Autobiography* (London: Transworld Ireland, 2009) pp. 228–29. Reynolds claims that the company was then controlled by his son while he was in government, and so he had no knowledge of the interest of the Masri family in investing in his company.
13. Collins, *The Power Game,* pp. 296–99, for background on Ahern; Byrne, *Political Corruption in Ireland,* pp. 174, 185; Colm Keena, *Bertie: Power and Money* (Dublin: Gill and Macmillan, 2011) p. 3.
14. Keena, *Bertie,* pp. 99; Michael Clifford and Shane Coleman, *Bertie Ahern and the Drumcondra Mafia* (Dublin: Hachette, 2009) pp. 117, 125, 127, 153, 192, 194,238.
15. Clifford and Coleman, *Bertie Ahern and the Drumcondra Mafia,* pp. 156, 193, 247, 251. Friends of his would raise money to pay for his separation settlement and to pay for his apartment.
16. Ibid., pp. 255–65 on Burke, pp. 265–66, 276, 278–79. Dermot Ahern later became the Irish foreign minister.
17. Keena, *Bertie,* pp. 106, 138, 154; O'Toole, *Ship of Fools,* pp. 75, 79.
18. Clifford and Coleman, *Bertie Ahern and the Drumcondra Mafia,* pp. 300–301, 303, 310–11.
19. Ibid., pp. 212, 324–25, 344, 358–59, 363, 369; Keena, *Bertie,* p. 67.
20. Byrne, *Political Corruption in Ireland,* pp. 103, 193, 205, 211;
21. Ibid., pp. 225–26; O'Toole, *Ship of Fools,* p. 183.
22. Byrne, *Political Corruption in Ireland,* pp. 220–21, 232, 238.
23. Heather K. Crawford, *Outside the Glow* (Dublin: University College Dublin Press, 2010), p. 169.
24. Ibid., pp. 191, 195; on the demographics of post-independence Ireland see Marcus Tanner, *Ireland's Holy Wars* (New Haven, CT: Yale University Press, 2001), pp. 290–93, 312–23.
25. See Charles M. Sennott, *The Body and the Blood* (New York: Public Affairs, 2001) for a discussion of this problem in the Middle East as a whole with an emphasis on Egypt, Jordan, Lebanon, and Palestine.
26. The years were 1932–48, 1957–1973,

Notes — Chapter Five

and 1997–2010. The biggest period of competitiveness was in the 1970s to the 1990s, with the most turnovers from 1981 to 1992.

27. Collins, *The Power Game*; Donal O' Shea, *80 Years of Fianna Fail* (Castlebar, Co. Mayo: Manlo, 2006); Noel Whelan, *Fianna Fail: A Biography of the Party* (Dublin: Gill and Macmillan, 2011).

28. O'Shea, *80 Years of Fianna Fail*, pp. 14–23; Collins, *The Power Game*, pp. 13–17.

29. O'Shea, *80 Years of Fianna Fail*, pp. 31–33; Collins, *The Power Game*, pp. 17–19; Tim Pat Coogan, *Eamon De Valera* (New York: HarperCollins, 1993), p. 470.

30. The Progressive Democrats (PDs) emerged just around Christmas 1985 and the Workers' Party had their breakthrough election in 1989, only to have all but one of the TDs leave the party for the splinter Democratic Left in 1992.

31. O'Shea, *80 Years of Fianna Fail*, pp. 34–41; Collins, *The Power Game*, pp. 18–21; Catherine O'Donnell, *Fianna Fail, Irish Republicanism and the Northern Ireland Troubles 1968–2005* (Portland, OR: Irish Academic Press, 2007), pp. 11–12; Coogan, *Eamon De Valera*, pp. 489, 493; Dermot Keogh, *Twentieth-Century Ireland: Nation and State* (New York: St. Martin's Press, 1994), pp. 96, 98, 101; Dermot Keogh and Andrew McCarthy, *The Making of the Irish Constitution* (Cork: Mercier, 2007), pp. 83, 126–27, 134–36.

32. Collins, *The Power Game*, pp. 14–15. The Irish language and the requirement are a frequent topic in the Irish press. The author met students on a train in Ireland in 1984 who resented having to learn Irish and among Protestants it is resented.

33. Collins, *The Power Game*, pp. 20–22; Keogh, *Twentieth-Century Ireland*, p. 287; J.J. Lee, *Ireland: Politics and Society 1912–1985* (Cambridge: Cambridge University Press, 1989), pp. 223–24.

34. Conor Cruise O'Brien, *Ancestral Voices* (Chicago: University of Chicago Press, 1995), pp. 148, 153.

35. O'Donnell, *Fianna Fail*, pp. 21–29; Collins, *The Power Game*, pp. 55–61.

36. Collins, *The Power Game*, pp. 62–93; Bruce Arnold, *Haughey: His Life and Unlucky Deeds* (New York: HarperCollins, 1993), pp. 80–92; T. Ryle Dwyer, *Short Fellow: A Biography of Charles J. Haughey* (Dublin: Marino, 2001), pp. 98–114.

37. On Blaney and Boland, see Kevin Rafter, *Neil Blaney: A Soldier of Destiny* (Dublin: Blackwater Press, 1993), pp. 100, 103, 110; Collins,

The Power Game, pp. 96, 105–11; O'Shea, *80 Years of Fianna Fail*, pp. 83–87; Justin O'Brien, *The Arms Trial* (Dublin: Gill and Macmillan, 2000), pp. ix, 214–24; Cruise O'Brien, *Ancestral Voices*, p. 162.

38. O'Donnell, *Fianna Fail*, pp. 36–41; T. Ryle Dwyer, *Nice Fellow: A Biography of Jack Lynch* (Dublin: Mercier, 2001), pp. 260–78; John Peck, *Dublin from Downing Street* (Dublin: Gill and Macmillan, 1978), pp. 44–45, 134, 136–37.

39. Collins, *The Power Game*, pp. 74–75. On the Official IRA ceasefire and the emergence of the INLA, see Henry McDonald, *INLA: Deadly Divisions* (Dublin: Poolbeg, 2010).

40. Dwyer, *Nice Fellow*, p. 283; Peck, *Dublin from Downing Street*, pp. 3, 11.

41. Henry Patterson, *Ireland since 1939* (London: Penguin, 2006), pp. 239–41; Cruise O'Brien, *Ancestral Voices*, p. 166; Conor Cruise O'Brien, *Memoir: My Life and Themes* (New York: Cooper Square Press, 2000), pp. 250–52; Garret FitzGerald, *All in a Life: An Autobiography* (Dublin: Gill and Macmillan, 1991,) pp. 210–27.

42. Patterson, *Ireland since 1939*, pp. 242–44.

43. Collins, *The Power Game*, pp. 117–20.

44. Ibid., pp. 143–44; Arnold, *Haughey*, pp. 173–74; Dwyer, *Short Fellow*, p. 186.

45. Dwyer, *Short Fellow*, pp. 229–32; Arnold, *Haughey*, pp. 198–99.

46. FitzGerald, *All in a Life*, pp. 326, 360; Stephen O'Byrnes, *Hiding Behind a Face: Fine Gael under FitzGerald* (Dublin: Gill and Macmillan, 1986), pp. 18, 20–30, 42.

47. FitzGerald, *All in a Life*, pp. 463–69, 478–84, 487–90, 497–555; John Hume, *A New Ireland* (Boulder, CO: Roberts Rinehart, 1996), pp. 62, 64.

48. Eamon Delaney, *An Accidental Diplomat* (Dublin: New Island, 2001), pp. 287–88, 290; Dwyer, *Short Fellow*, pp. 299–300; Arnold, *Haughey*, p. 227.

49. FitzGerald, *All in a Life*, pp. 496, 515; Margaret Thatcher, *The Downing St. Years* (New York: Harper Collins, 1993), pp. 391, 396, 400–402, 410, 413, 415.

50. FitzGerald, *All in a Life*, pp. 339–40, 602; Dwyer, *Short Fellow*, p. 165; Collins, *The Power Game*, p. 141; Kevin Rafter, *Martin Mansergh: A Biography* (Dublin: New Island, 2002), p. 175.

51. Rafter, op. cit., pp. 182–86. 190.

52. Ibid., pp. 25–46, 66–68, 311.

53. Ibid., p. 169.

54. Ibid., p. 194.

55. Pat Leahy, *Showtime: The Inside Story of Fianna Fail in Power* (Dublin: Penguin Ireland, 2009), pp. 42–44; Rafter, op. cit., p. 128; O'Shea, *80 Years of Fianna Fail,* p. 127.

56. Collins, *The Power Game,* pp. 191, 216, 220–24.

57. Ibid., pp. 229–33; Reynolds, *Albert Reynolds,* pp. 148–49; Whelan, *Fianna Fail,* p. 273; FitzGerald, *All in a Life.* In the beginning FitzGerald relates a story of how at age six he realized that his mother was a Protestant.

58. Collins, *The Power Game, p.* 215; also see Tim Ryan, *Reynolds: The Longford Leader* (Dublin: Blackwater, 1994); and Reynolds, *Albert Reynolds,* for his background.

59. O'Donnell, *Fianna Fail,* pp. 88–91; Eamonn Mallie and David McKittrick, *The Fight for Peace* (London: Mandarin, 1997), pp. 128–46; Reynolds, *Albert Reynolds,* pp. 184–96.

60. Fergus Finlay, *Snakes and Ladders* (Dublin: New Island, 1998), p. 112; Collins, *The Power Game,* pp. 246–48.

61. Sean Duignan, *One Spin on the Merry-Go-Round* (Dublin: Blackwater, 1995), pp. 57–66.

62. Finlay, *Snakes and Ladders,* pp. 1, 136, 140, 161; Quinn, *Straight Left,* p. 263. See also Stephen Collins, *Spring and the Labour Story* (Dublin: O'Brien Press, 1993), pp. 104, 216, 218, for more background on Spring.

63. O'Donnell, *Fianna Fail,* p. 92; Reynolds, *Albert Reynolds,* pp. 293–95; Rafter, op. cit., pp. 197, 208–16; Duignan, *One Spin,* pp. 96–106.

64. Reynolds, *Albert Reynolds,* pp. 306–11; Duignan, *One Spin,* pp. 118–28; O'Donnell, *Fianna Fail,* pp. 106–11; Rafter, op. cit., p. 217; Mallie and McKittrick, *The Fight for Peace,* p. 268.

65. Delaney, *An Accidental Diplomat,* pp. 325–29, 347; O'Donnell, *Fianna Fail,* p. 95.

66. Delaney, *An Accidental Diplomat,* pp. 342–43; Reynolds, *Albert Reynolds,* pp. 316–62, 364–77.

67. The best short account of this is Duignan, *One Spin,* pp. 129–35, 153–72; see also Reynolds, *Albert Reynolds,* pp. 378–417; Finlay, *Snakes and Ladders,* pp. 217, 246–73; Quinn, *Straight Left,* pp. 310–18.

68. Collins, op. cit. pp. 298–301; Finlay, *Snakes and Ladders,* pp. 271–73, 277; John Downing, *"Most Skilful, Most Devious, Most Cunning": A Political Biography of Bertie Ahern* (Dublin: Blackwater, 2004), pp. 135–38.

69. Collins, op. cit. p. 292; Duignan, *One Spin,* pp. 164–65; Reynolds, *Albert Reynolds,* p. 405.

70. Reynolds, *Albert Reynolds,* pp. 413–15.

71. Finlay, *Snakes and Ladders,* pp. 278, 280, 283; Henry McDonald, *Trimble* (London: Bloomsbury, 2001), pp. 143–46.

72. Mallie and McKittrick, *The Fight for Peace,* pp. 349–50.

73. Rafter, op. cit. pp. 230, 234; Finlay, *Snakes and Ladders,* pp. 289, 293, 300–301.

74. Mallie and McKittrick, *The Fight for Peace,* p. 368; David Sharrock and Mark Devenport, *Man of War, Man of Peace* (London: Pan, 1998), pp. 396, 399–401.

75. Leahy, *Showtime,* pp. 58–98, for a journalistic account of the election campaign and analysis of the results; Michael Marsh and Paul Mitchell, eds., *How Ireland Voted 1997* (Boulder, CO: Westview, 1999), pp. 174–75, 177; Whelan, *Fianna Fail,* p. 256.

76. Rafter, op. cit. p. 244.

77. McDonald, *Trimble,* pp. 195–97; Patterson, *Ireland since 1939,* p. 336.

78. McDonald, *Trimble,* pp. 203–4, 206; Downing, *"Most Skilful, Most Devious, Most Cunning,"* pp. 188–90; Bertie Ahern, *The Autobiography* (London: Hutchinson, 2009), pp. 210–30; Ken Whelan and Eugene Masterson, *Bertie Ahern: Taoiseach and Peacemaker* (London: Mainstream, 1998,) pp. 198–205. A text of the old and new Articles 2 and 3 is on p. 202.

79. Rafter, op. cit., pp. 198, 248–50, 252; O'Donnell, *Fianna Fail,* p. 149; Reynolds, *Albert Reynolds,* p. 188; Patterson, *Ireland since 1939,* p. 338; David Andrews, *Kingstown Republican* (Dublin: New Island, 2007), pp. 271–72.

80. Rafter, op. cit., p. 283.

81. Andrews, *Kingstown Republic,* p. 283.

82. O'Toole *Ship of Fools;* see the appendices for the economic information.

83. R.F. Foster, *Luck and the Irish* (New York: Oxford University Press, 2008), pp. 61–62, for the above-mentioned cases and in general terms, pp. 37–66; Chris Moore, *Betrayal of Trust* (Dublin: Marino, 1995), for details on the Brendan Smyth case, p. 5, on the damage it caused the church; Byrne, *Political Corruption in Ireland,* p. 227, on mass rates; on the scandals and the effects that they had on the Church's image see Tanner, *Ireland's Holy Wars,* pp. 396–410.

84. Dick Walsh, *Dick Walsh Remembered* (Dublin: TownHouse, 2003) p. 38.

85. See Foster op. cit. pp. 1–6 for this theme; John Ardagh, *Ireland and the Irish* (London: Penguin, 1995), pp. 305–44 for this theme.

86. O'Donnell, *Fianna Fail.*

87. O'Shea, *80 Years of Fianna Fail,* p. 89; Collins, op. cit. p. 99. There were also other

minor instances of loyalist terrorism in the border counties of Cavan and Monaghan in the 1970s.

88. Patterson, *Ireland since 1939*, p. 270; Jim Cusack and Henry McDonald, *UVF* (Dublin: Poolbeg, 1997), pp. 131–36, for their dismissal of the British conspiracy theory. The conspiracy is discussed in J. Bowyer Bell, *In Dubious Battle: The Dublin and Monaghan Bombings 1972–74* (Dublin: Poolbeg, 1996). For a refutation see David Ervine quoted in Ed Moloney, *Voices from the Grave* (New York: Public Affairs, 2010), pp. 347–49. I personally did not find Bell's argument at all convincing.

89. See McDonald, *Deadly Divisions*, for details.

90. Garda Jerry McCabe: Gerry Adams and Martin McGuinness claimed that it was an unauthorized killing by a renegade unit. McCabe's widow was not convinced and spoke out against the IRA and Sinn Fein for years after the murder.

Chapter Six

1. Ghada Karmi, a Palestinian doctor living in London, is typical of Palestinians in arguing in her one-state advocacy — she argues like an attorney *in the alternative* that modern Jews aren't really the descendants of ancient Israelites, and even if they are, this doesn't give them the right to settle in modern Palestine. Ghada Karmi, *Married to Another Man: Israel's Dilemma in Palestine* (Ann Arbor, MI: Pluto, 2007), pp. 67–69.

2. Ephraim Nimni, ed. *The Challenge of Post-Zionism* (New York: Zed, 2003); Thomas G. Mitchell, *Native vs. Settler: Ethnic Conflict in Israel/Palestine, Northern Ireland, and South Africa* (Westport, CT: Greenwood, 2000), pp. 9–11; Tom Segev, *One Palestine, Complete* (New York: Henry Holt, 2000), pp. 161–63.

3. Segev, *One Palestine*, pp. 377, 380; Benny Morris, *Righteous Victims* (New York: Alfred Knopf, 1999), p. 123.

4. Christians sometimes also have problems with this dual definition of Judaism.

5. Bat Ye'or, *Islam and Dhimmitude: Where Civilizations Collide* (Madison, WI and Teaneck, NJ: Fairleigh Dickinson University Press and Associated University Presses, 2003), for the concept.

6. Michael Bar-Zohar and Eitan Haber, *The Quest for the Red Prince* (New York: William Morrow, 1983,) p. 35.

7. Morris, *Righteous Victims*, pp. 124; Benny

Morris, *One State, Two States* (New Haven: Yale University Press, 2009), p. 102.

8. Bar-Zohar and Haber, *The Quest for the Red Prince*, p. 39. The five were, presumably, Qadir al-Husayni, the leader in the Jerusalem area; Aref Abd-al Razek and Abu Kamal, rival chiefs in the coastal plain; Hassan Salame, the leader in the Lydda (Lod) district under al-Razek; and Fawzi al-Kawakji, a Lebanese veteran of the Ottoman army who led a group of foreign volunteers from Iraq and Syria. This is based on a close reading of Bar-Zohar and Haber, pp. 26–30; Morris, *Victims*, pp. 127–28.

9. Bar-Zohar and Haber, *The Quest for the Red Prince*, pp. 30, 43–44; Morris, *Victims*, pp. 145–46, 150, 151, 153.

10. Bar-Zohar and Haber, *The Quest for the Red Prince*, pp. 46–53.

11. Ibid., p. 72. Abd al-Qadir al-Husayni was the son of Musa Kazim al-Husayni, another leading nationalist figure until his death in 1934.

12. Ibid., pp. 47, 59, 67–68, 73.

13. Ibid., pp. 77–78, 84, 86, 89; Robert Fisk, *The Great War for Civilisation* (New York: Vintage, 2007), pp. 363–64; Benny Morris, *1948* (New Haven, CT: Yale University Press, 2008), p. 196.

14. Morris, *Victims*, p. 159. For a reverse of the figures of killed by Arabs and by colonial forces, see Baruch Kimmerling and Joel S. Migdal, *The Palestinian People* (Cambridge, MA: Harvard University Press, 2003), p. 131.

15. Bar-Zohar and Haber, *The Quest for the Red Prince*, p. 43; Segev, *One Palestine*, pp. 416–17, 433.

16. Morris, *1948*, pp. 396–402; Segev, *One Palestine*, pp. 509–10; Morris, *Victims*, p. 248.

17. Barry Rubin and Judith Colp Rubin, *Yasir Arafat: A Political Biography* (New York: Oxford University Press, 2003), pp. 25–26.

18. Janet Wallach and John Wallach, *Arafat: In the Eyes of the Beholder* (New York: Lyle Stuart, 1990), pp. 71–72, 75, 85, 95.

19. Wallach and Wallach, *Arafat*, pp. 110–11; Rubin and Rubin, *Yasir Arafat*, p. 31.

20. Wallach and Wallach, *Arafat*, pp. 120–24.

21. Wallach and Wallach, *Arafat*, pp. 208–9; Michael C. Hudson, *Arab Politics: The Search for Legitimacy* (New Haven, CT: Yale University Press, 1977), pp. 354–55; James Lunt, *Hussein of Jordan* (New York: William Morrow, 1989), pp. 124–27, 131–33.

22. Wallach and Wallach, *Arafat*, pp. 270–71, 273; Rubin and Rubin, *Yasir Arafat*, pp. 40–43.

23. Rubin and Rubin, *Yasir Arafat*, pp. 35–36.
24. Many of the Palestinian intellectual leadership is based in the West in Paris, London, New York and Washington, D.C. They are doctor, lawyers, economists, university professors, and businessmen.
25. Sari Nusseibeh, *Once upon a Country* (New York: Farrar, Straus, and Giroux, 2007), p. 142.
26. Rubin and Rubin, *Yasir Arafat*, p. 70; Wallach and Wallach, *Arafat*, p. 160.
27. Rubin and Rubin, *Yasir Arafat*, pp. 69–70; Morris, *One State*, pp. 167, 169.
28. Morris, *One State*, pp. 104–7; Wallach and Wallach, *Arafat*, pp. 310–14, 318–30.
29. It was rumored that the driver had deliberately caused the "accident" to avenge a couple of Israelis who had been murdered shortly before. Such a rumor fed into both the conspiracy mentality and blood feuds of Arab culture.
30. Rubin and Rubin, *Yasir Arafat*, pp. 110–11; Glenn Frankel, *Beyond the Promised Land* (New York: Touchstone, 1996), pp. 43–45, 75–77; Nusseibeh, *Once upon a Country*, pp. 266–67, 268–79, 281–82, 295–96.
31. Rubin and Rubin, *Yasir Arafat*, pp. 113–17, 121–22.
32. Frankel, *Beyond the Promised Land*, pp. 308–11, 348–52; Nusseibeh, *Once upon a Country*, pp. 346–52, 360–63, 368–72.
33. Matthew Levitt, *Hamas* (New Haven, CT: Yale University Press and WINEP, 2006), pp. 20–21, 24.
34. Mosab Hassan Yousef, *Son of Hamas* (New York: Tyndale, 2010), pp. 19–20; "Hamas," *Wikipedia*, accessed Oct. 14, 2012; "Hamas," *Mideast Web*, accessed Oct. 14, 2012. Levitt gives the founding date as December 1987, but notes that its structure had existed since 1967 in the form of the Muslim Brotherhood in Gaza.
35. Izz al-Din al-Kassem was a Syrian preacher educated in Egypt who organized a guerrilla organization, the Black Hand, which opened its campaign in November 1935 after a clandestine shipment of rifles and ammunition intended for the Hagana was discovered the previous month. Several Black Hand veterans went on to play a major role in the Arab Revolt and ironically, al-Kassem was a hero of Yasir Arafat when he was younger.
36. Paul McGeough, *Kill Khalid* (New York: The New Press, 2009) pp. 68, 104–9; Levitt, *Hamas*, pp. 11–12; Robert Slater, *Rabin of Israel* (New York: St. Martin's Press, 1993), pp. 445, 446–49.
37. McGeough, *Kill Khalid*, pp. 367–68; Levitt, *Hamas*, pp. 172–78.
38. Levitt, *Hamas*, pp. 32, 107–42; McGeough, *Kill Khalid*, pp. 231–34 on Hamas-Fatah competition; on PA corruption see Said K. Aburish, *Arafat: From Defender to Dictator* (New York: Bloomsbury, 1998), pp. 306–8.
39. Shlomo Ben-Ami, *Scars of War, Wounds of Peace* (New York: Oxford University Press, 2006), pp. 210–11; Efraim Karsh, *Arafat's War* (New York: Grove Press, 2003), p. 121; Dennis Ross, *The Missing Peace* (New York: Farrar, Straus and Giroux, 2004), p. 261.
40. Karameh was a battle in March 1968 when the IDF invaded Jordan following an Israeli school bus being blown up by a land mine. The Jordanian army fought alongside the Fedayeen organizations and caused most of the Israeli casualties, which were extensive. But naturally, Fatah claimed the "victory" for itself.
41. Mark Matthews, *Lost Years: Bush, Sharon and Failure in the Middle East* (New York: Nation Books, 2007), pp. 237–38, 263; Nusseibeh, *Once upon a Country*, p. 465; Charles Enderlin, *The Lost Years: Radical Islam, Intifada, and Wars in the Middle East 2001–2006* (New York: Other Press, 2007), pp. 185, 192, 201, 203–5.
42. The policy actually began under Shimon Peres in the mid–1990s but was used much more sparingly and against military and not "civilian" terrorist leaders.
43. Paola Caridi, *Hamas: From Resistance to Government* (New York: Seven Stories Press, 2012), pp. 161, 163–64.
44. Ibid., pp. 167, 170, 172.
45. McGeough, *Kill Khalid*, pp. 317–18, 320–25, 330; Enderlin, *The Lost Years*, pp. 270–71; Matthews, *Lost Years*, pp. 412–14; Caridi, *Hamas*, p. 194.
46. Caridi, *Hamas*, pp. 196–98, 212; Morris, *One State*, p. 171.
47. McGeough, *Kill Khalid*, pp. 369–82; Caridi, *Hamas*, pp. 241–58.
48. McGeough, *Kill Khalid*, p. 416; Aaron D. Miller, *The Much Too Promised Land* (New York: Bantam, 2008), pp. 359–60; Itamar Rabinovich, *The Lingering Conflict* (Washington, DC: The Brookings Institution, 2011), pp. 177–80.
49. McGeough, *Kill Khalid*, pp. 412–13; Morris, *One State*, pp. 194–96.
50. Caridi, *Hamas*, pp. 267–73.
51. APN political analyst Yossi Alpher made this point on a number of occasions in his weekly column for APN. Alpher was formerly a senior Mossad analyst and a political advisor to Ehud Barak.

52. Bar-Zohar and Haber, *The Quest for the Red Prince*, pp. 145–77; Simon Reeve, *One Day in September* (New York: Arcade, 2011).

53. Bar-Zohar and Haber, *The Quest for the Red Prince*, pp. 219–20.

54. The British appeasement of the Palestinians in the form of the May 1939 White Paper severely limiting immigration and land purchases strengthened Ben-Gurion's hand in the subsequent fights over Zionist policy during World War II and immediately afterwards. While both supported Israeli independence and Ben-Gurion was willing to settle for partition in both 1937 and 1947–48, Weizmann would have been more open to compromise provided that the Palestinians had offered something.

55. Notably the Great Revolt of A.D. 66–70 and the Bar Kokhba Revolt of A.D. 132–35.

56. A cousin of Jamal al-Husayni signed an agreement with Ihud supporting a bi-national solution. Shortly afterwards he was assassinated for this and Jamal supported the murder. Walter Laqueur, *Dying For Jerusalem* (Napierville, IL: Sourcebooks, 2006), p. 179. Both Karmi, op. cit. and Abulima cite Ihud without however mentioning the Marxist-Zionist youth movement HaShomer HaTzair (The Young Guard), which had many more members and was the basis of the Mapam Party in 1948.

57. Caridi, *Hamas*, p. 337.

58. "Mahmoud Abbas interview with Channel 2 provokes controversy," *You Tube*, Nov. 4 2012.

59. Caridi, *Hamas*, pp. 170, 172.

60. Ibid., p. 339.

61. Ibid., p. 330. Siegman made clear that he didn't condone that terrorism.

62. Morris, *One State*, pp. 5–6.

63. Ibid., pp. 49, 57, 89. Unlike Ihud, HaShomer HaTzair always wanted a Jewish majority in Palestine. This abandonment may have been due to a change in Soviet policy towards Zionism in 1948 or due to the Arab invasion or to both. Technically Ahdut ha'Avoda was then Faction B, a group that split off from Mapai in 1944 and would split off from Mapam in 1954 over disagreements about the Soviet Union.

64. Ibid., pp. 185–86, 188.

Chapter Seven

1. Howard M. Sachar, *A History of Israel From the Rise of Zionism to Our Time* (New York: Alfred Knopf, 1996), pp. 47–64; see also Conor Cruise O'Brien, *The Siege* (New York:

Simon & Schuster, 1986), first chapter for a similar narrative.

2. Ibid., pp. 96–111.

3. Ibid., pp. 189–90.

4. Ibid., pp. 195–278.

5. Stalin was reportedly on the verge of declaring an anti–Semitic purge in the "doctors' plot" when he died in 1953.

6. Ibid., pp. 489–93.

7. Steven L. Spiegel, *The Other Arab-Israeli Conflict* (Chicago: University of Chicago Press, 1985), pp. 5–9.

8. Ibid., pp. 311–12.

9. Ibid., p. 474; Patrick Tyler, *Fortress Israel* (New York: Farrar, Straus, and Giroux, 2012), pp. 71–73.

10. Patrick Tyler, *A World of Trouble* (New York: Farrar, Straus, and Giroux, 2009), pp. 55, 58–62.

11. Ibid., p. 66; Tyler, *World*, pp. 116–33 passim, 142–43.

12. Tyler, *World*, pp. 112, 120, 123. The Eisenhower administration allowed Israel to purchase some recoilless rifles from the U.S. but had the Europeans sell Israel most of the weapons it needed.

13. Col. Eliezer Cohen, *Israel's Best Defense* (New York: Airlife Publishing, 1994); Ehud Yonay, *No Margin for Error: The Making of the Israeli Air Force* (New York: Pantheon, 1993), for history of transition.

14. Tyler, *Fortress*, pp. 164–83; Tyler, *World*, pp. 96–98; William B. Quandt, *Decade of Decisions* (Berkeley: University of California Press, 1977), pp. 53–59. Quandt argued that Johnson tried to restrain Israel but was unable to give the leadership the assurances they needed to delay striking, Tyler disagrees and argues that Johnson never intended that Israel should attack.

15. These can be found in the Watergate tape transcripts in which he makes anti–Semitic references. See Robert Dallek, *Nixon and Kissinger: Partners in Power* (New York: HarperCollins, 2007), pp. 170–71.

16. Ibid., pp. 34–59.

17. Henry A. Kissinger, *Years of Upheaval* (Boston: Little Brown, 1982), pp. 196–201, 202–3.

18. Dallek, *Nixon and Kissinger*, pp. 223–27.

19. Samuel M. Katz, *Soldier Spies: Israeli Military Intelligence* (Novato, CA: Presidio Press, 1992), pp. 203–18; Spiegel, *The Other Arab-Israeli Conflict*, p. 5. The Mossad managed to persuade an Iraqi MiG pilot to defect to Israel with his MiG-21 jet fighter in 1966

by gathering as much information as possible about the ethnic composition of the MiG-21 squadrons in the Iraqi air force and then looking at all those from Christian backgrounds to see who would be most persuadable. On this Dan Raviv and Yossi Melman, *Every Spy a Prince* (Boston: Houghton Mifflin, 1991), pp. 141–43.

20. Virginia Tilley, *The One-State Solution* (Ann Arbor: University of Michigan Press, 2005), p. 93.

21. Benjamin Beit-Hallahmi, *The Israeli Connection: Who Israel Arms and Why* (New York: Pantheon, 1987), pp. 38–107.

22. Tyler, *Fortress*, pp. 199–200. The Cold War was an important factor in American Middle East policy since the creation of the state of Israel, but until after the 1956 Suez War the United States took a backseat role in the region compared with Britain and France. It was starting with the 1969–70 War of Attrition that Arab-Israeli wars became superpower proxy conflicts, something which was definitely not the case in 1948 and 1956 and was much less important in 1967.

23. Ira M. Sheskin, *Recent Trends in Jewish Demographics and Their Impact on the Jewish Media* (Dallas: American Jewish Press Association, June 2011).

24. Wolf Blitzer, *Between Washington and Jerusalem* (New York: Oxford University Press, 1985), pp. 120–35.

25. Ken Flower, *Serving Secretly* (Alberton, Canada: Galago, 1987), p. 31; David Welsh, *The Rise and Fall of Apartheid* (Johannesburg: Jonathan Ball, 2009), pp. 5, 17.

26. J. Bowyer Bell, *Terror Out of Zion* (New York: Discus, 1978), pp. 79–80, 129–44, or any biography of Begin.

27. Tyler, *Fortress*, p. 188; Tom Segev, *1967* (New York: Henry Holt, 2007), pp. 386, 568–70.

28. Michael Bar-Zohar and Eitan Haber, *The Quest for the Red Prince* (New York: William Morrow, 1983), pp. 33–66. Salame infiltrated back into Palestine in November 1944 to carry out a sabotage mission.

29. Mark Matthews, *Lost Years: Bush, Sharon and Failure in the Middle East* (New York: Nation Books, 2007), pp. 142–44.

30. The author was an intern in the Foreign Policy Analysis section of AIPAC in 1995 and so is aware of its main themes from personal experience as well as having read *Near East Report*, its newsletter, on a regular basis from 1984–90.

31. Robert Slater, *Rabin of Israel* (New York:

St. Martin's Press, 1993), pp. 242–47; Quandt, *Decade*, pp. 269–70, 272–74.

32. Spiegel, *The Other Arab-Israeli Conflict*, pp. 347–49.

33. Tyler, *World*, p. 208.

34. Blitzer, *Between Washington and Jerusalem*, pp. 238–42.

35. Tyler, *World*, pp. 257–58, 269–71, 284–85, 294–95. Shultz used his economic background to help advise Peres how to end Israel's ruinous inflation in the mid–1980s.

36. Ibid., pp. 260–62; Blitzer, *Between Washington and Jerusalem*, pp. 126, 136; Spiegel, *The Other Arab-Israeli Conflict*, p. 398.

37. Blitzer, *Between Washington and Jerusalem*, pp. 110, 245.

38. Tyler, *World*, pp. 273, 280–81, 283–85; Blitzer, *Between Washington and Jerusalem*, pp. 54–57.

39. Blitzer, *Between Washington and Jerusalem*, pp. 121, 157, 206. By 2012 Egypt was in fifth place behind Israel, Afghanistan, Pakistan and Iraq with "only" $1.6 billion per year, compared with $3.08 billion for Israel, "U.S. Foreign Aid by Country," *Huffington Post*, accessed Oct. 17, 2012; by 2012 Israel had received $115 billion bilaterally from the U.S. according to a U.S. congressional report, "U.S. Foreign Aid to Israel: 2012 Congressional Report," *Journalist's Resource*, Joan Shorenstein Center at the Harvard Kennedy School.

40. Frankel, *Beyond the Promised Land*, pp. 332–33.

41. For his bio see his memoir, Martin Indyk, *Innocent Abroad* (New York: Simon & Schuster, 2009), pp. 5–6.

42. Tyler, *World*, pp. 388–90; Frankel, *Beyond the Promised Land*, pp. 299–304.

43. See Stanley Greenberg, *Dispatches from the War Room: In the Trenches with Five Extraordinary Leaders* (New York: Thomas Dunne, 2009), pp. 286–88.

44. Tyler, *World*, p. 528; Matthews, *Lost Years*, pp. 11–25 passim.

45. Tyler, *World*, pp. 525–26; Matthews, *Lost Years*, p. 75; Clayton E. Swisher, *The Truth about Camp David* (New York: Nation Books, 2004), pp. 404–5.

46. Tyler, *World*, pp. 538–39; Nir Hefez and Gadi Bloom, *Ariel Sharon* (New York: Random House, 2006), pp. 367–72; Baruch Kimmerling, *Politicide* (New York: Verso, 2006), p. 202; Uri Dan, *Ariel Sharon: An Intimate Portrait* (New York: Palgrave Macmillan, 2006), p. 189.

47. Aaron D. Miller, *The Much Too Promised Land* (New York: Bantam, 2008), pp. 347–49; Matthews, *Lost Years*, pp. 193, 216–27, 231–40.

48. Matthews, *Lost Years,* p. 263; Miller, *The Much Too Promised Land,* pp. 353, 359–60.
49. Dallek, *Nixon and Kissinger,* pp. 178–79, 223.
50. Tyler, World, pp. 182–94; Miller, *The Much Too Promised Land,* pp. 160–72.
51. The J Street website has attached to it a Brit Tzedek memorial project that dates the organization from April 2002.
52. Marcia Freedman, *Exile in the Promised Land: A Memoir* (Ithaca, NY: Firebrand, 1990).
53. The author received a mailer from the organization in October or November 2002.
54. Leonard Fein wrote about these in the Jewish newspaper *Forward.* He also discussed it in his role as moderator of *The Conversation,* his blog on the Americans for Peace Now website.
55. The merger was announced at J Street's first conference in October 2009 and took place a few months later.
56. Charles Boustany of Louisiana's seventh district.
57. Communication with a senior figure within J PAC.
58. AIPAC attracted 13,000 to its conference three weeks earlier. Joshua Hersh, "Pro-Israel J Street Group Faces Growing Pains at Annual Convention," *Huffington Post,* March 28, 2012.
59. The author attended AIPAC's annual conference in May 1995 and J Street's first conference in October 2009.

Chapter Eight

1. Theresa Papenfus, *Pik Botha and His Times* (Pretoria: Litera, 2010) pp. 609–12.
2. Although a few Boers did settle in Namibia during the thirstland trek of the 1890s, this wasn't considered sufficient to establish an Afrikaner claim on the territory as part of the boerestaat.
3. For a discussion of F.W. de Klerk's thinking see David Welsh, *The Rise and Fall of Apartheid* (Cape Town: Jonathan Ball, 2010) pp. 344–49, 354–60, 379–87; and F.W. de Klerk, *The Last Trek : A New Beginning* (New York: Macmillan, 1998).
4. He mentioned this saying at the time of Shamir's death in 2012.
5. Israeli Palestinians do not want to accept the status quo that leaves them as both de facto and de jure second-class citizens. They want Israel to be a "state of all its citizens." Meretz has proposed a compromise of recognizing Israel as both a Jewish state and a state of all of its

citizens i.e. individually Jews and Arabs would be on an equal basis but collectively Jews would be favored.
6. James Lunt, *Hussein of Jordan* (New York: William Morrow, 1989) pp. 115–17, 118–43.
7. Janet and John Wallach, *Arafat: In the Eyes of the Beholder* (New York: Lyle Stuart, 1990) pp. 230–46.
8. It was part of the plan presented by the Zionist delegation at the Versailles peace conference.
9. The point here is that both the A.mericans and the Boers generally lacked a united national native opponent comparable to the Palestinians, and the Palestinians have considerable foreign support, which both the American Indians and the native peoples of South Africa lacked. See Thomas G. Mitchell, *Native vs. Settler: Ethnic Conflict in Israel/Palestine, Northern Ireland and South Africa* (Westport, CT: Greenwood, 2000) for a discussion of the differences.
10. The Palestinian Charter said that Palestine could only be liberated through armed struggle, which in Palestinian usage is almost synonymous with terrorism.
11. For a discussion on the Palestinian authority that discusses the corruption comparable to that outlined for Ireland and Fianna Fail see Barry Rubin and Judith C. Rubin, *Yasir Arafat: A Political Biography* (New York: Oxford University Press, 2003) and Said K. Aburish, *Arafat: From Defender to Dictator* (New York: Bloomsbury, 1998).
12. Stephen Collins, *Breaking the Mould : How the PDs Changed Irish Politics* (Dublin: Gill and Macmillan, 2006) pp. 31–32.
13. The four leading Irish-American politicians (Sen. Daniel Moynihan of NY, Gov. Hugh Carey of NY, Sen. Edward Kennedy of MA, Rep. Tip O'Neill of MA) were known collectively as the Four Horseman and in 1977 John Hume made a connection with them on a trip to the United States. They supported the SDLP as an alternative to violence. Starting in the 1980s the international arm of the Democratic Party started providing training to SDLP activists in electioneering and other party political skills.
14. Martin Meredith, *The Past Is Another Country: Rhodesia — UDI to Zimbabwe* (London: Pan, 1980) pp. 242–93; see Joshua Nkomo, *The Story of My Life* (London: Metheun, 1984) for a short description of his conversation with Kissinger.
15. Itamar Rabinovich, *The Lingering*

Conflict (Washington: The Brookings Institution, 2011) pp. 177–80.

16. Dennis Ross, *The Missing Peace* (New York: Farrar, Straus and Giroux, 2004) pp. 573–90; Clayton Swisher, *The Truth About Camp David* (New York: Nation Books, 2004) pp. 112–23, 127–30.

17. This is the thesis of Barry Rubin, *The Truth About Syria* (New York: Palgrave Macmillan, 2007). But Rubin is not honest about Barak's 2000 offer to Assad.

18. On intellectual opinion in Egypt and Jordan see Fuad Ajami, *Dream Palace of the Arabs: A Generation's Odyssey* (New York: Vintage, 1999). On the Syrian revolt see Ajami, *The Syrian Rebellion* (Palo Alto, CA: The Hoover Institution Press, 2012).

19. National unity governments can make war and settlements but not peace as this would lead to their collapse.

20. See Thomas G. Mitchell, *When Peace Fails: Lessons from Belfast for the Middle East* (Jefferson, NC: McFarland, 2010) pp. 206–23 for other lessons of relevance from Northern Ireland and past peace processes for the Middle East peace process.

21. Arthur Hertzberg, *Jewish Polemics* (New York: Columbia University Press, 1992) pp. 16–27; Glenn Frankel, *Beyond the Promised Land* (New York: Touchstone, 1996) pp. 212–33.

22. Gershom Gorenberg, *The End of Days* (New York: Oxford University Press, 2000) for a look at some of the Christian fundamentalist supporters of Israel.

23. For a discussion of the differences see Kevin P. Phillips, *American Dynasty: Aristocracy, Fortune and the Politics of Deceit in the House of Bush* (New York: Penguin, 2004).

24. Although it is more likely that he would have caved in to the Israeli supporters in his own camp and supported Netanyahu.

25. But notably his sole foreign election trip was to England, Israel and Poland in July 2012.

26. It is telling that James Mann in his book on the Obama administration's foreign policy, *The Obamians* (New York: Viking, 2012) hardly mentioned the Middle East peace process only really covering the Cairo speech.

27. See Leon Hadar, *Sandstorm* (New York: Palgrave Macmillan, 2005) for an exploration of this theme.

28. Mitchell, *When Peace Fails*, pp. 208–10.

29. Kissinger also relied heavily on Joe Sisco, the Assistant Secretary of State for the Near East, for advice.

Bibliography

Israel/Palestine

Arian, Asher. *The Second Republic: Politics in Israel.* Chatham, NJ: Chatham House, 1998.

Arian, Asher, and Michal Shamir, eds. *The Elections in Israel, 2003.* New Brunswick, NJ: Transaction, 2005.

_____. *The Elections in Israel, 2006.* New Brunswick, NJ: Transaction, 2008.

_____. *The Elections in Israel, 2009.* New Brunswick, NJ: Transaction, 2011.

Bar-Zohar, Michael, and Eitan Haber. *The Quest for the Red Prince.* New York: William Morrow, 1983.

Beit-Hallahmi, Benjamin. *The Israeli Connection: Whom Israel Arms and Why.* New York: Pantheon, 1987.

Blitzer, Wolf. *Between Washington and Jerusalem.* New York: Oxford University Press, 1985.

Boutros-Ghali, Boutros. *Egypt's Road to Jerusalem.* New York: Random House, 1997.

Caridi, Paola. *Hamas: From Resistance to Government.* New York: Seven Stories Press, 2012.

Cohen, Mitchell. *Zion and State.* New York: Basil Blackwell, 1987.

Dan, Uri. *Ariel Sharon: An Intimate Portrait.* New York: Palgrave Macmillan, 2006.

Dayan, Moshe. *Breakthrough.* New York: Alfred Knopf, 1981.

Elazar, Daniel, and Shmuel Sandler, eds. *Who's the Boss in Israel.* Detroit: Wayne State University Press, 1992.

Enderlin, Charles. *The Lost Years: Radical Islam, Intifada, and Wars in the Middle East 2001–2006.* New York: Other Press, 2007.

Eytan, Freddy. *Ariel Sharon: A Life in Times of Turmoil.* Paris: Studio 9, 2006.

Frankel, Glenn. *Beyond the Promised Land.* New York: Touchstone, 1996.

Freedman, Robert O., ed. *Contemporary Israel.* Boulder, CO: Westview, 2009.

_____. *Israel's First Fifty Years.* Gainesville: University Press of Florida, 2000.

Friedland, Roger, and Richard Hecht. *To Rule Jerusalem.* Berkeley: University of California Press, 2000.

Hefez, Nir, and Gadi Bloom. *Ariel Sharon.* New York: Random House, 2006.

Kaplan, Eran. *The Jewish Radical Right.* Madison: University of Wisconsin Press, 2005.

Karmi, Ghada. *Married to Another Man: Israel's Dilemma in Palestine.* Ann Arbor, MI: Pluto Press, 2007.

Katz, Samuel M. *Soldier Spies: Israeli Military Intelligence.* Novato, CA: Presidio Press, 1992.

Kessler, Glenn. *Confidante: Condoleeza Rice and the Bush Legacy.* New York: St. Martin's Press, 2007

Levitt, Matthew. *Hamas.* New Haven, CT: Yale University Press, 2006.

Lochery, Neill. *The Difficult Road to Peace: Netanyahu, Israel and the Middle East Peace Process.* Reading, UK: Ithaca, 1999.

_____. *The Israeli Labour Party: In the Shadow of the Likud.* Berkshire, UK: Ithaca, 1997.

Mahler, Gregory S., ed. *Israel after Begin.*

Albany: State University of New York Press, 1990.

_____. *Politics and Government in Israel.* New York: Rowman & Littlefield, 2004.

Matthews, Mark. *Lost Years: Bush, Sharon and Failure in the Middle East.* New York: Nation Books, 2007.

Morris, Benny. *1948.* New Haven, CT: Yale University Press, 2008.

_____. *One State, Two States.* New Haven, CT: Yale University Press, 2009.

_____. *Righteous Victims.* New York: Alfred Knopf, 1999.

Netanyahu, Benjamin. *A Durable Peace: Israel and Its Place among the Nations.* New York: Warner Books, 2000.

Peleg, Ilan. *Begin's Foreign Policy, 1977– 1983: Israel Moves to the Right.* Westport, CT: Greenwood, 1987.

Peretz, Don, and Gideon Doron. *The Government and Politics of Israel.* Boulder, CO: Westview, 1997.

Rabinovich, Itamar. *The Lingering Conflict.* Washington, D.C.: The Brookings Institution, 2011.

Reich, Bernard. *A Brief History of Israel.* New York: Checkmark, 2008.

Rolef, Susan Hattis, ed. *Political Dictionary of the State of Israel.* New York: Macmillan, 1987.

Ross, Dennis. *The Missing Peace: The Inside Story of the Fight for Middle East Peace.* New York: Farrar, Straus and Giroux, 2005.

Rubin, Barry, and Judith C. Rubin. *Yasir Arafat: A Political Biography.* New York: Oxford University Press, 2003.

Sandler, Shmuel, Manfred Gerstenfeld, and Hillel Frisch, eds. *Israel at the Polls, 2009.* New York: Routledge, 2011.

Segev, Tom. *One Palestine, Complete: Jews and Arabs under the British Mandate.* New York: Metropolitan, 2000.

Shapiro, Yonathan. *The Road to Power: Herut Party in Israel.* Albany: State University of New York Press, 1991.

Sharon, Gilad. *Sharon: The Life of a Leader.* New York: HarperCollins, 2011.

Shindler, Colin. *A History of Modern Israel.* New York: Cambridge University Press, 2008.

_____. *Ploughshares into Swords?* New York: I.B. Tauris, 1991.

_____. *The Land beyond Promise: Israel, Likud and the Zionist Dream.* New York: I.B. Tauris, 2002.

_____. *The Triumph of Military Zionism.* New York: I.B. Tauris, 2010.

Silver, Eric. *Begin: The Haunted Prophet.* New York: Random House, 1984.

Sofer, Sasson. *Begin: An Anatomy of Leadership.* New York: Basil Blackwell, 1988.

_____. *Peacemaking in a Divided Society: Israel after Rabin.* Portland, OR: Frank Cass, 2001.

Spiegel, Steven L. *The Other Arab-Israeli Conflict.* Chicago: University of Chicago Press, 1985.

Spruyt, Hendrik. *Ending Empire: Contested Sovereignty and Territorial Partition.* Ithaca, NY: Cornell University Press, 2005.

Temko, Ned. *To Win or to Die.* New York: William Morrow, 1987.

Tyler, Patrick. *A World of Trouble: The White House and the Middle East from the Cold War to the War on Terror.* New York: Farrar, Straus, and Giroux, 2008.

Wallach, Janet, and John Wallach. *Arafat: In the Eyes of the Beholder.* New York: Carol Publishing, 1990.

Weizman, Ezer. *The Battle for Peace.* New York: Bantam, 1981.

Yousef, Mosab Hassan. *Son of Hamas.* Carol Stream, IL: Tyndale House, 2010.

South Africa/Namibia

Bridgland, Fred. *The War for Africa: Twelve Months That Transformed a Continent.* Gibraltar: Ashanti, 1990.

Cawthra, Gavin. *Brutal Force: The Apartheid War Machine.* London: IDAF, 1986.

Crocker, Chester A. *High Noon in Southern Africa: Making Peace in a Rough Neighborhood.* New York: W.W. Norton, 1992.

Dominguez, Jorge I. *To Make a World Safe*

for Revolution. Cambridge, MA: Harvard University Press, 1989.

Geldenhuys, Jannie. *At the Front.* Cape Town: Jonathan Ball, 2009.

Hamann, Hilton. *Days of the Generals.* Cape Town: Zebra Press, 2006.

Heitman, Helmoed R. *War in Angola: The Final South African Phase.* Gibraltar: Ashanti, 1990.

Holt, Clive. *At Thy Call We Did Not Falter.* Cape Town: Zebra, 2005.

Jaster, Robert S. *South Africa in Namibia: The Botha Strategy.* Lanham, MD: University Press of America, 1985.

_____. *The Defense of White Power: South African Foreign Policy under Pressure.* New York: St. Martin's Press, 1989.

Jaster, Robert S., et al. *Changing Fortunes: War, Diplomacy, and Economics in Southern Africa.* New York: The Ford Foundation, 1992.

Lord, Dick. *From Fledgling to Eagle: The South African Air Force during the Border War.* Johannesburg: South Publishers, 2008.

Malan, Magnus. *My Life with the South African Defence Force.* Pretoria: Protea, 2006.

Nortje, Piet. *32 Battalion.* Cape Town: Zebra, 2004.

Onslow, Sue, ed. *Cold War in Southern Africa.* New York: Routledge, 2009.

Papenfus, Theresa. *Pik Botha and His Times.* Pretoria: Litera, 2010.

Pottinger, Brian. *The Imperial Presidency: P.W. Botha, the First 10 Years.* Johannesburg: Southern Book Publishers, 1988.

Price, Robert M. *The Apartheid State in Crisis: Political Transformation in South Africa 1975–1990.* New York: Oxford University Press, 1991.

Ramsden, Tim. *Border-Line Insanity.* Victoria, Canada: Trafford, 2007.

Shubin, Vladimir. *The Hot "Cold War": The USSR in Southern Africa.* Ann Arbor, MI: Pluto Press, 2008.

Shultz, George P. *Turmoil and Triumph.* New York: Charles Scribner & Sons, 1993.

Steenkamp, Willem. *South Africa's Border War, 1966–1989.* Gibraltar: Ashanti, 1989.

Weiland, Herbert, and Matthew Braham, eds. *The Namibian Peace Process: Implications and Lessons for the Future.* Freiburg, Germany: Arnold Bergstraesser Institute, 1994.

Ireland

Ahern, Bertie. *Bertie Ahern: The Autobiography.* London: Hutchinson, 2009.

Andrews, David. *Kingstown Republican.* Dublin: New Island, 2007.

Arnold, Bruce. *Haughey: His Life and Unlucky Deeds.* New York: HarperCollins, 1993.

Brown, Terence. *Ireland: A Social and Cultural History, 1922–2002.* London: Harper Perennial, 2004.

Bryne, Elaine A. *Political Corruption in Ireland 1922–2010.* New York: Manchester University Press, 2012.

Clifford, Michael, and Shane Coleman. *Bertie Ahern and the Drumcondra Mafia.* Dublin: Hachette, 2009.

Collins, Stephen. *Breaking the Mould: How the PDs Changed Irish Politics.* Dublin: Gill & Macmillan, 2006.

_____. *Spring and the Labour Story.* Dublin: O'Brien Press, 1993.

_____. *The Haughey File.* Dublin: O'Brien Press, 1992.

_____. *The Power Game: Fianna Fail since Lemass.* Dublin: O'Brien Press, 2000.

Coogan, Tim Pat. *Eamon De Valera.* New York: HarperCollins, 1993.

Crawford, Heather K. *Outside the Glow.* Dublin: UCD Press, 2010.

Delaney, Eamon. *An Accidental Diplomat.* Dublin: New Island, 2001.

Desmond, Barry. *Finally and In Conclusion.* Dublin: New Island, 2000.

Downing, John. *"Most Skillful, Most Devious, Most Cunning": A Political Biography of Bertie Ahern.* Dublin: Blackwater, 2004.

Duignan, Sean. *One Spin on the Merry-Go-Round.* Dublin: Blackwater, 1995.

Dwyer, T. Ryle. *Nice Fellow: A Biography of Jack Lynch.* Dublin: Mercier, 2001.

_____. *Short Fellow: A Biography of Charles J. Haughey.* Dublin: Marino, 2001.

Farrell, Brian. *Sean Lemass.* Dublin: Gill & Macmillan, 1991.

Finlay, Fergus. *Snakes and Ladders.* Dublin: New Island, 1998.

FitzGerald, Garret. *All in a Life: An Autobiography.* Dublin: Gill & Macmillan, 1991.

Foster, R. F. *Luck and the Irish.* New York: Oxford University Press, 2008.

Hume, John. *A New Ireland: Politics, Peace and Reconciliation.* Boulder, CO: Roberts Rineheart, 1996.

Keena, Colm. *Bertie: Power and Money.* Dublin: Gill & Macmillan, 2011.

_____. *Haughey's Millions.* Dublin: Gill & Macmillan, 2001.

Keogh, Dermot. *Jack Lynch: A Biography.* Dublin: Gill & Macmillan, 2008.

_____. *Twentieth-Century Ireland: Nation and State.* New York: St. Martin's Press, 1994.

Leahy, Pat. *Showtime: The Inside Story of Fianna Fail in Power.* Dublin: Penguin Ireland, 2009.

Lee, Joseph J. *Ireland: Politics and Society 1912–1985.* Cambridge: Cambridge University Press, 1989.

Mansergh, Martin. *The Legacy of History: For Making Peace in Ireland.* Cork: Mercier, 2003.

_____. *The Spirit of the Nation: The Speeches and Statements of Charles J. Haughey, 1957–1986.* Dublin: Mercier, 1986.

Marsh, Michael, and Paul Mitchell, eds. *How Ireland Voted, 1997.* Boulder, CO: Westview, 1999.

Moore, Chris. *Betrayal of Trust.* Dublin: Marino, 1995.

O'Brien, Conor Cruise. *Ancestral Voices.* Chicago: University of Chicago Press, 1995.

_____. *Memoir: My Life and Themes.* New York: Cooper Square Press, 2000.

O'Brien, Justin. *The Arms Trial.* Dublin: Gill & Macmillan, 2000.

O'Byrnes, Stephen. *Hiding behind a Face: Fine Gael Under FitzGerald.* Dublin: Gill & Macmillan, 1986.

O'Donnell, Catherine. *Fianna Fail, Irish Republicanism and the Northern Ireland Troubles 1968–2005.* Portland, OR: Irish Academic Press, 2007.

O'Shea, Donal. *80 Years of Fianna Fail.* Castlebar, Ireland: Manlo Publications, 2007.

O'Toole, Fintan. *Ship of Fools.* New York: Public Affairs, 2010.

Patterson, Henry. *Ireland since 1939: The Persistence of Conflict.* New York: Penguin, 2007.

Quinn, Ruairi. *Straight Left.* Dublin: Hodder Headline, 2005.

Rafter, Kevin. *Democratic Left.* Dublin: Irish Academic Press, 2011.

_____. *Martin Mansergh: A Biography.* Dublin: New Island, 2002.

_____. *Neil Blaney: A Soldier of Destiny.* Dublin: Blackwater, 1993.

Reynolds, Albert. *Albert Reynolds: My Autobiography.* Dublin: Transworld, 2009.

Ryan, Tim. *Albert Reynolds: The Longford Leader.* Dublin: Blackwater, 1994.

Thatcher, Margaret. *The Downing Street Years.* New York: HarperCollins, 1993.

Walsh, Dick. *Dick Walsh Remembered.* Dublin: Town House, 2003.

Whelan, Ken, and Eugene Masterson. *Taoiseach and Peacemaker.* Edinburgh: Mainstream, 1998.

Whelan, Noel. *Fianna Fail: A Biography of the Party.* Dublin: Gill & Macmillan, 2011.

Index

Abbas, Mahmoud 8, 19, 47, 75, 77, 79, 81, 166, 170; becomes PLO leader 75, 145; negotiations with Israel 47, 71, 76, 78, 146–47, 174
Abu Ala'a *see* Qurei, Ahmed
Abu Mazen *see* Abbas, Mahmoud
Adams, Gerry 119, 122, 123, 126–27, 141
African National Congress 86, 92, 93
Ahern, Bertie 121, 125, 126; corruption and finances 102, 103, 106–7, 108; peace process, role in 102, 107, 108, 127–28
Ahern, Dermot 107
AIPAC 9, 47, 158, 160–65, 167, 168–69
Al-Abbas, Mahmoud Abou 142
Allon, Yigal 14, 18, 36
Allon Plan 19, 54
Anglo-Irish Agreement 118–19
Angola 4, 5, 86–89, 91, 170, 172; RSA negotiations with 98–99; SADF in 92, 93, 94–98, 99, 100, 191n, 192n
Angolan army *see* FAPLA
Apartheid 4, 86, 91
Arab Peace Plan of 2002 173
Arafat, Yasir 8, 15, 44, 56, 62, 65, 67, 70, 75, 77, 79, 81, 137, 138–39, 141–47, 149, 150–51, 160, 166, 170–72, 177, 187n, 191n
Arens, Moshe 20, 42, 43, 63, 65, 186n
Articles 2 and 3 (Irish constitution of 1937) 8, 111, 127, 128, 173, 195n
Ashkenazi Jews 14

Barak, Ehud 18, 20, 44
Baram, Uzi 18, 19
Begin, Benny 42
Begin, Menachem 14, 17, 20, 46, 49; at Camp David 59–62; images of Arabs 51; intellectual influences 50–51
Beginism 40–41
Bennett, Naftali 178
Bi-bloc system 12, 13
Blair, Tony 178

Botha, Louis 16
Botha, Pieter Willem (P.W.) 87–88, 91, 93
Botha, Pik 86, 91
British mandate 28, 31
Bruton, John 125, 126, 178
Burg, Avram 18–19
Burg, Yosef 64
Burke, Ray 107
Bush, George H.W. 142, 169, 179
Bush, George W. 76–77, 145, 147, 157, 165–67 169, 177, 179

Camp David summit (1978) 60–62
Camp David summit (2000) 60, 179
Carter, Jimmy 46, 53, 56, 58, 59–62, 63, 64, 65, 67, 89, 160–63, 167, 169
Casey, Eamonn 129
Castro, Fidel 98, 99–100
Catholic Ireland 129
Celtic Tiger economy 108, 128–29, 175
Center Party 21, 183
Cleary, Michael 129
Clinton, Bill 47, 61, 65, 67, 108, 124, 125, 126, 165–66, 169, 177, 179–80, 183
Contact Group 90–91
corruption 8, 21–23, 38, 79, 102–3, 105, 109, 114, 120, 124, 144, 146, 149, 193n; beef tribunal 105–6, 122; flood tribunal 107; Mahon tribunal 106–8
Crocker, Chester 91, 99
Cuba 91, 92, 94, 97–99
Cuito Cuanavale 95–96, 99–100

Dayan, Moshe 11, 14, 18, 36, 38, 39, 52–55, 59, 63, 64
Dayan, Uzi 72
Dayan, Yael 19
Dayan Plan 54
decommissioning of arms 20, 123, 125–26, 127
Democratic Movement for Change 21, 22, 26

207

Index

Malan, Magnus 96
Mansergh, Martin 83, 119–20, 122–23, 125, 126, 127, 128, 178
Mapai 12, 14, 30, 35, 36, 45, 54, 55, 189n
McCain, John 179
McGuinness, Martin 127
Meretz 9, 11, 18, 19, 21, 24, 65, 67, 69, 74, 75, 168, 178; electoral performance 21, 23, 24
military politicians 14–18
Milo, Ron 42
Mitchell, George 47, 108, 126
Mizrakhim 12, 14, 157
Mofaz, Shaul 23–24, 178

Namibia 4; decolonization 100–1; early colonization 84; legal status 85–86; political parties 90, 100; South African conquest 84–85
Nashishibis 134
National Party (South Africa) 88, 92
National Religious Party 25, 27
Netanyahu, Benjamin "Bibi" 18, 24, 26, 42, 43, 170, 178
New Ireland Forum 117–18
Nixon, Richard 9, 80, 155–56, 162, 167, 169
Northern Ireland 1, 4, 8, 102, 109, 110, 112, 113, 117, 119, 126, 129, 130, 175, 180; Irish policy towards 112, 114, 115, 117–18, 120; peace process 1, 7–8, 9, 20, 47, 81, 102, 119–20, 121–22, 123, 125, 127–28, 173, 175, 178, 181
Nusseibeh, Sari 1, 149

Obama, Barack 23, 46, 47, 83, 148, 159, 165, 168, 169, 179–81
official IRA 114
Olmert, Ehud 20, 22, 46
Oslo Process 44

Palestine Liberation Organization (PLO) 142, 144, 145, 146, 148, 151, 160, 170, 171–74; creation 138; phases strategy 140–41
Palestine National Council (PNC) 146
Palestinian Islamic Jihad 15, 76–77, 79, 132, 143, 144, 145, 146, 148, 149
Peres, Shimon 17, 18, 19, 20, 42, 44
Peretz, Amir 20
Princes (in Likud) 42–43
Progressive Democrats (PDs) 105, 120–21, 122, 173

proportional representation 11–12; reform attempts 13, 26
provisional IRA 114

Qurei, Ahmed 145

Rabin, Yitzhak 17, 18, 19, 42, 179
Ramon, Haim 22, 27
Reagan, Ronald 91, 93
religiosity 109, 129, 175
Revisionist Party 28, 29
Revisionist Zionism 28
Reynolds, Albert 121, 178; beef scandal 104–5, 122; peace process 121–24
Rogers, William 36
Romney, Mitt 179
Russian Jews 27, 151, 165

Salame, Hassan 135–36, 160
Scott, Winfield 15
Sephardic Jews 14
Shamir, Yitzhak 25, 32, 34–35, 37, 40, 41, 51, 63, 150, 171; background 41; foreign minister 39, 41; Likud leader 39; prime minister 40, 41, 42, 45, 48, 83, 142, 159, 165
Sharon, Ariel 46, 48, 49, 66, 179; Al-Aksa Intafada 46; and disengagement 66–80; foreign minister 44; forms Likud 37–38; forms Shlomzion 38; invades Lebanon 39; legal difficulties 71; prime minister 66–80, 83; targeted killings 69–70
Shas 14, 23, 27, 83, 178, 187n
Shinui 76–77, 177–78
Sinai 1, 3, 4, 7, 9, 37–38, 40, 50, 51, 54, 56, 65, 66, 76, 82, 83, 152, 154, 170, 171; negotiations 52, 59–61, 161; withdrawal from 3, 64
Sinn Fein 20, 83, 110, 113–14, 115, 118, 119–20, 122–23, 125–27, 150
Smuts, Jan 16, 18
Smyth, Fr. Brendan 124, 129
Social Democratic and Labour Party (SDLP) 115, 116, 117, 118–19, 122, 126, 173, 200n
South African Defense Force (SADF) 87, 89, 92
Spring, Dick 122–23, 125–26
SWAPO/PLAN 86, 88–89, 90, 91, 92, 93
Syria 5, 8, 20, 39, 41, 45, 50, 53, 56, 82, 95, 131, 135, 138–39, 142, 144, 156, 171, 175; civil war 175, 180; track 82, 167, 171, 175

209